"*Love's Way* is a simple, but not simplistic, map to the inner working of the heart as it expresses love through relationship. It can help guide the reader through the tangle of (pseudo) relationships built on projection and traumatization. One of Brenda Schaeffer's unique contributions is bringing in the role of the living, knowing spirit in the body. Without this rooting, our relationships are built on a house of cards."

—Peter A. Levine, Ph.D., author of
Waking the Tiger, Healing Trauma

"This book will be a great help to those who have been truly afraid: the betrayed people who now fear to love."

—Patrick J. Carnes, Ph.D., clinical director of
Sexual Disorders Services at The Meadows

"Who wrote the Book of Love? Now along comes Brenda Schaeffer to give us a timely rendition of the age-old questions and answers about Love . . . *Love's Way*—well done!"

—Jeremiah Abrams, author of *Meeting the Shadow*

"Our main task in life is to learn how to love ourselves and each other. Brenda Schaeffer's wise and intelligent words can help you heal a wounded heart. You may even come to see your wounds as gifts, magical ciphers that illuminate the often mysterious ways of the heart."

—Eric Utne, founder of the *Utne Reader*

Love's Way

The Union of Body, Ego, Soul, and Spirit

BRENDA SCHAEFFER

HAZELDEN®

INFORMATION & EDUCATIONAL SERVICES

Hazelden
Center City, Minnesota 55012-0176

1-800-328-0094
1-651-213-4590 (Fax)
www.hazelden.org

ISBN: 1-56838-623-0

Library of Congress Cataloging-in-Publication Data

Schaeffer, Brenda.
    Love's way : the union of body, ego, soul, and spirit / Brenda
Schaeffer.
        p. cm.
    Includes bibliographical references and index.
    ISBN 1-56838-623-0
    1. Love. I. Title.

BF575.L8 S34 2001
152.4'1—dc21

00-054210

Author's note
The vignettes in this book are composites of actual situations, and those created by the author are for illustrative purposes only. Any resemblance to specific persons, living or dead, or specific events is entirely coincidental. Those
who wrote the autobiographical sketches have given permission to appear in
this book. Their names and some circumstances have been changed to ensure their privacy.

05 04 03 02 01   6 5 4 3 2 1

Cover design by Lightbourne
Interior design by Elizabeth Cleveland
Typesetting by Stanton Publication Services, Inc.

For Heidi and Gordy, who have quietly and deeply shared Love's Way with me for years. Thank you for the opportunity to be your mother.

The day will come when after harnessing the winds, the tides, and gravitation, we shall harness for God the energies of love. And on that day, for the second time in the history of the world, man will have discovered fire.

—Pierre Teilhard de Chardin

Contents

Acknowledgments

I feel most grateful to Love for showing up and being so persistent in getting my attention. This book would not be what it is if it had not done so. Thanks too for the hard lessons love has given to me and the push and pull not to give up on love as I sought the bigger definition. And to the lovers in the book whose gripping stories give us the courage to believe and move forward, thank you. To my wonderful and gifted children, Heidi and Gordy, I thank you for the opportunity to deeply know and love you. A very special thank you to Jon Spayde, my editor, for mentoring me through the dark night of the writer's soul. Your spirit is in this book in many ways. Thank you, Tom Tiegs, for your good humor, research, and patience as you assisted me. And for your invaluable support, careful reading, and comments, heartfelt thanks go to Dr. Bart Knapp, Peter Richards, Karen Lyons, Holly Schuck, and Steve Wilson. Special thanks to Karen Chernyaev, Hazelden editor, for supporting what this book is about. Beyond that I want to thank Mystic and Sage, my canine pals, who patiently sat by my desk and insisted I take walks in the woods at predictable times. And to the spirits of the land where I listened and wrote, you affirmed that love is everywhere and available any time of the day or night. And to the men and women who, over the years, have opened your hearts to me and kept them open, thank you. To those who opened and then closed them, I thank you, too. There have been lessons in it all.

The author and publisher graciously acknowledge the following individuals and organizations for allowing us to reprint their material:

The excerpts on pages 16, 18, 22, and 170, from *The Prophet* by Kahlil Gibran ©1923 by Kahlil Gibran and renewed 1951 by Administrators C.T.A. of Kahlil Gibran Estate and Mary G. Gibran, are reprinted by permission of Alfred A. Knopf, a Division of Random House, Inc.

The excerpts on pages 26–27, from *The Art of Happiness: A Handbook for the Living* by Dalai Lama and Howard C. Cutler © 1998 by H H Dalai Lama and Howard C. Cutler, are used by permission of Putnam Berkley, a division of Penguin Putnam Inc.

The excerpt on pages 115–116, from *Mama I Love You* by William Saroyan © 1956 by Little, Brown, is reprinted by permission of the Trustees of Leland Stanford Junior University.

The poem on pages 154–155 is reprinted with the permission of Nina Watts.

The poems on pages 192 and 211, from *The Essential Rumi* by Coleman Barks © 1995 by HarperSanFrancisco, are reprinted with the permission of Coleman Barks.

"This Thing of Goodness," on pages 228–229, is reprinted with the permission of Alison Luterman.

The poem on page 246 is reprinted with the permission of Lila-Qadrya.

Introduction

When I was a little girl I felt happy much of the time. I had my family, my friends. They were all I needed. I learned to tie my shoes when I was three so I could wake up before the others and go outside and watch the sunrise and feel the morning dew on my skin. I was so alive. And when I did this, a very "big something" rushed through my body that seemed to start right at my heart. And it was good. I didn't question this much, I just trusted it. I liked to watch tadpoles in the crystal clear pools in the crevices of the rocks on the shore of Lake Superior. They were my friends, too. And I noticed as I watched them, this "big something" rushed through my body again. It started in my heart. And it was good.

Sometimes my mother would hold my hand and walk with me. We would be quiet. I could hear her talking to me without any words. She said, "I love you." And when she did, this "big something" was in me, and all around me. And it was good. Sometimes my dad would take me fishing. I would lie on the bottom of the boat, merge with the rocking motion of the waves, take in the warm rays of the sun, and smell fish smells. My dad would check on me, smile, and talk to me without words. He said, "I love you." I said, "And I love you." The "big something" filled me again. It started in my heart. It seemed as if I went up to the sun and down to the bottom of the lake. And I felt good. I felt safe and happy. One day, when I was five and I was selling church raffle tickets, I went to my grandpa and grandma's house. I loved my grandpa. He smiled at me and without words he would say, "I love you." And that "big something" would be there again.

Grandma did not like children. She did not have to tell me that. I heard her without words. She would check my hands to see if I was clean enough to come into her house. I noticed that the "big something" wasn't there when she talked to me. I missed it. I felt scared. And when I was scared, I noticed that my heart was different. Sometimes it hurt.

I asked my grandpa if he would buy a church raffle ticket. He said, "Yes, come in, Honey." I liked it when he called me "Honey." That "big something" was always there. And I felt good. Grandpa began to write his name on the raffle ticket as he was supposed to do. Grandma got mad at him; I don't know why. She said in a mean voice, "Give me that pen! You don't know how to write your name!" That "big something" started to leave again. I felt very sad and tears were starting to come into my eyes. I ran outside and hid in the bushes. I cried for a very long time. But my "big something" did not go away. I told it not to.

I learned the "big something" had a name. Its name was love. I was very confused, though. In my mind I looked around at all the grown-ups who used the word "love," who said they loved each other and even said they loved me. I saw and heard many things. Sometimes grown-ups would laugh at each other or call each other names. Sometimes they would swear or yell. Sometimes one of them would be afraid of another and try too much to please the other. Sometimes they wouldn't listen or answer. Or when they spoke, they would try to prove they were right and the other one was wrong or stupid. Sometimes they would try to make the other one jealous. Sometimes they would touch each other in icky ways. I promised myself right then and there that when I grew up I was going to learn more about this word *love*. I also promised myself that when I grew up I would not say or do those things that hurt my heart and sometimes made that "big something" go away.

I grew up, fell in love, got married, had two beautiful children, and planned to live happily ever after. I forgot what I had committed to, until one day I saw that some of the things I promised myself I would never have in my life were happening. The fullness in my heart wasn't there as often. I missed it. It was as though I had lost my way. And then I remembered my promise.

LOVE'S WAY

Love. A small word for such a spacious and elusive phenomenon. Of all the mysteries that enchant us, love may be the one we seek with the greatest passion. Love, of course, is a huge topic every day in my practice of therapy. Clients ask me: "How can I love myself more?" "How can we have a more loving relationship?" "How can I heal from this failed love affair?" "If he loves me, why does he betray me with endless sexual affairs?" "Am I in love or am I in an addiction?" When I ask outright, "What is love?" clients stop dead in their tracks. Though it seems to be something they are chasing, they seem not to be able to identify that which they are looking for. "Well, I don't really know, but I know the phenomenon when it is there—I think," they often respond. It is as though they once knew Love's Way, and now they are lost.

Oprah and Sally Jesse and Ricki Lake talk about love on television. The soaps talk about love daily. Music, movies, and novels talk about love. Talk, talk, talk. We talk too much about love. As much as we talk about it, we seem to hardly get it at all.

Love cannot be found by talking about it. Love is much greater than that. It is an experience. It is huge. It is like the very air we breathe. Without the air we die. As the air gets polluted, we want to know why and what we can do to clean it up. We talk and talk about it. Then we put it aside and go about our daily business. Sometimes we forget the air is polluted and we get sick. We wonder why. Gradually we lose sight of the fact that we are sick and we begin to think sickness is life. And in our ignorance we die. Not only did we die taking air for granted, we died in polluted air. So it is with love.

You would think that all this talk about love implies respect, even reverence, for it. Yet as a society we have trashed love. We act embarrassed or ashamed of it. We are afraid to look someone in the eye and say, "I love you." At other times we treat it flippantly: "I love my new car." "Don't you just love this new book?" "How much do you love me?" "Do you love me as much as you love her?" Sitcoms talk more about scoring in love than they do about love itself. People are used as objects of love and not a way to experience love. We use the word in such a sloppy way that it has come to mean nothing or everything.

The truth is that love, like air, is simple, but its way is hard and steep. Just when we think we understand it or have it, it eludes us. Why? Perhaps because we have been bombarded with definitions and how-tos from an endless variety of sources. Biology has its definition. Psychology does, too. Culture has some very distorted perceptions. Spiritual teachings claim to have the right answer. In these opinions, and in the hundreds of how-to books on love—how to find love, how to keep love, how to make love, how to do love, and how to grieve love—there is an underlying arrogance that we know what love is.

Do we? On a recent book tour I was asked over and over again, What is love addiction? As I began answering the question with definitions and signature symptoms of this relationship disease, the overwhelming response was, "Well, if that is love addiction, what is love?"

Pondering the question later, I told myself that if I were to write yet another book on love it would not assume that readers know what love is. I knew I would ask readers, If you do know what love is, are you living it? Love may be the most haunting of life's experiences and the most frequently used word in the world. But what in the world is it, really? Whether I was conscious of it or not, I have been searching for an understanding of the word *love* for a very long time. What was this "big something" and why was it present sometimes and other times totally gone? It was as though it was always there and went into hiding. That is why I kept chasing after it. It was home and I missed it. If love had a way, I wanted to find it. If it had a yellow brick road, I wanted to be on it. And if I was the one blocking my path to love, I wanted to know that too.

Love is home; it is not a destination. And we all to some degree keep ourselves from coming home. As a child I experienced love and nonlove directly. So did you. In order to get back on love's track, my personal and professional journey became a process of elimination. To get to the purity of love requires getting rid of the glut and clutter of definitions and programmed "love maps," understanding the power of human trauma and releasing its impact, embracing and healing fear, and surrendering my will to Love's Way.

But what I can tell you is that love is real. Love is alive. I knew that as a child and I know it again now. When I am in love, it does not matter whether I have an object of my affection—having one is a bonus, a unique and special opportunity to share love on a body, ego, soul, and spirit level. I can be in love without a love object, and so can you. What I had to discover along the way to love was what love was not. I would like to share that discovery with you. This is important because the more time we spend in fictitious love, the less time we have for being in real love. And we do not have a lot of time to learn Love's lesson. What love is not:

It is not dependency,
it is not a feeling,
it is not a mental construct or thought,
it is not a behavior,
it is not a role,
it is not romance,
it is not a set of biochemical responses,
it is not sex,
it is not a commodity,
it is not something we earn,
it is not something we learn,
it is not dependent on an object,
it is not limited,
it is not a neat little package,
and it is not a relationship!

No, it's not a relationship. Don't assume that because you are in relationship you are in love, or that you need a relationship to experience love. As we are well aware, we can be in a relationship and not experience love at all. In fact, relationships can zap us of our life energy and literally make us sick.

Relationships are neutral places that can provide the opportunity to experience love or not to experience it. In our human relationships we have the opportunity to experience a profound love, that overwhelming feeling so evident in my childhood. We also have the opportunity to withhold love. It is really up to us.

It's also true that it is in our human relationships that we seem most humbled by love's lessons. Love relationships are the places we go to look for love's promise and keep hitting pain and sorrow. But there are reasons for that. In relationship we will experience

ourselves in all ways, whether we like those ways or not. We have
a biology we will keep bumping into. We have cultural love maps
that guide us to dead ends. We have a psychological history that
has not met our emotional needs. We have a personal story filled
with mental and emotional constructs that have skewed our definitions about love. And we have had trauma.

Though it is intended to be a special gift, the fact that we can
experience love in many ways has been a great challenge to living
Love's Way. It is my belief that we bring a reactive body, an adaptive ego, a curious soul, and a lofty spirit to *every* relationship we
are in. When these four facets are fused and run through the
heart, our relationships thrive. Each has a gift to offer our love
relationships.

For too long we have kept body, ego, soul, and spirit separate
when it comes to love. Many talk or write about the chemistry of
love and leave it there. Others view it strictly as a problem of the
ego and search for "how to" do it right. Some have said that it is
the soul's time to enjoy the desires and urges of love's call. Forget
ego and spirit, they say. There are those who say the search for the
Beloved is what counts. It is in the face of those we love that we
find God. Spirituality is greater than body, ego, or soul.

But love says, "Don't fence me into any one mode. Each of
these has its rightful place." Love's Way is to play them all, not in
a trivialized game, but in a comprehensive and fulfilling way.
And why not? We are multidimensional lovers. What a trip this
earth life offers us. We get to bring love into the total human experience and into all aspects of self. Body, ego, soul, and spirit are
meant to be in love together, not to have one made more important than the other. And we need to get this message now. If
Love's Way has one major emphasis, it is that we must stop putting these aspects of ourselves into a competition.

Because we are multidimensional, we live in two worlds: the
sacred and the secular. Each person, as well as each love relationship, has the possibility to live in both. If we had caregivers who
provided us with even a little safety, we knew this as children. We
understood that love was everywhere—in us, around us, above
us, and below us. We understood what mystics and even now science is telling us. We are one cell in this great ocean called love.
And the heart is the portal of entry. There is no separation, and

anything that causes separation immediately takes us out of love and into illusion. We are in need of a new psychological paradigm confirming that this is so. We need specialists working in the arena of love relationships to stop fragmenting us.

Some phenomenal things happened as I wrote this book. It had a working title and an outline. A book needs one. But the book kept changing. The publisher did not like the working title. The book was not following the outline. My editor began seeing other things surface in the words. We twisted it this way and then that way. I felt frustrated and at times exhausted. I fought the changes. I wanted to quit. I hit what poet and essayist Gloria Anzaldua (drawing on Aztec myth) calls *nepantla*, the writer's dark night of the soul. My editor understood, patiently extended his hand and pulled me out of the dark. He smiled a knowing smile.

And then I realized that I was a mere messenger and I'd better get out of the way. Something was attempting to birth itself, and it was bigger than any outline I could have come up with. And it was far greater than me. "Be still and listen," I told myself. "You did it as a child and it always worked." This book was alive, and I was in relationship with it. It was as though there was a ball of energy bubbling up and taking form. I let it take over; I was in for a ride. The energy developed a voice. It was separate from my ordinary voice. It was to the point, supportive, and strong. It started sending memos. The first memo came out of the blue. It was not in my original plan. I wondered if there would be more. There were. They always came when I was still or in meditation.

I have attempted to do justice to the voice and to stay out of the way as much as is humanly possible. At one point I asked, "Who is writing this book, anyway?" I was clearly told: "We both are. I need your practical human experience to validate what I am saying. You have the information and the human voice needed. Every experience you have had and are now having has been leading you to here." I knew the voice was right. It does not matter to me if the voice is my creative imagination or a power much greater. The voice is wise, all-knowing, caringly detached, compassionate, and universal. And I knew the primordial energy oozing through me was the energy known as love. It was the "big something" I had quested for since childhood. Love has something in store for us. It has a way of being in the world and yet not of this world. If you listen carefully, you realize that love is willing to speak through each one of us. And it only speaks to us when we are in our heart.

When they were little, my children would ask me to read "What Color Is Love?" by Joan Walsh Anglund. At the end of the story a long pause and an inquisitive expression alerted me to the fact that they were going into the recesses of their minds to find the answer. By age four or five, having surveyed the world of grown-ups, children sense that the face of a love relationship has many colors. Some days it is pink and soft, some days it is red and angry, some days it is green and growing, some days it is gray and gloomy, and some days it is yellow and warm. They end up very confused. As children, we watch how significant grown-ups relate. We learn to respond to certain gestures, smells, idiosyncrasies, styles of dress, and manners. We become accustomed to styles of living, to order or chaos. And we learn the definitions of love and power and what it means to be a man or a woman; definitions that become locked in our psyche and interpreted in adulthood as universal truths. These early experiences will determine whom we love, how we love, and the color of our love. We learn more about what love is not than what love is.

As we grow, love gets no easier. We want to love. We fear love. We want to know ourselves and we forget who we are. We want to change our story lines and we keep reenacting them. We touch our souls; we give them up. We strive to be spiritual and we are consumed by ego distractions. We want to stop and rest and life keeps going faster and faster.

Sometimes we truly open our hearts to love, pour forth love and become a receptacle to receive it. And when we do, it feels magnificent. We feel catapulted into a reality that has a vague familiarity, one that lets us know who we really are and what really matters. A moment that says, "This is it, this is life, this is God!" But soon we begin empowering the objects of our love as the master key holders, and when they threaten to leave or begin to close their heart to us we become angry, resentful, and scared, and we up the ante with power plays, victimization, depression, and anxiety attacks, forgetting once more who we are and what we are in this life to do. We are left with despair, longing, and confusion that we convince ourselves *is* reality. This is as good as it gets. The

splendid moment was only a dream, we might convince ourselves. Let's get back to reality, we say. This zigzag path drives us
crazy. It leads us further into the depths of loneliness, the number
one disease underlying addiction, compulsive habits, and unhealthy relationships. As destructive as these means of coping
are, they can also be viewed as a friend that helps us deal with the
loneliness. They are predictable, they tune out pain temporarily,
they are what we know, and they help us feel alive momentarily.
There is, oddly enough, a sense of safety in these maladaptive
friends that we cannot seem to find in our human love stories.

As I work with people recovering from sex, love, and romance
addiction, coaddiction, codependency, depression, anxiety, post-
trauma, and other emotional and behavioral illnesses, I see that
giving up the destructive behavior or negative experience only
makes the loneliness more apparent. After the euphoria of stopping a negative habit, belief, or feeling passes, fear presents itself.
People are often shocked to discover this. When we stop the self-
medicating we are raw.

It has been said that there are two ways of living—from love
and from fear. Paradoxically, when fear arrives we have an opportunity to know love in a profound way. We must be willing to surrender our life of illusion and pretense, humble ourselves, walk to
the razor's edge, fall into the all-knowing abyss, or omniscient
universe, and trust that love is real and will sustain us. Being in
love requires both deep psychological and spiritual work.

All my spiritual teachers taught me that there are two essen-
tials to progressing: the first is clear intention, and the second is
absolute faith in the possibility. If your intention is to know love
and live it and you believe it is possible, then so it shall be! And it
may require hard work. We live in two worlds—the sacred and
secular, the within and without. We are the bridge. As we clear
out the glut and clutter we have accumulated in our human story,
we will discover that we also contain the connection to a higher
wisdom that we can tap into and bring to all our relationships. Be
forewarned. Life as we know it will not make this easy.

At one time the words "falling in love" greatly disturbed me.
The words "falling madly in love" disturbed me even more. When
Harper subtitled my book *Falling into Healthy Love*, I cringed. Ah,
but now I get it. If, as science is validating, the universe contains

an intelligence known as love, it is a matter of allowing ourselves to open the gates protecting our heart and allowing ourselves to fall into it. In a new love relationship, whether it be with our newborn baby or with another adult, we allow ourselves an openness that momentarily allows us to step off the razor's edge. The truth is that we are in love already! And we do not need an object of love to know that. To repeat: Love is everywhere—in us, around us, above us, below us. Everywhere!

These truths are not new. Every religion, great philosopher, wisdom teacher, poet, and artist has spoken to the force of love. Love is not something founded by the Greeks nor was romantic love begun in the Middle Ages. Love is power. Diane Ackerman writes: "It is the great enabler that allows us to commune with every aspect of being alive, with people and objects, animals and cities. One needs love to feel harmonious, to feel part of the rich landscape of one's life."[1] We are intended to be in service of love. And if you consider it, all human suffering results from denial or resistance to this responsibility. On the contrary, human happiness, awe, and passionate living result from adhering to this principle. Love is a rainbow, a prism of colors that can warm hearts, heal bodies, and bring out the true color of our souls. Wounded or confused, we forget this. We need a large enough community of people to really understand what love is and is not, to do the necessary heart work, and to be willing to heal the wounds of the heart so the ethereal blood of love can flow on this earth freely. Science is now demonstrating what the mystics have always known. We must move our world from a grid of fear to one of love. This is no myth. It is not even an option. If we do not do it, life may be over. If we do it, we will evolve as a species.

This book is attempting to say:

Love is real and it is time to expand our definition.
Love is trying to get our attention in a big way.
We have been spending too much time in the illusion of
    love.
It is time to be the multidimensional lover we were born
    to be.
We can be in love in body, ego, soul, and spirit, and it is
    time to stop separating them.

The heart is intelligent.
And we need to get busy and put love on the streets.

Each chapter begins with a personal message from Love itself. Love has given the body, ego, soul, and spirit each an assignment. I have attempted to support the messages with personal stories and authenticating data. There are many brave hearts out there "walking the point," as soldiers say, and helping us believe in the power of love. I have been witness to miracles. I think you will be impressed by their stories and hard work. I cannot thank them enough for their bravery. They venture forward in a world that is inviting us to step back and lend us courage and modeling we so desperately need in order to believe in love relationships. I have included relevant myths, research, or studies that support my premise and that may pique your interest.

Chapter 1, "What Is Love?" provides an expanded definition of love based on research and sacred wisdom and shows embodied versions of down-to-earth human love relationships. It explains how body, ego, soul, and spirit are unique and what is meant by each of them in the context of this book.

If love is so powerful, why does it continue to elude us? Chapter 2, "The Illusions of Love," tackles that question by explaining the many versions of trauma we are likely to experience in our lifetimes and how that relates to closing down our hearts and living in fear of intimacy (often without being aware of it). We are meant to be in relationships and so use melodrama as a substitute way to stay connected. Dependent love, sex, and romance addiction become all too attractive. Having stepped out of Basic Trust because of betrayal, we must discover it again to be in love.

Chapter 3, "The Body in Love," chapter 4, "The Ego in Love," chapter 5, "The Soul in Love," and chapter 6, "The Spirit in Love," begin with specific assignments from Love. The chapters contain poignant stories to authenticate that each of these facets contributes immensely to our love stories. Each has intelligence. Each can work in service of love or against it. And each of these chapters contains a recipe for a vibrant love life and a meditation to help you into closer communion with these aspects of love.

The body is essential to physical bonding and contains the

chemicals you need to interact with life. Yet these same chemicals can result in addictive and compulsive habits. The body is the storehouse of trauma. The ego's job is to see to it that you have emotional intimacy and that your material life runs smoothly. You will learn how it adapts to the world to get its needs met. It writes a story that contains the beliefs and decisions that contribute to what is going on in your love relationships. It has been taught what it means to be a woman and a man and what a love relationship is. Because it has been betrayed, it will both want and fear emotional closeness. You will learn how the soul relates to love. It thrives in love's mystery and passionate living. It is not afraid of pathos nor does it need to know the future. It goes for the deep and the evocative and it lives the Bigger Story. Like a wild child it can get lost in dark places and needs the wisdom and guidance of the spirit. You will learn how soul and spirit are unique and why it is important to not confuse them. Your spiritual self is not as interested in your love story as you are and can easily get bored with mundane living. It would much rather merge with the Beloved and has been known to bypass wounds and in so doing gets in trouble.

Chapter 7, "The Realm of the Heart," pulls it all together as it shows with supportive data that to have the vital love relationships we yearn for we must unify all aspects of ourselves by living from the heart. When we have done so, we become what I call the multidimensional lover. The heart is more than a physical organ. It has an intelligence that is beyond IQ or emotional intelligence. Love makes clear that the heart is its port of entry. But because of the human condition and trauma it may not be all that easy to relax our hearts and let love in. A dramatic opening story alerts us to the fact that trauma is the perennial challenger.

Chapter 8, "Taking Love's Way to the Streets," reminds us that we are all in this love story together and that what each of us does or does not do makes a difference. Now that we have heard the assignments, the supportive stories, and the data, it is time to do the work. This is a self-help chapter, chock full of guided exercises, assessments, and data that can help you continue or get started living Love's Way. It provides the weary traveler with guidance to heal body, ego, soul, and spirit, along with ways to live in the realm of the heart.

Love says: "*Be kind to yourself as you sift through your love stories. If I am not there to the degree that you want me to be, it is because your heart has been injured. Every relationship is a teacher and will provide you with opportunities to recreate the hurt or heal the wound. You must be a willing student, however, and remove your false self and show your nakedness—wounded heart and all. Remember, though, if you do not learn the lesson, the teacher will come back.*"

Memo

To: You

From: Love

I imagine you are surprised to hear from me. I can understand. I have been trying to get your attention for a long time, and though many of you hear me on good days, I cannot wait any longer for all of you to get my message. I am deeply concerned. Rather than getting closer to me, you seem to be moving away from a full understanding of me. Your definition of me has become far too narrow and constricting. You act as if I am eluding you. I am not. You have even become rather desperate in your search to find me. You must stop the foolish search. You see, I am right here at your fingertips. The only thing between you and me is your limited view of me. I am here to remind you that I am everywhere and just waiting for you to remember me. More important is that humanity is in desperate need of you to do so.

You knew my grandeur and simplicity as a child. You experienced my safety and power. You saw me in a smile, sensed me as you held your mother's hand. I was in your joy as you built sand castles, rode on the back of your horse, and climbed your favorite tree. I was there when someone wiped away your tears and told you that life meant you no harm and that it was good. I was in the rising sun and the starry nights. I rushed into your heart and when I was there you felt bigger than life itself. But then you started going to sleep and put me in a little box and placed me on a shelf. You have all but forgotten what I am. I am here to remind you.

I am here to expand your definition of me. What the spiritual teachers have been telling you has been the truth right along. Now that science is validating what they have always known, maybe you will believe me. I am enormous and my power is beyond your comprehension. I am readily available and eager to be used.

You have been given a special gift. Yours is the only species on earth with the capacity for multidimensional love. You can know me in many ways, not just one. You have a body with which to sense me. You have an ego that can direct you to bond with others in loving ways. You have a soul that knows passion. And you have a spirit that can elevate me. Each has been given an important assignment. You must become familiar with these assignments and live them. Sadly, these dimensions have become separated, and they even feud with each other. You must give each its importance and bring them together harmoniously into your love life.

Being vulnerable, staying open to me, is your greatest task. You started out open. You believed in me. You had every intention of harnessing me and putting me into life. And then in a moment of intimacy you got hurt. You felt a pain in your heart and your heart began to shut down. It just happened. Though you want to know me, you are handicapped in your ability to do so. You see, the heart is my portal of entry. Without your willingness to open and then listen from the heart, your ability to know me again is limited. I need you to let me in. It is time. Look around.

When you use the words "in love," you are speaking a truth beyond your ordinary comprehension. I encourage you to see me as the miracle of life in everything and everyone around you. Therein lies your challenge.

Everything in the universe is related. You cannot *not* be in relationship. I am the great force that cements everything together. I am here to help remind you what I am and what I am not and to review the assignments given to you. Whether you do them is up to you. Humanity's fate is in your hands. You can continue to live in fear or you can live my way. I am trusting that as you hear the stories you will get the urgency of what I am here to tell you and will choose Love's Way. It is life.

Good luck.

CHAPTER ONE

What Is Love?

◘ ◘ ◘

When love beckons to you, follow him,
Though his ways are hard and steep.
And when his wings enfold you yield to him,
Though the sword hidden among his pinions may wound
  you.
And when he speaks to you believe in him,
Though his voice may shatter your dreams as the north wind
  lays waste the garden.

For even as love crowns you so shall he crucify you. Even as
  he is for your growth so is he for your pruning. . . .
But if in your fear you would seek only love's peace and love's
  pleasure,
Then it is better for you that you cover your nakedness and
  pass out of love's threshing-floor. . . .
—Kahlil Gibran, *The Prophet*

Love is enormous. It is an amorphous, intangible state of being,
an immutable presence that's pure and simple and seems to have
a spirit of its own. It is an expansive energy that needs no object. It
runs the universe, fills all spaces. It cannot be quantified. Though
we think we know love by experience, true communion with love
is rare, and very different from the biochemical high of romance.
Love is a power. Even a brief experience of love in a personal relationship can transform a human life forever. It can open our
hearts so wide that we have a distinct sense of having stepped out
of ourselves into an endless presence.
  When I, personally, am in it, I sense that it arises from deep

within me—from a place I cannot clearly define, though it feels like the heart talking to each cell of my being. I enter a timeless, inexplicable zone—a zone where there are no boundaries yet I remain aware of myself. It is as if I am falling into an abyss. People undergoing near-death experiences talk about this same experience. It is as though some spirit in me is catapulted into another realm of experience. It is not a "body" experience, though I remain in body while it's happening. Perhaps I could call it an out-of-body experience that's totally in body.

Love pulls me out of myself to connect with something bigger than me—a something that is in me, around me, above me, and below me. It draws me to want to reach out and touch life in good ways, to nourish and protect. In it I feel full, strong, luminous, green, and growing.

Love encourages me to experience every aspect of being alive, of what it means to be human. In love I deeply touch everything—other people, the natural world, souls, bodies, minds, hearts. It is what opens me to my possibility, mirrors back who I am to others. It encourages me to see the miracle of life in everything and everyone around me. The passionate, alive, on-fire power of love motivates me to cut through life's entanglements.

Love is about experiencing God, Buddha, Christ Consciousness, Creator, Yahweh, the Beloved, or Light in everything and everyone. It is about experiencing a profound intimacy with all of life. I believe that fairy tales, legends, epics, and mythology are trying to tell us that love is essential—not only to our existence, but to what we can become as a species. Though religion speaks to it, love is not cloaked in any dogma. It is free and available to all and everyone. Love does not care what you look like, what you believe, whether you are married or single or in a relationship at all. It couldn't care less whether you are prince or pauper, sinner or saint. When you gather but a small portion of this Kingdom of Heaven, as Jesus referred to it, and put it into the world, miracles happen. And science is catching up and figuring out why.

Love is an energy as distinct as mental energy. The sensation of warmth in our hearts for a loved one is perhaps the nearest we can come to experiencing its power physically. We must not confuse this with sentimentality or physical love. It is far greater. It is like a food. It nourishes. Sometimes we stop the energy;

sometimes we further it. Sometimes we want to share it with someone else, and the other person isn't open to it. When that happens we experience a sorrow, a pain in the heart. But in love we remain open—keeping the heart supple. At these times love is a sweet sorrow with no judgment, an understanding that acknowledges the words of Kahlil Gibran: "Your joy is your sorrow unmasked."[1]

Earlier I stripped love of the many things we have taken for granted as belonging to it. I said that love is not a dependency, a romance, or a feeling. Nor is it a mental construct, a behavior, or a biochemical reaction of the body. It is not dependent on an object, and it can't be bought or earned. I said this so that you would, just maybe, begin to understand how small-minded we have been. How little our ego has made love to be. The problem is not that there is not enough love to satisfy our yearnings, it is that we are such a small container. And our pettiness, fear, trauma, limiting beliefs, and ignorance cut off what we are capable of containing.

Many people are praying for love, thinking it will be dropped into their lives in the form of the mythical perfect mate. What they do not understand is that the great creative force wants us to receive this great energy and live it. It is a gift of life. It is our destiny! It is a power of such magnitude that we are challenged to become a strong enough container to receive and retain it, and then we must be careful to not dissipate the energy foolishly. That requires some dedication and hard work.

BRINGING LOVE DOWN TO EARTH

Love is a transcendent mystery, but it is also a down-to-earth experience. How love manifests itself in its earthly form has been the subject of endless streams of mythology, legend, spiritual teaching, psychology, and scientific research. On earth we have elevated love in art and song and at other times have used the word *love* in such a sloppy manner that it has come to mean almost everything and nothing at all. The word we use for the enormous power has been known to spark wars and shape history, create national scandals, justify crimes of passion, turn strong men and women into weaklings, and make fools out of kings. And perhaps because of these same things we are embarrassed by love. We blush when we talk about love, we feel weakened when in it, ashamed we have fallen, and reluctant to admit to it. The English language has dozens of words to talk about how we hurt and hate and far fewer to describe the faces of love. Love defies all words. It is indescribable. When it is present, no words are necessary.

It seems we were given the commandment "You shall love" and then dumped on earth trusting we would be shown how to do it. Some days frantic, other days tranquil, we limp through life never giving up on love's possibility. In fact it is an enchanting mystery to which we are secretly attached. If we get this one, we understand all. Human life will, of course, put up an obstacle course.

The anonymous Frenchman who coined the phrase "Love makes the world go 'round" was probably not thinking of quantum physics or the intelligence of the heart when he made the statement. He must have known that love is the most important thing in our lives, the something that would motivate a mother to die for her child and a comrade to risk his life for the life of a friend, the passion that keeps artists at their tasks and love relationships alive. What a great motivator love is.

If we were angels we would be swimming in love; it would be the easiest thing in the world. But we live on earth. It is dense here. Love has a hard time getting in, let alone out, of us. Love is perfect. Humans are not. When perfect and imperfect meet, frustration and confusion are the result. On some days it feels like a bad joke. We have the consciousness in us to have glimpses of perfect love, yet we are trapped in bodies and egos that prevent us from achieving it.

How do we step love down into human form? Through *relationship*. Relationship with self, relationship with family, relationship with friends and lovers, relationship with the four-legged and the winged ones, with the elements, the sky, and the earth. Relationship with everything.

To relate means to connect, and while it is true that we exist in a massive web of interconnections, we do not always experience a whole lot of love in these relationships. Often the experience is that of fear, anguish, hate, and longing. You don't have to tell someone who's suffering from a love affair gone bad that "relationship" and "love" are not the same thing.

While it is true that fear can crowd love out—that our attachments to the object of our desires can result in disillusionment, obsession, anxiety, and despair—we must not forget that love relationships are also our greatest teachers. Relationships initiate us. They may put us through the fires of torment and hell and test us to our limits. If we pass the test we come out an entirely new form. That is alchemy. Relationships are a great matrix in which we can wither or ascend. For most of us, spiritual development doesn't mean hiding in a hermitage but rather engaging in solid, everyday, down-and-dirty human relationships. Everything we need to know about ourselves—good, bad, and indifferent—we will discover in our love life.

And love life takes many forms. There is mother love, father love, and family love. There is love of a friend. There is romantic love. And there is profoundly spiritual love. Each, in its unique way, challenges us. Will we collapse into our vices or will we ascend into a more elevated species? Will we give up because love demands too much of us? Intimacy with friends, family, partners, children, lovers, and the earth itself requires at times hard work but provides us with amazing opportunities to know ourselves and do love right. And *right* is not to be understood as some inflexible standard. Right is vibrantly alive.

Romantic and sexual relationships can be sacred places but we often abuse them. Romance is more than a temporary psychosis or a psychobiological reaction based on neurochemical and hormonal processes to ensure the survival of the species. Keeping it at the level of chemistry, as we'll see, has justified our using and abusing people. Considering rape as a way for males to spread their seed or pass on their genes or dismissing the sexual promiscuity of our leaders, which endangers our cultural integrity, with "Boys will be boys" keeps us at a primal-brain level.

We now know that our brains are capable of much, much more. To quote Dr. Paul MacLean: "Nature added something to the neocortex that for the first time brings heart and a sense of compassion into the world. . . . As humans, we seem to be acquiring the mental stuff of which angels are made. Perhaps it is time to take a fresh look at ourselves and act accordingly."[2] Our romantic, sexual, and love relationships are the places where we sentient beings can develop loving hearts, where we can look at our foibles and failings and virtues. A "yoga of relationship" and a new understanding of love have become indispensable.

VARIETIES OF LOVE

Eros

Almost all great love stories metaphorically speak to the passion that brings us together and, when mishandled, brings suffering and even death. This blazing passion, which longs for union, is Eros. Eros was the Greek god of love. Considered the capricious child of Aphrodite and Hermes, he was so compelling that it was said that no mortal could resist his charms. A beautiful and serious youth, he gave gifts to mortals. The philosopher Plato best summed up his nature: "Love—Eros—makes his home in men's hearts but not in every heart, for where there is hardness he departs. His greatest glory is that he cannot do wrong or allow it: force never comes near him. For all men serve him of their own free will. And he whom Love touches not walks in darkness."[3] Eros was often represented blindfolded, perhaps to suggest that love is often acted out in blind melodramas.

And in the throes of drama, Eros shows us that what we poor humans are looking for is a way to meld paradoxical realities, to bring opposites together into fusion and mutuality. In that timeless zone we are free of life's constraints and, perhaps for just a moment, find ourselves. In Eros we have a clarity and strength that allows us to let go of our armor and become completely vulnerable to love's great mystery, perhaps even become willing to die for it. In those instants we get a glimpse of our possibility.

As science is validating, love points us to the real meaning of transformation, toward the possibility of mortals becoming goddesses and gods. Love stories speak to our own inner birth, the birth of our souls. Looking for the Beloved, we are really searching for ourselves and love and, if God is love, then union with God.

The romantically infused person, the devotee of Eros, displays a nobility of character in which virtues flourish. The romantic is like a mother in love with her newborn, a person grieving the death of a beloved friend, a child reveling in the birth of kittens. When people belong—romantic or otherwise—however they belong, everything seems to fall in place, even in times of chaos and doubt. When intimacy is this profound, something inside of us says, "Life doesn't get any better than this."

Romance in and of itself has an important place in our human life. If we consider romance as a state of ecstasy, it's clear that we do not require an object of passionate love to experience it. We can be romantically propelled all by ourselves. I knew this blissful state when I held each of my two children for the first time. I connect with it sitting in my favorite spot in the woods. I know passion as I let the words filter through me to this page. All of these experiences can be euphoric and orgasmic and hurl us into a blissful state of satisfaction. As one newly single friend said to me, "The woman to whom I can say, 'I don't need someone else to be in love,' and she says, 'I know exactly what you mean—that's how I feel, too,' is the woman I am interested in."

Slipping into that all-knowing abyss brings out the best in us. Not knowing that we are the conduit to these experiences and having limited access to them because of our human stories, we empower the objects of our love for what it is we are experiencing. When our hearts are not free, which they often are not, we cling to these experiences and the method of transport. When our hearts are open and we unite pleasure and deep joy that only the soul knows, spirit enters our human experience and romantic love becomes a different experience. Look at yourself when you have been newly in love. As Rumi expressed it, "In this world of love we are the hidden treasure, we are the owners of eternity."[4]

Agape

> And let there be no purpose in friendship save the deepening
> of the spirit.
> For love that seeks aught but the disclosure of its own mystery
> is not love but a net cast forth: and only the unprofitable is
> caught.
>
> —Kahlil Gibran, *The Prophet*

Agape is the Greek word for another kind of love—profound, nonerotic love for a friend or a neighbor. Many writers in the nineteenth century considered the love of a good friend as more pure and noble than the love of the opposite sex. It was not uncommon to use the word *lover* to mean a friend. In an 1841 essay Ralph Waldo Emerson writes, "High Thanks I owe you, excellent lovers, who carry out the world for me to new and noble depths, and enlarge the meaning of all my thoughts." In his essay "Friendship," Emerson asserted that "friendship, like the immortality of the soul, is too good to be believed."[5] To poet Walt Whitman, friendship could be an experience that was both ethereal and physically intimate. And he saw intimate friendship as the very spirit of democracy. "For You, O Democracy / I will make the most splendid race the sun ever shone upon, / I will make divine magnetic lands, / With the love of comrades."[6]

Another important form of agape is profound love of our family. With the breakdown of communities over time the web of life has been altered. "Community is the spirit, the guiding light of the tribe, whereby people come together in order to fulfill a specific purpose, to help others fulfill their purpose and to take care of each other," writes West African author Sobonfu Somé.[7] We must not bury our heads in romantic liaisons and forget our community. Too often I have been witness to child neglect when single parents were preoccupied with their romantic pursuits, ignorant of the fact that the opportunity for love was right in front of their eyes.

I am convinced that single parenting can succeed when the parent has a loving community to support her or him, maintains a strong sense of family, and expresses deep love. Yet we are programming single-parent families with the belief that they cannot generate enough love to have healthy children. And what does that say to those children? This programming also fosters what I have defined as addictive love, emotionally dependent relationships in which the child takes care of the parents' fears and insecurities rather than the other way around. And it encourages jumping into relationships before the heart wounds have been understood or healed. Of the clients I see, 90 percent were raised in two-parent households. It is not the roles we play but the love we put into those roles that matters. Without love in our communities, all relationships are at risk.

But how do we put love into a community? By some simple

actions that can have profound results. Ed Robins, an anthropologist friend, told me that when he was a consultant in Burkina Faso in West Africa, he noted how important greetings were to the Burkinabe. Following is a paraphrase of our conversation:

> For them a morning greeting was more than a perfunctory hello. It was a way to renew the relationship each day, to remind the self how much they needed each other. To type A driven Americans, the ritual seemed a waste of good time. It interfered with production.
>
> The Burkinabe would insist on at least a shake of the hand, a warm smile and preferred much more. They wanted to be informed as to what had happened between now and the day since they had last seen you. They understood how important each person is to the whole community. They understand that we are in this together. They would grieve together, celebrate together. If someone died, the entire community would all go to the funeral and support the family and feel the loss. We Americans might send only a single delegate; we couldn't justify sending the entire office, and missing most of a workday, to attend something as "minor" as a funeral. In our obsession with mere accountability, we Americans seemed to miss what community is all about.

Amour

Hints of a new kind of love, a love that implied deep partnership between the sexes, appeared at the beginning of the twelfth century, when courtly or passionate love for another, rather than being considered sinful, began to be viewed as emanating from the soul. Eros, our longing for physical union, united with agape, the universal, spiritual love of our neighbor, and became *amour,* a deep personal love relationship. This profound feeling preceded any physical union; often the yearning was more important than the actual physical coupling. Touch and sexuality were rendered sacred and often never took place in courtly love. One lover would leave so he could hold the longing, could stay in the first stage of a romantic relationship. This experience was in complete contrast to euphoria or the sexual high. There, pleasure of the body and ego only was the goal. In courtly love the senses were honored and respected as a meaningful part of the love relationship.

In her book *A Natural History of Love,* Diane Ackerman points out that courtly love in the Middle Ages brought with it a shift from unilateral love to mutual love. This was an avant-garde and dangerous idea, given that the Church preached that there was one solitary love and that was love of God. Love of another human being could be interpreted as idolatry.

That didn't stop the troubadours, traveling folksingers, who invented the love song and became the Middle Ages' equivalent of gossip columnists. Affairs of the heart, adventures, and adventurers filled the musicians' repertoires and brought love down to earth where they thought it belonged. For the troubadours, humans could see the face of God in the face of another. Seeing the divine in them reminded us of our own divinity and virtue. In fact, courtly love was more about virtue than anything else.

The culture was now getting closer to the truth that divine love, the Eternal Source, is everywhere, including within us. We have souls, we have within us the reflection of the divine, and we are larger than our bodies and personalities. For these inspired singers, love dwelt on earth and could be experienced in our physical hearts.

The impact of Muslim mysticism, which entered the Western world through the cosmopolitan court of medieval Sicily, may have had something to do with seeing God in the face of another. The Sufi Muslim mystics understood that religious ecstasy and the ecstasy of lovers had a lot in common— great insights, vows, all-consuming passion, rituals that led to bliss, and an experience of primordial oneness. The *in love* experience was the same whether its object was a human or a deity.

Amour even upset the politics of the time, implicitly challenging a feudal system in which men served lords and women served their men. To elevate woman to an equal and virtuous status was unthinkable—except to the love-besotted troubadours.

Remnants of amour remain in modern-day romantic love, although there seems to be much less concern today about love bringing out our virtues. As we see, the contrary has actually happened: over time the virtues of romantic love have turned into the pains of dependent love and love addiction—using the other to "get" and "consume" love.

Compassion

> All happiness there is in this world comes from thinking about others, and all suffering comes from preoccupation with yourself.
>
> —Shantideva, *Awakening the Buddha*

There is another form of love that seems to be filtering into the planet right now in a big way. This love is bigger than amour, more encompassing than agape. And it guarantees happiness. It is called *compassion*. In the Tibetan language, *compassion* translates as "nobility or greatness of heart."[8] A compassionate person is one who sees and feels with all of his heart and embodies open-hearted wisdom.

Compassion implies love without any human strings attached. There is one requirement, however. To become compassionate, you must stop your preoccupation with yourself and take down the walls barricading your heart. And when you do so you discover what spiritual masters know: You are nothing and you are everything.

Compassion implies a love that is bigger than romantic love, and it has a ring of spirituality that romance does not. But perhaps the two are closer relatives than we think. Courtly love dared to say that love can live on earth, in our human relationships, and that passion is our birthright and a gift of the soul. No more leaving God up there in the clouds indifferent to human suffering. Life is to be celebrated and enjoyed. There is enough natural suffering here to contend with, said the troubadours.

Compassion, too, is interested in suffering and living in a more wide-awake manner. It too refuses to divide spirit from the mundane world. In *The Art of Happiness*, His Holiness, the Dalai Lama, says: "Compassion can be roughly defined in terms of a state of mind that is nonviolent, nonharming, and nonaggressive. It is a mental attitude based on the wish for others to be free of their suffering and is associated with a sense of commitment, responsibility, and respect towards the other."[9]

Compassion is not only for the other. It knows that the other is but a reflection of our own divinity, and it wants for us what it wants for others. Compassion, then, includes a wish for good things for oneself and the wish for oneself to be free of suffering. The freer we are, the more naturally we cultivate compassion and extend it to others.

According to the Dalai Lama, if we give compassion expecting something in return—love, for example—the relationship is unstable. A relationship based on genuine compassion, however, is unshakable:

> Genuine compassion is based on the rationale that all human beings have an innate desire to be happy and overcome suffering, just like myself. And, just like myself, they have the natural right to fulfill this fundamental aspiration. On the basis of the recognition of this equality and commonality, you develop a sense of affinity and closeness with others. With this as a foundation, you can feel compassion regardless of whether you view the other as a friend or enemy. It is based on the other's fundamental rights rather than your own mental projection. Upon this basis, then, you will generate love and compassion. That's genuine compassion.[10]

Compassion has a spiritual loftiness that is detached from suffering while being genuinely present to another's suffering and the suffering in the world, whether or not there is a personal relationship involved. Compassion is available in any circumstance. It is strong, wide, and durable, and it goes beyond the human realm. Driving home from a meeting one evening, a friend and I came upon a large and badly injured turtle in the middle of the road. We stopped traffic, even though many gestures of harried irritation greeted us. We wrapped up the frightened animal and spoke to it in a loving way, assuring it that, at the very least, we would provide it a peaceful death. As we spoke the turtle relaxed, closed its mouth, and let us carry it to a sacred place near land and water. We blessed it and thanked it for the many ways it contributed to life. The turtle was our kin and we experienced its pain. The caring had no desire, no attachment; only a profound and loving presence that contained a tinge of sorrow.

Awareness of suffering in the natural world enhances our ability to open our hearts. When we bring love in through our hearts to care about pain and suffering we experience compassion. The Dalai Lama prompts us to step out of the indifference and the deadness we often experience in response to real world suffering. Developing a feeling of unbearableness at the sight of suffering is developing our humanity. It gets us out of denial and narcissism to remind us that we are all related and as one person suffers, in a manner, so do all others. To reduce the suffering in the world, we must first be willing to see it in its many shapes and forms and then let the suffering warm, not close, our hearts.

Compassion is living without attaching to fear and pain and moving toward trust and joy. But to live in nonattendance to pain, paradoxically, you must allow for its possibility. As you make room for suffering, you let it be without giving it a charge. You do not condone it; you do not choose it. You figure out what place it has in your life and that is it. You choose to put your energy elsewhere.

Something else that compassion teaches us is that it is not enough to stop or avoid negative thoughts, feelings, and actions; we must also actively choose positive thoughts, feelings, and actions and put them into life. And it emphasizes that we cannot afford to wait to do so. Sometimes we vow to be more positive or to do a "good deed," but we are just too harried and stressed-out to act. "It can wait till tomorrow when I am not so rushed and I can think straight," we say to ourselves. We postpone goodness just as we postpone balancing our checkbooks or starting our exercise programs. But tomorrow never comes. Love is always a *now* experience.

When I use the word *suffering* I am not referring to the manipulative, self-generated patterns of suffering we can become attached to in our ego life. That type of suffering is a sort of emotional racketeering in which we concoct dramatic scenarios to get to a specific painful payoff and keep people around. It is also important that we recognize when others are caught up in their pain or victimization and are inviting a rescuing response from us. If we step into that swamp we will soon discover ourselves stuck in muck knee high. And it may not be all that easy to get out. In our grief we can choose to believe that this is necessary suffering as we say good-bye to someone we love, or we can add needless suffering by clinging to a person who probably is not good for us anyway or hanging on to a belief such as "I am un-lovable" and perpetuate our pain.

Even in these situations, though, we can choose a compassion-ate response. And our compassion is not about the specific suffer-ing with which we're dealing; it's about the fact that the sufferer has been led to believe that he or she needs to use pain and drama to be connected.

Compassion adds a strong dose of wisdom to love. Consider these scenarios: In desperation your best friend calls you up to borrow money but has not paid back a previous loan. Your part-ner promises to stop his use of pornography but does nothing about it. Family members want your sympathy but continue to be hurtful, abusive, and unkind. You reach out to your children but they do not reach out to you. When you stand still or give into these emotionally abusive patterns you are practicing what Trungpa Rinpoche coined "idiot compassion."[11] To not take care of yourself is immature love—which in my lingo is love addic-tion. Love addiction is always based on fear: fear of rejection, fear of anger, fear we won't get what we want, just to name a few. And because it is easier to do what we always have done, we do it.

You can recognize the difference between genuine compassion and pseudo- or "idiot compassion" in several ways.

First, note where the energy is coming from in your body. If you feel warmth in the heart and poise in your body and mind, you are in genuine compassion.

Second, notice whether you feel tired or in some way ener-gized by the experience. Love generates energy.

Third, note if you are alert and fully present or dull and want-ing to move away.

Fourth, is your caring free of judgment, irritation, and fear? If you are unclear, simply go to your heart and ask it if genuine compassion is being called for in the situation. Your heart will an-swer, and, of course, it will be right on target.

COMPASSION AND PERSONAL
RELATIONSHIPS

We must learn what it means to give with a pure and unselfish heart. And while this may be more easily understood in universal terms, the great challenge is doing so in our one-on-one, intimate relationships. Compassion is essential to them.

We each bring into our relationships a body filled with trauma experiences that we are still trying to release. We often reenact those traumas in an attempt to get closure, and we are usually not aware we are doing it. We have an ego with years of conditioning to contend with. We have a soul that has normally been relegated to a back seat. We have a spiritual self, and our spirit often feels dead. Given all of these factors to contend with, we can see that although love is simple, it is not easy.

Compassion, seeing from the heart, understands that we are multidimensional lovers—body, ego, soul, and spirit—with a lot to contend with. We must be kind to ourselves, our symptoms, and our resistance to change. Though we do not have to like it, we must love our self that lives the illusions of love, not beat it up. We must hear its story, consider how it views life, and invite it rather than force it to change. We must love it to death.

Bringing compassion to ourselves helps us be compassionate with others. We must listen to another's story from deep within our souls. When we do, we do not try to change them. We note how difficult it is to be who they are. There is no shame in not being able to help those we love as we give that task back to them. All they really want is to be deeply heard—without judgment or criticism. Being heard naturally brings release and healing.

You might be thinking: "All well and good, Brenda. It is easy to love a turtle, but how do I bring compassion into my love life?" To be compassionate, we must become aware. And building that awareness is the task. Love's task isn't always easy, but it is possible. Listen to Steven and Lynn's story.

STEVEN AND LYNN'S STORY

It was wonderful seeing him smile again. It had been a long time coming. He gently reached over and touched her hand as he introduced me to her.

"This is my friend, Lynn. I wanted you two to meet."

I reflected on Steven's story and the many misguided experiences he'd had with love—so misguided that he had fallen into a deep depression after years of an emotionally, sexually, and spiritually empty marriage. Adopted at the age of two weeks by a couple who felt incomplete without a child, he began life feeling alone and controlled. Treated like a "something" and not a "someone," he soon learned to play back what they asked for.

He had to be the perfect child to assure his parents that they were good parents. According to them, he failed miserably. His normal curiosity and aliveness was deemed wicked and was squelched early on. He became the easy scapegoat for the marital problems and alcoholism in the family. He felt confused by the religious epitaphs that preached love, yet he did not see or experience it anywhere. Like many children, he personalized the emotional neglect and concluded that there was something wrong with him; he was discarded goods. In fact, he had in many ways been told that his soul was bad by a grandfather and a father who had never bonded with him.

He would remain quiet and obedient until he could no longer contain the suppressed energy. Then there would be the outbursts of anger and rebellion. His life seemed to be taken up with trying to get out of his mother's grasp. Seduction and emotional incest, followed by verbal battering, occurred over and over again. Motivated by loneliness and emptiness, his mother covertly seduced Steven to put her needs and wants first. He was to take care of her. Feeling used and trapped and having no other choice, he silently agreed. But he could never satisfy her emptiness. A warped sense of love and intimacy were modeled daily, leading him later to warped relationships with women. For years he had love and hate feelings for himself and the world. But he felt a longing to find himself, to know who he was and where he came from.

His zest for life diminished early. It was gone for sure the day his bike was stolen. He found the culprit and fought for his rights. With his bike and a sense of personal pride he returned home. But his mother was not eager to see him, having learned of his behavior. Severely punished, he decided to temper his instincts for life. He felt soulless. "There is no God," he said to himself, "and if there is, he abandoned me."

Guidelines, red lights, and the freedom to learn from mistakes were what he needed. Instead he got senseless rules and control that generated fear. As an adult he would get highly motivated to make needed changes in his career and relationships, only to be greeted with anxiety that put the stoppers on him. Fear ran his life, and no one was to know. In his nighttime dreams he would experience a desire to run but be immobilized by fear. When Lynn showed up, he knew a relationship with her was what he wanted, what he had asked for, but he could not initially step up to the plate.

He gave up on love and spirituality very young. He became an atheist. Instead of God, he chose alcohol, drugs, and sex. He was never without a relationship. Though he did not know much about love, he understood intense anxiety when a relationship ended and would jump into one after the other. When the time for marriage came, he plunged into one that looked good on the surface. He even thought he was happy from time to time as he reviewed his well-groomed lawn, his asset portfolio, and his affluent lifestyle. He experienced safety *and* loneliness in this ideal-looking arrangement. After all, it was not safe to get close to a woman, and he had found one who fit the bill. He could not blame her for his choice. She was what she was.

Yet he could not deny the growing discontent. A persistent emptiness pushed him to look for his biological parents. He succeeded in finding them. But in the find he learned something of importance: He had been conceived *in love*. This news shocked him. Unable to marry at the time, his mother and father went forward with their lives with an ache in their heart for each other and him. He would be their only child together. Years after Steven's birth, they found each other and married.

Something changed for him when he discovered his father and mother and the story of his conception. It was as though he could give up the shackles that had bound him to a life of loneliness. He was not discarded goods. *He was loved.* Thinking of himself as lovable and worthy freed him to look at outdated patterns and beliefs that limited him and his love relationships. He reached the nil point. He stopped and examined everything. It was like letting go of layers and layers of skin. He was raw but free. Spirituality appeared. So did love—self-love first. He saw an image of the innocent child who had come to earth to learn about love and whose soul was so eager to immerse itself in life. His heart opened to him and he wept. He moved into Basic Trust as he reflected on the drama he had lived. He saw how moving from love to nonlove was necessary to his arriving at this point in his relationship with Lynn. Every experience had a place and a meaning. There was no judgment. In fact, he felt grateful for it all. He lived in the peaks and valleys. He alchemized the experience and came out in a new form. "Life may be a dream," he said, "but it's my dream."

I smiled at them both as I returned to the here and now. "This is no small deal," I said to myself as I reflected upon the story.

Proceeding with the interview eventually led to Steven telling me, "There's something very special about this relationship. And I do think I love her."

"I love him, too," Lynn commented. "It's different. We are truly friends first."

"What is love?" I asked them.

The question took them by surprise. Their eyes widened and their mouths fell open. For a minute they remained speechless.

"Well, I don't know. . . . I mean, I never really thought of or answered this question before," he replied.

"A very good question," she said. "No one ever asked me this so directly, and this is important for us to really understand, given our histories."

Each of them paused. He went first. "I don't know if I can describe it. I know when I am in it. The way it shows up in our relationship, I guess, is as a feeling of closeness, even in quiet. It's a meeting of the minds, a connection. There is mutual respect. It's a friendship where there is a physical attraction. We walk beside each other. It is spiritual. Mostly though, it is the safe feeling I have to be myself when I am with Lynn. It was never safe to show who I was because I had been told that I was a 'bad seed' and some part of me bought into it, and I was scared to death of being found out and rejected. I may get rejected again. I have no control over her half of the relationship. Only mine. Oh, it would break my heart for a while, but I have a strong heart. I know who I am now, and I have one determined spirit that has taken years to free. The issue is no longer what she thinks of me, it is what I think of me."

She spoke next. "Love is much bigger than our relationship. I have to agree. I have never felt as safe as I do in this relationship. When I feel safe, love just wants to pour out of me. I do not quite understand it. And that poured-out love nourishes both him and me. Strange. I am growing at my age. Yet, I know I feel scared at times and fear getting hurt again. When that happens I feel my heart shutting down. It seems to be an automatic response at times, and knowing that it comes from my history helps calm me and I open up again. My former partner started out saying he loved me and later became possessive and jealous. Frankly, he became abusive. Steven and I are hopefully more mature. We've done a lot of work and soul-searching. We appreciate what love is helping our relationship shape into. What I learned from the 'awful' in my past is that relationships are not the problem; they're the places that reveal the problems. Likewise, they're not love but a place we can really experience it. It's as though our relationship is one big container that holds us. It's great. So, I guess I've not answered your question directly, have I?"

"You have done a great job contemplating the question," I replied. "You are wise to separate love from a relationship. Some relationships are mean and sting hard. Love is, as you struggled to describe, much bigger than you or your relationship. It is a power that is in you, around you, above you, and below you. Some say it runs the universe. Some call it God. It is endless and always available to you. And as you have learned, happiness and joy are by-products of how we do our love relationships alone or with others. First we need to get out of the hypnosis of our conditioning that generates the fear we all seem to have buried. It comes with the package called life. Knowing what love is not is often trial and error. If you do not learn the lesson, the teacher keeps showing up till you get it. You both took the time to step into yourself. You listen to your inner voice that speaks your truth, and you have learned how the past defines your future and has kept you from the future you deserve. I truly believe that if you have a clear intention to live from the heart and are willing to be responsible for what you bring into the relationship *and to take care of it,* your relationship will thrive."

It was not as though they were infatuated teenagers. They had known each other for more than two years and were still discovering and growing. They understood that a love relationship is not a neat little package but an ongoing, vital, alive organism in itself, forever in motion and always becoming something different. Not only is it alive, it helps keep us alive and enlivens life.

LOVE AND HEALTH
There is growing scientific evidence to back up the claim that love
is good for your emotional and physical well-being. And there is
growing scientific evidence that some of the things we pass off as
love are bad for your health, too.

According to C. Norman Shealy and Caroline Myss, love of
others and being loved are key factors in improving the immune
system, adding to life expectancy, and creating overall happiness.
Their research shows that even bad habits like overeating and
smoking have less of an impact on those who have loving support systems.

A research project conducted by James House at the University of Michigan Research Center clearly demonstrated that doing
good deeds pays off. Those people who did volunteer work on a
regular basis and who interacted with others in a caring and compassionate manner dramatically increased their life expectancy
and overall vitality.

At Harvard University, a well-known experiment conducted
by psychologist David McClelland found that an increase in the
antibody immunoglobulin-A (IgA), which helps ward off respira-
tory infections, can be generated simply by watching a film of
Mother Teresa working among India's sick and impoverished
people.

People who are "in love" have fewer colds. The unconditional
love that pet owners receive from their animals helps lessen depression. In one study of Israeli men, high cholesterol and high
blood pressure were less important to health than the quality of
love in their marriages. Individuals who have close intimacy with
others have higher IgA antibodies and less serious illness. Children whose parents love them unconditionally thrive and have
good esteem and more zest for life.

Emotional health is improved, as well. Studies have shown
over and over again that caring about others induces feelings of
warmth, calm, and happiness, which significantly reduces depression. In fact, a study by Allan Luks found that 90 percent of
a group of volunteers reported a "high" from their volunteering
experience.[12]

*Love is the most cost-effective medical insurance policy and the
cheapest medicine there is. And there is no end to its supply.* In fact, the

more love you put out, the more it generates. And it attracts love to itself. It generates joy, happiness, serenity, esteem, vibrancy, kindness, appreciation, respect, laughter, generosity, tolerance, tenderness, open-mindedness, respect, care, affection, goodness, service, appreciation, compassion, awe, wonder, bliss, and trust, all of which have been proved scientifically to be good for your health.

It takes only one conscious act of love to get the healing juices of love flowing. And it does not even matter if the other person is conscious of your conscious act. All that matters is the willingness to put love out there. So do it!

LOVE AND THE WEB OF LIFE

Science tells us that we are the most highly evolved species on the planet. Some days I believe it. We are linked to each other in a very profound way, and as we evolve individually, we evolve as a species. We are each a part of a great cosmic web. The sustainability of this web of life depends upon the strength of each individual strand.

Our indigenous ancestors knew this well. Moving beyond staying close for survival, they valued the spirit of community. When someone was sick, they considered the community to be sick, so they all pitched in to restore the health of that person through prayer, ritual, and tender caring. Elders carefully observed the children and noted their special gifts. They knew who was to be the teacher, who was to be the medicine man. "It takes a whole village to raise a child" was an actual experience.

But what is it that holds the strands of the web together? We have been striving for the scientific answer that supports what mystics and spiritual masters have been telling us all along: "God is Love"; "He that loveth not knoweth not God";[13] "The Lord resides in the hearts of all beings"; "I am the God of Love"; and "Love is the essence of God."[14] According to the Sufis, "Love is the electromagnetic milieu in which we exist, which exerts various forces of attraction among all that it contains; the greatest transforming power: our experience of the spirit."[15] Some teachers of physics suggest that the divine mortar is none other than love. This concept views love as an energy as real as electricity, the electromagnetic power that cements the universe together.

And, as science is relearning, the human heart is the conduit. We have known this experientially and intuitively. But how can we verify this? And why do we need to?

Let's look at the last question first. The western mind is a skeptical mind. We are the technocrats of everything—including love, spirituality, mind, and matter. Though much of our questioning has been to answer the skeptic, exploring our questions and finding the answers has contributed immensely to our evolutionary process. While we can choose to use technology to bring about the collapse of humanity, we now have an opportunity to go beyond mind and emotional intelligence and come to a greater understanding of the intelligence of the heart. That intelligence that science is validating is none other than the heartbeat of the universe, love.

The more we know about what love really is and how to harness it more wisely, the more we contribute to our human destiny. We know loneliness and separation are creating more loneliness and separation. We realize that traumas are not healed and are perpetuated in violence and war. Domestic abuse is on the rise. Addictions, greed, and stress are everywhere. Though we are raging for the experience of love, we do not know how to activate this hidden power of the heart. Many have given up and settled for abuse or live in quiet despair. Does it not make sense to learn more about love and to start curing the loneliness?

If we really understand the power of love and use it, we can help bring about a fundamental shift in our collective human experience. By doing our part we can affect the whole force field of life. Violence, addiction, trauma, and dependent love are based on obsolete attitudes. If you change but one attitude or make one decision that generates love on this planet, you will be changing the planet for the better, because in love, we are all related and what one does affects the whole. If you agree to live in love, you will create an unmistakable elegance that puts out a welcome sign saying, "People walking through here are safe."

PAULA'S STORY
Yes, despite all of its pains and travail, love is not only worth it— it is the most worthwhile, powerful thing in the entire universe, and it changes everything. But don't take my word for it. Listen to

Paula. Rev. Paula Kuether is a personal friend and mentor. She
had moved to Arkansas and, until a recent phone call, we had not
spoken in months. She was busy living her life and I was busy
working on the manuscript. In our conversation she told me of a
recent close encounter with death. As she told me her story I was
astounded. What she was telling me was precisely what was coming to me as I wrote the book. Here is her story:

> Not long ago I nearly died. They discovered a hole in my in-
> testines that required emergency surgery, and in the course of
> that surgery I crossed over to the other side. Something in me
> changed that day. I heard my voice being called and it was as
> if my arms floated upward. I saw a purple light off in the dis-
> tance. In a split second a great force transported me into an-
> other dimension. This force was pure love. In a flash I was
> brought to spirit, where there was no time, no space, no think-
> ing, and no separateness. Only love existed. This love filled
> every square inch of space and carried me, lifted me to a place
> of absolute peace and bliss.
>
> When I woke up from the surgery, I still had the experience
> with me. I knew that love flows through the heart and can con-
> trol the mind if we let it, with consciousness and disciplined
> attention. I could hear, feel, and know the people around me,
> their thoughts and pain. I was connected to tubes and ma-
> chines and yet I was in utter peace.
>
> [Afterward,] some people were concerned about me. They
> were uncomfortable with my changes and wanted the old me
> back. I can never go back knowing what I know—but the
> opinion of others does not matter now. I do not judge them be-
> cause that would put me out of balance, and out of balance I
> am out of love.
>
> Before the surgery I really thought I was in touch with
> love, the divine flow. I was, but only in a small way. You see, I
> am a spiritual teacher, an ordained minister who preached
> love and healing. I had a great relationship with my husband
> and my daughter. My life was dedicated to giving to others. I
> felt happy and fulfilled.
>
> But now, after crossing over and coming back, I have a new
> awareness of love. I do not walk with it just some of the time;

it is present to me all of the time. Everything I do is affected. I never run out of energy, physically, mentally, or emotionally. I am in action—producing, creating, and intuiting—no longer trying. And I know how we are all connected. All I know is that there is a divine intimacy, and as soon as I step out of it I step out of love.

I understand now that Love is asking us to be present to it and to walk it on earth. We must accept everything and sur-render to it. If we do not, we generate fear. Fear works against love. It separates, and when we are separate from love we try to control it, which is absolutely insane. Love is big and avail-able, and it is the same here on this earth as it is in heaven. Love is not a hardship but requires discipline and conscious intention to make it work in our lives.

How do we bring heaven to earth? All we need to do is say: "I am willing to receive." There is so much love we don't even have to think about it. It is about letting go of control. But we are like ants, scurrying around, always busy, always trying, al-ways doing things to try to make the outer world more conve-nient. We are already plugged in to love; we do not need to go searching.

We must step away from this antlike business. We get plugged in by doing less, not more. Love will lift us and nour-ish us if we let it. We must stay in the present. Each step of life has to be fully experienced. Accept everything. Surrender. Then believe there is something bigger that is guiding us—Love—and plug in to it. Listen. Love the body, ego, soul, and spirit. Stay connected. Love, but do not do so at your expense or the expense of another. That is the illusion of love.

Paula's story confirms that love is enormous and close at hand. But if love is a power and it is everywhere, why does it seem to elude us? Why is there such pain and suffering in our love life? What went wrong? On some days it does feel like a bad joke, that we were given an assignment but not the tools. Wrong. We do have everything we need, and love is personally asking us to pay attention. We started out as believers and then lost our way. We forgot our assignment. Having forgotten Love's instruc-tions and needing to connect, we began living the illusion and called it love. Like Steven, Lynn, and Paula, we arrived on planet Earth in innocence and with an open heart, and we need to recapture both. But to do so we need to recognize the many ways we delude ourselves and why. That is what we will get to next. It is imperative that we know what love is not.

BODY, EGO, SOUL, AND SPIRIT

Beyond paying attention to the illusions that have been created for us or by us, the stories point out the gift of multidimensionality that allows us a love experience unequaled by anything experienced by any other species. We love with the body, the ego, the soul, and the spirit. Love wants us to stop acting as if they were separate. In the chapter on the body, we'll look at chemical, neurological, and other physical sides of healthy and unhealthy love. In the three chapters that follow it, though—those on ego, soul, and spirit—we'll be dealing with trickier concepts. Ego is widely misconstrued, spirit sometimes means far too much, and soul is rarely understood at all in our modern world.

So here are some rough distinctions to guide us through the rest of the book. Though there are many definitions for these words, these are the meanings I have given them for our purposes.

Body refers to our biological makeup, our chemistry, our senses, and our physical vehicle of transportation in the world of matter. It has its own unique intelligence, which allows it to interrelate with all life forms. It is home to our heart and our brain and contains our genetic makeup. It allows for profound physical intimacy that is the touchstone and foundation of love on earth.

The body is the self that bubbled up as matter evolved into the physical species known as the humanoid. It has a triune brain: the reptilian brain, the mammalian brain, and the neocortex. Its main task is to identify physical needs so it can survive in a competitive world. To do so it senses, reacts, thinks, and mobilizes energy to take effective action. It has specific needs that must be met or it will die: food, water, air, space, rest, elimination, shelter, temperature control, health, movement, stimulation, and touch. It is essential to the full expression of love, and in the scheme of this book it has been given the assignment of bringing sensuality, sexuality, physical bonding, and energy to our love relationships. It lives in symbiotic relationships with others. When it matures it is self-sufficient and exchanges its energy with others.

Some words we use when we talk about the body include *somatic, sensual, sexual, energy, biological, reactive, conditioned, habitual, compulsive, primal, athletic, sick, healthy, uptight, graceful, strong, aroused, satiated, euphoric, frozen, terrified, alive,* and *dead.*

Ego is that part of a person that lives in the material world and is defined by it. It is great at organizing the mundane life, it is told by the authority figures what to do, what to believe, what to feel, and what to think. It belongs to the masses. It has basic survival needs that must be met or it will die. It adapts to the world to get those needs met, and, as we'll learn, some life adjustments are healthy and serve it well. Other adaptations limit it. How it adapts will determine its human presentation.

The ego lives in a physical body, has an emotional life, and grows through specific stages of development. Its life is more or less outwardly focused; it looks to externals for validation and direction. Sometimes it gets lost, not only in the external world but also in image, glamour, and drama. It can self-medicate pain with addictions, compulsive habits, adornment, and being adored. It lives in roles and has a life script filled with traumatic events. Sometimes it believes that this secular world is all there is and so attempts to control it. Compared to spirit or soul, it is dense and its energy moves slowly. It confuses doing with being and can easily get lost in stereotypical roles. When therapists or spiritual teachers work with the ego, their goal is to help it become a well-integrated personality structure by means of which the soul can be on earth and live.

Ego is limited, but that doesn't make it bad. In fact it is essential to our human love stories. It feels, it thinks, and it nourishes and protects those we love and ourselves. It is emotionally intelligent and desires intimacy and connection. It can be autonomous, antidependent, or dependent. Other words we often associate with ego include *personality, image, drama, glamour, roles, emotions, neurotic, psychotic, well-adjusted, fragmented, depressed, passive, dependent, likable, mean, needy, critical, nurturing, controlling, analyzer, intellectual, driven, addictive, selfish,* and *appreciative.*

Spirit refers to that part of us that aligns with the divine. It is that immutable self that we often experience as detached from life, in an observer position. It is the internal force that pulls us toward growth. Whether it is recognized or not, it is always working in us. It can view life as mundane, secular, and temporarily distracting. Often referred to as our higher self, it is more interested in "becoming" than in living. It seeks enlightenment, spiritual highs, and is definitely heaven-bound. Seeking union with a God force, it is always striving upward.

Spirit is idealistic, creatively inspiring, and wise. It is evolutionary in nature and seeks not only to learn lessons but also to transform and transcend them. It has strong inner intent and absolute faith; it expresses the higher emotions of compassion, gratitude, and humility. It is the philosopher and mystic in us. In our human life it is sometimes considered lofty, ascetic, detached, overly serious, even pedantic and intolerant. It can even be self-deceptive and limit soulful living. It is on a path to the Beloved and is determined to be with the Beloved for eternity. Bent on divine perfection and truth, it exalts both the soul and the ego to it. Spirit brings heart into matter and helps guide the soul.

Spirit words include *generosity, compassion, grace, luminosity, gratefulness, forgiveness, joy, pure, all-knowing, detached, truth, sacred, divine, wise, cosmic, enlightened, higher self, Self, observer self, gratitude, transcendence, universal,* and *energy.*

Soul refers neither to ego nor to spirit, but to the glue between them. It is earthbound and brings depth to raw experiences. Earthy and primal, it speaks through symbols as it explores life's mysteries. It loves ritual and ceremony, art, and music. It is the creative muse, the generator of intuitive knowing. It jumps into life and devours all of it, the dark and murky as well as the light. It is our personal medicine, our unique essence, and our authentic self.

Soul lives now and now only. It does not care about a path and can be easily distracted. Think of it as the spirit's inner child. Words associated with soul include *raw, wet, juicy, deep, earthy, mysterious, melancholy, longing, vivid, organic, zestful, mythological, sensual, erotic, nostalgic, passionate, awe-filled, ecstatic, brave, exquisite,* and *serene.*

It is perhaps the most alive part of who we are. It brings passion and depth to our love life. It needs the food of experience and takes it in and magically changes it to something new. Often it is referred to as the mediator or middle principle. Some say the body is in the soul; others say we have a soul-infused body. It is the soul that can bridge the two realities, heaven and earth, the sacred and the secular. It materializes spirit and spiritualizes matter. The soul is unique and yet is at one with other souls. It is greater than ego or personality and is said to use the personality to express itself. The soul needs the ego to recognize it and give it its rightful place. And it is the soul's job to bring spirit into the world.

We must never think of these four as separate entities at odds with each other. Intrinsically intertwined and often overlapping, body, ego, soul, and spirit make for an exalted human and for exalted love. To make their relationship a little clearer, let's consider how each faculty relates to a chocolate bar. The body sees the chocolate bar and craves it. The ego gets attached to the craving and acts to get its need met: it begins eating the bar. The soul relishes the delicious taste of the chocolate and the delightful mess it's making on its chin. The spirit simply observes the process without judgment and lets the craving rise, persist, and then pass away. And if the others persist in the cravings to a point of overdose, it will intervene as a wise and loving parent and say, Stop, you are hurting yourself.

To be fully alive and available to love we must own all four aspects of ourselves. We have pleasure chemicals that keep us aroused and invite cuddling. Our ego supports our need to live in relationships and experience emotional bonding. Passion is a soul experience and spirit adds that dose of wisdom that reminds us that we are all in one big love story. When we recognize the intricate intelligence they each bring we have the potential to live and love deeply "on earth as it is in heaven."

Recognizing that we are multidimensional, however, doesn't guarantee that we will bring love into our love life. There is one more ingredient to turn us into multidimensional lovers—heart. Without heart, love does not enter. Our biological drive, our psychological development, our soul yearning, our spiritual quest— all were intended to help us embrace the vast quality of love. But our hearts have been broken, we have felt betrayed by love's promise, and we have closed down our hearts. Fear and ignorance reign. Our life is lost to safeguarding, calculating, planning, projecting, searching, or waiting. And then death arrives.

Yet, as Carlos Castaneda says, "Death may be the best advisor you have."[16] When you lose someone important to you or realize that your own death is impending, you may understand that your life has been a dream, a play that you have written and produced. All the things you made important were not important after all. What you thought was reality was a dream. The dream of love fulfilled was reality—a reality that, for the most part, you have missed. At that magic moment, you recognize that you will not be remembered for how much wealth you have accumulated, how many sexual encounters you have had, how much you have accomplished, how much you have pleased others, but how much love you have put into your relationships and life.

In the face of death you realize that the pleasures of the material world felt good but they did not ensure love. Never knowing what others will do, you have put up walls. You realize that most of what you had been told about love was a lie. Surrendering, your heart opens and you find yourself filling with an energy that you recognize as love. You are home. For you, there is no death. In love, out of love, in love again. You came into life with an open heart. Something happened and you recoiled. At death you lay down your arms and love is in you, around you, above you, and below you. You remember. That is Love's Way.

Memo

To: You

From: Love

I'm what you need to experience every aspect of being alive, all the facets of what it means to be human, and I give myself to you with no strings attached. With me you will touch everything deeply—other people, the natural world, your soul, your body, your mind, and your heart. I am in you and around you at all times but because you have closed down you will not always know that.

I have given you another gift: love relationships. Because of your confusion, fear, and forgetting, you have designed some clever ways of trying to know me. These are called love illusions. And though I show up from time to time even in those illusions, you must stop deluding yourself. These delusions are not love. They may be exciting, euphoric, predictable, or dramatic, but what you will discover is that they are not love. Based on fear, they allow you to be in a relationship without ever having to sustain your vulnerability. I know your heart has been broken and that you have felt betrayed, but that does not excuse your keeping your heart closed.

When you live in fear and in the memories of your trauma, you forget about me. Think of it. How many times do you stop and thank the people who love you? Who, in spite of the pain and betrayal they have endured, have been strong enough to let you in? How many times do you think of your relationships with these people as gifts and not burdens? How often do you stop and really reflect on how rare and important a love relationship is? How much time in a day do you give to your love relationships? How often do you reach out and say, "I love you" or "Thank you for your love"?

When in fear or indifference, you do not. Your mind is elsewhere. You wallow in your pain; you think of what others have done to you. You say, "Not now, I'm busy," or "I'm too depressed, too angry, too afraid." You think of your children as a burden, pushing them aside when they threaten to interrupt your busy day. What you are really saying is, "I do not have time to love you." You take a love relationship, the very thing that nourishes you and makes life bearable, for granted. You abuse it, you ignore it, you betray it, you refuse it, or you make it unimportant in the scheme of things.

You are even suspicious of a love relationship when you live in past and painful memories. How many times have you trashed your love relationships, put down the people who were there for you? How often have you chased that illusion, the "lover" who abuses you and makes your life miserable? How often have you thought, "I'd rather make another dollar, have an affair, another drink, watch pornography, go hang out with my guru, sleep in"? How often have you said, "I won't receive your love and caring because it makes me feel vulnerable"?

In fear and stress, you become lazy when it comes to love. How often do you simply think of all of the people in your life in loving ways? How many times do you reach out, look someone in the eyes, and really see them? How many times have you cried when a loved one has gone away or died?

Take an inventory. Have you refused to accept responsibility for your own lack of love, your own laziness, your own failure? You are not paralyzed. Your heart still beats. Open your eyes and see me—love. Open your ears and hear me—love. The past is the past. There are no more excuses.

How many more messengers do you need to hear from before you will believe that you are love in disguise and that you have everything you need within you to enjoy the magic of many love relationships, not just one? It is time to be mindful of love, to take the counsel about love you have accumulated over the years and to put it into action. I have told you what love is. And I have told you that I, love, am everywhere. I pass through the darkness, trickle through the universe, and find my way to your heart.

Yes, a love relationship is a precious gift, and too often you live in fear or indifference and do not acknowledge that gift until it is gone. Then you realize how much you have missed, how selfish you have been, how many wonderful opportunities have passed you by. A real love relationship is rare. It needs to be nourished, protected, not taken for granted. You need to think about your love relationships and give them their rightful place. You need to be willing to stick with the uncomfortable parts of love and work them out.

You must stop tossing people away as if they were consumer products. You must stop judging and picking at others. Love relationships are sticky at times, messy and painful. But they will also teach you, heal you, and fulfill the need to belong and connect. They are the mirrors you need to grow into more evolved men and women. And since you have millennia of trauma and confusion to tend to, you must love with noticeable intent. Being human, you won't find the task easy. Yet it is possible. Your love can mature, and the more you love, the more it expands.

I ask you to step out of your illusions and fear, stop trashing the people who love you, who are not afraid to give to you—your children, your friends, your lover, your partner. You can't afford to wait for them to change or appreciate you. Go out of your way. Tell them you value them. Give where it is not noticed, too.

In the cases where you have made love unimportant, go and make amends. A love relationship is not a showplace, a place to take out your aggression, a place to hide your insecurities. It is real, vital, and alive, and it is the very reason you are alive on this planet right now. You do not need to go into solitude to find me. Opportunities are right here in front of you. Everything you need to know about yourself you can learn in your love life. Take advantage of that opportunity.

Your fear will surface, yes. So will your selfishness, your projections, and your insecurities. What a wonderful opportunity a love relationship is, even in its pain and sorrow. If you agree to be in love relationships, you will experience it all. Accept the gift, now. Make the choice to be a person someone can feel safe with.

I am an unfathomable, endless mystery. You have not come close to experiencing your love quotient. You have barely scratched the surface. Don't be afraid to jump in. Yes, sometimes I burn, but I also heal.

Maybe you fell into the swamp. Get up and start climbing the mountain. When you were little, no one had to tell you when it was time to hold your head up, stand on your own two feet, and take your first step. You knew it was time. And you probably fell a few times, felt disappointment, and cried. But you did not stop. You responded to that inner urge to be and become who you are:

upright, mobile, independent. And now if I asked you how it is you walk, you would laugh at me; it's so natural and easy. And so it is with me—love.

Good luck.

CHAPTER TWO

The Illusions of Love

□ □ □

Life seems to fear love itself because the moments of experiencing its safety, freedom, and power have been so scarce. Perry's story is eloquent testimony to this truth.

Lying on the closet floor in musty darkness, a four-year-old boy ties his feet together with an old tie of his father's and feels the beating of his heart. A strange feeling of arousal charges through his body. He waits in anticipation for someone to come and find him, jerk him by the arm, or pull him by the leg—and, once again, beat him. He knows he was bad. Bursting with energy and excitement he could not contain, he had once again left the confines of the yard his parents had told him never to leave, in order to climb his favorite tree. His mother's piercing screams got his attention, and, terrified, he ran home. She grabbed him and scolded him, "Wait till your father gets home; he'll take care of you!" He knows the meaning of those words. He goes to his room and into the security of his closet. Fear races through his small body and mind. He ties himself even tighter.

"I wonder when he will be home?"

"How bad will it be this time?"

"Maybe she won't tell him how bad I was."

"Why can't you love me?"

"No, I can't cry."

"I can't be afraid."

Perry enters a world where there is no time. He is at the top of the closet watching himself. No more fear, no more tears. He has gone to a place where no one can touch him, where he is *safe*.

For what seems like eternity there are no sounds, no feelings.

The unmistakable sound of his father's car coming up the driveway jerks him back into his body and reality. The familiar sound of footsteps walking to the closet door confirms that the time has come. Frozen in terror, Perry waits for the punishment due a "bad child." He doesn't have to wait long, and he is glad. Once it is over with, he can fall into a state of relief—one he has begun to look forward to. Father takes off his belt, pulls down Perry's pants, and wallops him again and again and again. Mother peeks from the kitchen, and though she winces, she says nothing.

He feels totally alone, abandoned by both of his parents. His heart, once open to love for his parents, is beginning to hide. He can't help it. It just happens. Deep inside is a loving, vibrantly alive child who will grow up and be compelled to do unto others what has been done unto him.

Perry had all but dismissed the experiences or told himself that they were a normal part of childhood. He grew up, as most children do, with unhealed fear and grief. He did not realize that his emotions were frozen in his body. What got him to therapy was his love for his little daughter. He loved her free spirit and her exuberance for life, and was confused by the rageful feelings that came up inside him, the competition he felt. "I couldn't be a kid, why should you?" he heard himself say to her in his mind. Often he felt numb and could not feel the love for her he knew he had. And he did not seem in charge of these experiences.

The spiritual work he had done remained his anchor and directed him to seek help. He was concerned for himself and his daughter. He did not feel safe within himself, and, when his daughter pulled away from him in fear, he knew she did not feel safe, either. He knew from his spiritual practice that there are two ways of living: in fear or in love. "*Where there is fear, love does not enter.*"

This story has a good ending. In a therapy session he began to reenact the earlier story he had all but forgotten. As he followed the sensations in his body he imagined himself in the closet, his childhood place of refuge. Rather than leaving his body this time, he stayed with the sensations. Instead of arousing himself by tightening the knot he untied himself. He left the closet and let out the anger he felt. "Stop hitting me. I am your little boy. You should love me. I am not bad, I am curious. I am your only son.

Love me, Daddy." The anger turned to deep sobbing. When the sobs subsided, in his mind Perry turned to his mother and exclaimed: "And where were you? You said you loved me. You should have stopped him. He gets crazy and you let him."

This time, in his mind, his parents stopped and listened. They knew he was right. They could not look him in the eye. At that point he brought his wise adult self into the scene, who took young Perry by the hand and asked him if he was ready to leave his parents in their shame and come with the older Perry. He was. He had been locked in that closet long enough. Perry's body began to tremble, and when it was over he let out a sigh of relief. A smile came to his face. Placing his hand naturally on his heart, he felt deep love for little Perry. Tears of reconciliation filled his eyes. He felt safe once again.

Now his daughter could begin to trust him and feel safe, too.

A HEART BETRAYED

No sooner do we begin to know other people than we discover their broken heart.

—Jacob Needleman, *A Little Book on Love*

Young Perry's heart ached. He longed for a father and mother's love. When he realized it was not there he felt betrayed. Not having the words or perceived power to stand up for himself, he gave up. Love illusion began standing in fatally for the loss of trust. It usually does. How can it be otherwise? Trauma leads to betrayal leads to loss of trust leads to fear leads to broken heart leads to love illusion. Trauma moved him out of love.

I wish none of us had ever been traumatized. We were. I wish our hearts were more open to love. They are not. It is not our fault that we were traumatized, and we could not help but be affected. We are not crazy, but many of the adaptations we, like Perry, designed to reorganize our lives into some sense of normalcy after traumatic experiences seem crazy, and we can end up recreating old dramas that are crazy, too. (How often have you said and done things you promised yourself you would never say or do in your relationships? How many times have you said and done things that were done to you that you feared or hated?) It is as though we are in a rut and we cannot see our way out. Like Perry, we started out in life living Love's Way. Because of trauma we move to a life organized around fear and get trapped in a damage-control mode.

At the base of love relationship problems is a violation of trust. We have all experienced such violations in some form or another. Because of the betrayal of trust, we want and yet fear closeness. Our fear is both biological and psychological, and it runs deep. Since we are meant to be in relationship, we have no choice but to figure out a way to be involved with others. Love illusions become our answer. They are quite clever and often get passed off as the real thing. Sometimes you have to look very closely to notice the difference. But we really do know in our hearts and in our souls when we have been fooled, when we are fooling ourselves, and when we are just plain fooling around.

I do not need to tell you that our relationships are in trouble. Read the paper, listen to the daily news. I do not need to remind you that the rush of authentic love through our veins happens less often than we would like it to. Nor do I need to tell you that the rush of intoxicating feelings is not love. But I will, just for a reminder, speak to love illusions that I have written of before. But before I take that on, let's look at trauma, the culprit most likely behind the illusions we pass off as love. There are four kinds of trauma, and we are bound to have experienced at least one of them: post-traumatic stress, shock trauma, trauma of omission, and trauma of commission.

TRAUMAS OF ALL KINDS

When we hear the word "trauma," most of us probably think of a single, horrific experience that leaves us in terror: being in a serious accident, witnessing violence or a murder, being raped or physically assaulted, being kidnapped, or being in a war or a natural disaster such as an earthquake, flood, or tornado. Such life-threatening or chaotic events can overwhelm our psyches and flood us emotionally, and as a result we are likely to experience *post-traumatic stress disorder (PTSD)*. We are catapulted into another reality so quickly that we cannot process it adequately. Often thrust outside the range of normal human experience, the victim becomes an outsider watching the world go by. We feel alone and isolated from others by our unique experience.

Though often given less attention than PTSD, there are other seemingly routine life events that create *shock trauma:* surgeries, accidents, difficult prebirth and birth experiences, hospitalizations, sudden loss, peer shaming, school beatings, public shaming, or extended high-stress situations.

But even if we have not gone through such shattering events, we are likely to have suffered traumas of a different kind. As we have heard and will hear in the personal stories throughout this book, in our development as children there were specific tasks and experiences we all needed in order to ensure our ability to form loving relationships. We needed to hear certain words that affirmed it was okay to be who we are, feel what we feel, need what we need, think our own thoughts, do and explore, succeed in our own unique way, be important, trust and be close, separate and grow, be well, and be glad we are alive. We needed permission and role modeling on how to do all of those things safely. For many and varied reasons our caretakers could not or would not completely affirm all these experiences, and we began believing we had to earn or perform or deny in order to be loved. Whether this neglect was intentional or unintentional does not matter. Adequate nurturing, protection, and wise guidance from our caretakers are critical to forming healthy love relationships in our adult lives.

It is my belief that none of us got what we needed developmentally in just the way we needed it. That is part of the human dilemma. So be it. Yet these deprivations—call them *Trauma of Omission*—left us with unhealed wounds and negative belief structures about others and ourselves. We walk around oblivious to the holes in our psyches, pain in our bodies, and constrictions of our hearts—unfinished business we unknowingly strive to finish in our adult relationships. The object of our love is the one designated to fix us.

There is also *trauma of commission*—things said and done to children that never should have been said and done. Sometimes adults who have claimed to love them perpetrate these events on children. Children are beaten, screamed at, and told they are sick, stupid, and never should have been born. They are told to shut up and go away. They are abused sexually by people they trusted, or are left with unsafe caretakers who abuse them. Such traumas can have far more damaging consequences to our love relationships than the traumas of omission, as Perry's story clearly shows. Perry understood love. He knew his daughter was love. He also knew his behavior and violent tendencies did not generate a feeling of warmth and safety. It was as though something inside of him wanted to project outward. On a biological and psychological level, what was happening had an explanation.

Trauma generates fear and even terror. I have known people who panic when they think of a commitment to a love relationship. Their hearts are under lock and key. In a euphoric state of sexual excitement or romantic high, they may open up temporarily to feed the senses and then go back and lock them. In a therapy session a client so aptly put it: "I have seven gates around my heart. The closest I have let anyone get is to gate 3. Only I have the keys. The more they push to get in, the more I resist." At forty-five years of age and after two failed marriages and numerous romantic liaisons, he has not known sustained, committed love and views others pushing as the problem. In truth, he has old unhealed wounds and fear behind the gates. He may look at himself as a warrior, and until he has the courage to expose his heart, he remains in a self-imposed prison. This man may know sexual and romantic love, but until he unlocks the gates, he will not know sustained love. It is time for warriors to project the energy of love into the world. And in order to do that they may need to acknowledge their traumas of omission or commission and feel the primal fears, grief, and anger and put it to rest.

Many stay in toxic relationships out of fear. Others say yes when they want to say no. Some people would rather manipulate than ask directly for what they want. Still others become what others want them to be and don't make waves. All of these behaviors suggest the presence of an underlying fear. Too many people are stuck in fear as immobilizing as Perry's was. Many more do not even know it or will not admit to it and play on the edge of love. They fool themselves and others and believe they are in love.

We are programmed to avoid fear at all costs. And why not? When fear is present it feels as though we are losing control of our sanity, or perhaps of life itself. As I work with clients and unpeel the onion of fear, deeper and deeper levels are inevitably exposed. I have heard something like the following hundreds of times:

"Why are you afraid to tell him what you want?"

"I fear he may get mad at me."

"And if he gets mad at you?"

"I fear he will leave."

"And if he leaves?"

"I fear I will get very depressed."

"And if you get depressed?"

"I may never come out of it."

"And if you don't come out?"

"I will get sick or feel crazy."

"And if you are sick long enough, or feel crazy long enough, what do you fear?"

"Death."

THE ILLUSIONS OF LOVE

Until we are free from fear, we may climb the highest mountain, invent every kind of God, but we will remain in darkness.

—J. Krishnamurti, *On Fear*

Love and fear do not coexist. Though both are available to us, only one reigns at a time. It is as though fear is competing with love to control our heart and keep love out. Though love is greater, fear is fierce. We have been hurt, we have been betrayed, and we are determined not to be that vulnerable again. Come close, we say, but not too close. Come in, but only for a while. We put on a good face, we play a good game, and we think no one will notice. We have all experienced violations of trust; we have all undergone trauma. Out of these experiences, along with the many warped ideas we have been taught about love, we have built up powerful illusions about what love is. In many cases, these illusions are so deep, intense, and tenacious that we can call them addictions at their worst and unhealthy dependencies at their best.

In my previous writing I have gone into depth describing how sex, love, and romance have become dependencies and even addictions. Words we often associate with addiction include *obsessive, excessive, destructive, compulsive, habitual, attached,* and *dependent.* And when you think about it, some of those words are also used to talk about our love relationships. Now that we have an expanded definition of love we are no longer excused. Love is real—it is not an addiction. Our assignment is to identify and then do what we can to keep unhealthy dependency and addiction out of our love lives so that we can experience more *in love* moments. Let me stress one more time that love relationships are not black-and-white, either/or, but have elements of love and love's illusion. There are healthy and unhealthy dependencies. After all, we are all related.

In love illusion, which I have referred to as love addiction, we rely on someone external to the self in an attempt to resolve trauma, get unmet needs fulfilled, avoid fear or emotional pain, keep people around, and maintain balance. *The paradox is that in our attempts to gain control of our lives, we go out of control by giving personal power to someone other than the self.* Love addiction is often associated with feelings of "never having enough" or "not being enough." It attempts to satisfy our developmental hunger for security, sensation, power, belonging, and meaning. Love addiction is also a form of passivity in that we do not directly resolve our own problems but attempt to collude with others so they will take care of us. *We willingly take care of others at our own emotional expense, or we attempt to control others to meet our needs at their expense.*

No matter how it plays out, we look to others to "fix" our fear, pain, and discomfort and tolerate or inflict abusive behaviors in the process. We use and abuse. This other can be any important person in our life that we unconsciously hook up with: a child, a parent, a friend, a boss, a spouse, or a lover. Or, as in romance or sexual compulsion, it can be someone we don't even know personally.

Our dependency on others may or may not include a romantic or sexual component. When the object of love is, or has been, our romantic and sexual partner, the stakes run high. What we witness daily in the news confirms that the more extreme cases of sex, love, and romance addiction can be lethal. Homicide, suicide, stalking, rape, incest, AIDS, and domestic violence capture the headlines. Love addiction can range from an unhealthy dependency sanctioned by society to violence and abuse abhorred but nevertheless promulgated by that same society. If millions of people got high on the daily drama of the O. J. Simpson trial or the Clinton-Lewinsky affair on TV, one can begin to imagine what it is like to actually be in such a drama. The neurochemistry of melodramatic love can become a drug as difficult to get off as alcohol or cocaine.

A MYTH: TRISTAN AND ISEULT

Love stories have been around forever. They are filled with pathos and longing. During the Middle Ages, one of the most beautiful and tragic epic tales was the first story in Western literature to describe the mysterious terrain of love. It inspired many great love stories, including *Romeo and Juliet*. Traveling minstrels would sing the ballad of the handsome knight Tristan and his fatal love for the beautiful Queen Iseult.[1] As we will see, this great story is a classic illustration of the costs of love's illusion, perhaps even of love's addictions. Though love is there, too, at some point Tristan and Iseult lose their way.

Long ago, there was a beautiful maiden who fell in love with a brave and handsome knight; after many trials, she married him. In their deep love they conceived a child, whom the knight would not live to see. As is usual for brave knights, he was summoned to battle, never to return. The shock of his death was so great that the maiden fell ill, but she lived long enough to give birth to a son she named Tristan, which means "sadness."

After her death, her uncle, King Mark of Cornwall, adopted the child. Tristan grew up heroically and was prepared for knighthood. In a required test of his bravery, he killed a monstrous Irish giant, Morholt. But in the process he was wounded with a poisonous barb. Certain he would die, he asked to be set afloat with his sword and harp without oars or sail. His boat drifted near the coast of Ireland where he was rescued by the queen of Ireland herself and her beautiful daughter, Iseult the Fair. He told his tale to them both, with no mention that he had killed Morholt, whom he knew to be the queen's brother. Possessed with powers of healing, Iseult nursed Tristan back to health and sent him on his way home.

Time passed, and one day King Mark, standing at the castle window, saw a bird carrying a beautiful golden hair in its beak. So enthralled was he that he decided he must find the maiden to whom it belonged and make her his queen. Tristan was sent to find her. On perilous seas he found himself shipwrecked. He landed in Ireland, where once again he was in need of being nursed by Iseult. Only this time she learned that it had been he who had slain her uncle, and she determined to kill him. With sword in hand she went to the baths to kill Tristan, but seeing him in his naked beauty, she stopped short.

Tristan told her the nature of his mission, to find the fair maiden to marry his uncle the king. She said she was the very maiden the king sought and that she would like to be a queen. She laid down the sword and spared Tristan's life.

Tristan was on his way to bring the fair maiden to his uncle, the king. At sea, Iseult asked her maid to bring refreshments to her and Tristan. The maid grabbed a small flask filled with a powerful love potion prepared by the queen herself to ensure a great wedding night for her daughter and King Mark. Thirsty and unaware, Tristan and Iseult drank the love potion, and soon thereafter felt pangs of passionate love for each other. Absolutely inseparable in heart, soul, and flesh, in a moment their destiny was fixed and inescapable. Physical union was inevitable.

Despite the deep passion he felt for Iseult and the catastrophic betrayal of his uncle that union with her meant, Tristan was determined to honor the code of knighthood and see that Iseult got to King Mark. All went well. On the night of the wedding, Iseult's maid crept into the royal bedroom and consummated the marriage in her place.

It did not take long before the king's barons told him that Tristan and Iseult had been lovers. Angered by the betrayal, the king banished Tristan. The lovers continued their passionate meetings and, learning of Tristan's impending execution at the direction of King Mark, they hid in the forest. Their life was increasingly harsh and difficult.

Now it came to pass that, unbeknownst to them, the power of the love potion was set to wear off in three years. And when the three years passed, they began to feel guilt and discontent. Tristan began to miss the court life of a knight and Iseult began to miss being a queen. And so, after more travails and longing for the worldly pleasures, the couple decided to return to the king and ask for his forgiveness. They reestablished themselves in the good graces of King Mark.

Reinstated as a knight, Tristan set out on many brave adventures. Alone for some time, he gradually began to miss the company of Iseult the Fair, and, in a moment of nostalgia, he married a beautiful woman with her name, Iseult of the White Hands. Still longing for the original Iseult, he could not make love to his new bride.

Time passed. Tristan continued in knightly battles until one day he was seriously wounded. About to die, he asked to be reunited with his original love, Iseult the Fair. Upon being notified of his request, she set out at once, sending a message that her ship would carry a white flag. Knowing this, Tristan's jealous wife deceived Tristan and told him that the sail on the approaching ship was black as doom. Tristan felt despair and pined to death just as the ship landed. Iseult the Fair, tormented at finding Tristan dead, lay beside him and succumbed to death.

As this tale shows, "fatal attraction" is as old as time itself. Passionate stories, to stay hot, seem to need danger and agony. Passion, by its very nature, includes calamity. Passionate love of another may elevate us for a while, but it also afflicts us. In this myth, as in so many others, love arrives out of the blue. It hits Tristan and Iseult, and the rest of the story seems out of their control. Abducted by love itself, they cannot resist. Love has its own edicts and physical laws. The lovers feel anguish, not because they are in love, but because they are in love with being in love. What they need to maintain the melancholy of their love's illusions is their absence from one another, not their togetherness. When the potion wears off they are bored with each other and with life. Tristan and Iseult's story is not unlike the illusions of love we hear about today. Love, sex, and romance still seem to capture us. Though intended to help us get into love and show our virtues, we want to capture and hang on to the experience, and we believe it is love itself. We often die there—if not physically, then mentally, emotionally, and even spiritually. Love addiction shows up in all three ways in the story: dependent love, romance, and sex.

DEPENDENT LOVE
On an unconscious level dependent love is nothing but a misguided search to fulfill our unmet dependency needs. We attach

ourselves to others and take care of them at our own emotional
expense, or we try to control them so they'll meet our needs at
their expense. A key element in identifying dependent love is
how we feel when the person disapproves of us, disagrees with
us, moves away from us, or threatens us. An escalation of behaviors occurs when the love object threatens to leave us psychologically or physically.

Dependent love is always self-serving. It survives on myths: "I
will take care of your fears and inadequacies so you will take care
of mine." "If you fail me, I will do whatever it takes to keep you
around." "But since I do not know how to be intimate or I fear intimacy, I will allow only so much closeness before I push you
away." In dependent love the phrase "What a catch" has a whole
new meaning. My psyche will scan the prospects and catch the
partner who will assist me as I reenact my inner landscape. If I
believe men are never there when you need them most, I will find
that kind of man. If I need a woman who won't support me, I will
find her. Our attractions are psychological as well as physical.

ROMANCE ADDICTION

Romance addiction refers to those relationships in which the object of love addiction is also a romantic object. This person can be
a romantic partner or live only in someone's fantasies. The fix is
an elaborate fantasy life not unlike a romance novel or the euphoria of a new romance itself. The rush of intoxicating feelings experienced during the attraction stage of a romance becomes the
drug that can become a substitute for real intimacy. "Limerance,"
the pursuit of this high, can become an addiction in itself. Often it
becomes a dramatic obsession that results in the stalking of the
romantic love object by the obsessed. An internal fantasy life of
perfected love can drive a person.

Lisa, a client, admitted that she chose unavailable men, often
men who lived on other parts of the globe. When they were not
around, she would bathe herself in the soothing, often exhilarating biochemicals of romantic fantasies. She lived in a future of
perfected love. She was also in grief, having discovered that her
latest romantic love (of three intense weeks) did not see the future
in the same way and did not want to continue. She recognized a
sharp pain in her heart.

When I asked her what her fantasies did for her, she realized that they attempted to create the "perfect" childhood she never had. She also recognized that they were safer than risking not being wanted. Even though she professed grief for the relationship that was ending, the thought of entering a long-term relationship only to discover she would not be wanted was too risky for her. She not only carried her own legacies in her body and psyche, she carried the fears of her mother, who became pregnant to ensure that Lisa's father would stay.

I asked her if she was ready to give up the illusion of perfected love and simply be in the relationship now. The ineffable potency of sweet new love was not the problem, it was avoiding a frightful past and living in an all-consuming romantic future. It was a dead end. Though she escaped through a rich fantasy life, she would need to keep her suitors at arm's length. Lisa's fear has validity. It, as well as her pleasure chemicals, resides within. The drama of her unresolved childhood trauma will be repeated over and over. Little Lisa was still in search of the perfected childhood she never had.

Total immersion in the romantic relationship or fantasy can consume the addictive person. Since the romantic high is dependent on the newness of the relationship or the presence of a person, romance addiction is filled with victim/persecutor melodrama and sadomasochism. Living on the edge of love is a rush. Bizarre acting out behaviors are often a by-product.

Romance can be a double-edged sword. On the one hand, because we are so stimulated, we allow ourselves to open the gates, fall in love, show our soul, and let another see who we are. In fact, we may surprise ourselves with what we find: chivalry, kindness, nonjudgment, awe, passion, compassion, and a desire to connect, nourish, and protect.

Romance can also cut us off from our spirit and community when we become a bit crazy and obsess about the object of our love. We jump from the swamp to the tip of the mountain and want to stay there forever! When a romantic relationship ends, so do our virtues. Recently a client was in grief, having ended what he claimed was the most complete love relationship of his life. He felt desperate to be in yet another relationship so he could feel that way again. What I reminded him was that his lover had not put anything in him that was not already there. In a sense, the romantic relationship had given him permission to be his real self, and in that regard it was a gift. I asked him to reflect on how he was in the relationship that he liked. He responded: "I was free, I was more fun, I laughed, I enjoyed life, I was kinder." I then asked him how he was as a little boy. He recalled being sent to his room for being too exuberant. He rarely had fun, and open affection was frowned upon. He got the message. He did not have to wait for another person to open those gates. The experiences he had were potentially there all along and were his to energize as he so chose.

SEXUAL ADDICTION
The power of sexual love is unequaled. According to author Mark Laaser, normal sexual love is often distorted, repressed, or forbidden by religion or families, and sexual addiction can be the result. Laaser writes, "Sexual addiction is a sickness involving any type of uncontrollable sexual activity which results in negative consequences."[2] When obsessive-compulsive sexual behavior is left unattended, it causes distress and despair for the individuals, their partners, and their families.

Denial causes the sexual addict to distort reality, ignore the problem, blame others, and give numerous justifications for his or her out-of-control behavior. Perhaps the negative consequences of sexual compulsion will motivate society to take this problem more seriously. People are dying of AIDS, sexual violence continues, professionals are publicly shamed, and there are unwanted pregnancies, lost jobs, arrests, and broken relationships. Sexual exploitation by people in positions of power seems epidemic. The cost of this addiction to our society is more than financial. The fabric of our spiritual, emotional, and relational lives is affected as well.

A pioneer in the field, Patrick Carnes, stresses that sex is not about good or bad; rather it is the behaviors that accompany sex that determine whether or not it is an addiction. According to Carnes, sexual behavior that involves the exploitation of others, is nonmutual, objectifies people, is dissatisfying, involves shame, or is based on fear indicates the presence of sexual addiction.

His research points out grim facts. Of the sex addicts researched, 97 percent suffered emotional abuse, 81 percent experienced sexual abuse, and 72 percent reported physical abuse.[3] Childhood trauma among those who become sex addicts generates core beliefs that become the organizing principle of their relationships in adulthood: "I am basically a bad or unworthy person"; "No one would love me as I am"; "My needs are never going to be met if I have to depend on others"; "Sex is my most important need"; "Everyone is out for him- or herself." For sex addicts, these trauma wounds must be healed and trust restored before they can experience sacred sexuality that includes the experience of love.

THE ROLE OF CULTURE

We don't get our distorted views about love in a vacuum. To comprehend how and where we have learned erroneous ideas about love, romance, and sex, we must look beyond trauma and fear to examine our culture. The lessons that are available when we do so are both subtle and blatant. So extensive is this mass cultural phenomenon and so deeply internalized is it in our psyche that we often fail to see our culture's misguided direction. We use what we are hearing, seeing, and experiencing as the rationale for the hurtful and destructive behaviors we pass off as love. To ease our guilt and shame, we need to learn to recognize the many ways in which our culture reinforces destructive behaviors. Recognizing how relentlessly the ideas of love and other addictions are thrown at us every day of our lives can help us develop compassion for ourselves and for those we have hurt.

We live in a culture of image and ownership. We are measured by how good we look, how much we have, and whether we have someone by our side who supports a good image of ourselves. Fewer than 2 percent of the population fit the beautiful supermodel standards, and yet we strive to emulate those standards. Research shows that men constantly exposed to beautiful models are less satisfied in their own personal love relationships. We have, sadly, been groomed to look outside ourselves for happiness and love. Our obsession with love pervades every aspect of popular culture, from Madison Avenue to Disney World, from romance novels to rock and pop song lyrics. It even permeates great works of fiction, poetry, drama, and art.

Each day, in a variety of ways, our society encourages us to seek addictive relationships. Our culture idealizes, dramatizes, and models a dependency that says we cannot live without another person. Witness the plots of popular gothic romances or soap operas marketed to both men and women; typically they are odes to consumptive love.

Our need to share love is legitimate. The problem is that culture has instilled in us such an unrealistic need for others that we sometimes become dependent, addictive, neurotic, or parasitic. We let others dictate our happiness. We become dependent almost unconsciously. And then we resent our dependence. At times we may even become hateful, projecting the hate onto others. Our society trains us to be "effective" at getting what we want, and when we can't get others to give us what we want when we want it, we feel anxious, even to the point of violence. For proof, all we need to do is turn on the news: "Young woman ends abusive love relationship and is brutally murdered." "CEO charged with sexual harassment." "Coach sued for child support by a former lover." "Domestic abuse charges filed by wife of quarterback."

THE ROLE OF SPIRITUAL QUESTS

Many would say that experiencing our spiritual nature is as profound an experience as we humans can undergo. We are not talking about a specific religion, though religion can play a role. Spiritual pursuits may be defined as those that transport a person beyond material needs and worldly pleasures on a very personal, profound quest for meaning that aligns us with a higher purpose for our lives. Our spirit seeks to continue growing. Like the blade of grass that pushes through hard dirt to reach toward the sun, we too continue to quest for the experience of awe, wonder, mystery—union with God. In spirit, we can experience love everywhere and in everything. When we become intimately involved with something or someone we experience a growing love for that thing or person—the ocean, a sunrise, a painting, our children, our lover, our friend, our creative pursuits, and yes, even our enemy.

Spiritual questing is meant to guide us to stop looking outside of ourselves for happiness. Instead of regarding love relationships as our source of happiness, we are asked to see them as places to express our happiness as well as other higher emotions: compassion, sorrow, gratitude, and joy. Love is generated from within. We are mere conduits of love, and we desire to share it. When we experience such a shared moment, it is a moment of "oneness." We experience ourselves in the other.

Spiritually, we long to share our self. Once we know that we are capable of such a "divine experience," we seek it. Some even become addicted to the spiritual high of ecstasy, bliss, awe, and transcendence and choose to live more in that reality than in practical daily life. Though it is natural for us as spiritual beings to yearn for transcendent experiences through which we merge with something greater, this must come through a gradual and balanced process. Some people feel an urgency about these experiences, and their experiments result in highs not unlike those resulting from experimentation with chemicals. When the spiritual "turn-on" is the goal, a person can become addicted to it. They deceive themselves and call it spiritual love. The process of avoiding a painful reality by reaching for such highs begins to define a person.

Because few people have learned how to develop their spirituality, they may embrace love addiction in the misguided belief that dependent merging with another is the highest spiritual experience. And it's easy to understand how this confusion occurs, for at the beginning of a love relationship, one often feels euphoria and ecstasy of almost mystical proportions, and rational thought is subordinated.

Obsessive, erotic love is often a misplaced attempt to achieve that fusion we so deeply desire. We want to end the feelings of isolation caused by our learned restraints against true intimacy. In a sexually aroused state, one is often willing to suspend those restraints in order to merge with another. If the merger is dependent and immature, the result is love illusion. Life energy is directed toward the pursuit of gratification rather than toward growth. As Erich Fromm said in *The Art of Loving*: "This desire for interpersonal fusion is the most powerful striving in man. It is the most fundamental passion, it is the force which keeps the human race together . . . . Erotic love . . . is the craving for complete fusion. It is by its very nature exclusive and not universal."[4] Without agape, universal love of others, it remains narcissistic.

STEPPING OUT OF TRAUMA:
CREATING SAFETY

We have lived in grids of fear for thousands of years. We fear abandonment, we fear we are not enough, we fear surrendering. This force, fear, has been scientifically measured. Unlike the wave of love, fear's frequency stunts our growth. We are now collecting scientific evidence of this important fact. Transforming the energy contained in fear to an energetic love frequency is the greatest opportunity our relationships have to offer us. Nowhere but in our relationships will we be so greatly challenged.[5] It may be relatively easy to surrender to love while meditating alone on a mountain, holding our newborn child, or saying good-bye to one leaving us in death. We all know that the real challenge is to surrender our personal self to another member of the adult human species. After all, wasn't it other humans who betrayed or hurt us?

Even if another has not betrayed us, aren't we all prone to the belief that the world or life will let us down? Everyday life bombards us with reinforcement for these two "facts"—war, natural disasters, mass murders, corporate downsizing, and domestic violence. And as if this is not enough, we learn that our family or friends are talking about us behind our back, our partner has been sleeping with our best friend, our business partner has been stealing money from us. We are told there is only one path to God and we are not on it. We are verbally, mentally, sexually abused in a myriad of ways. We have developed a suspicion of others and of life without even realizing it. This suspicion becomes so well disguised that we begin to think that fear is our true nature.[6]

Given all of this, why would you expect to feel safe enough to entrust yourself to another? How many relationships have you had where you felt so safe that you were willing to be totally vulnerable to the other? Count them. How many people have let you down?

Fear, fear, and more fear. There is no end to it. Fear is in our bodies, fear is in our psychological beliefs, fear is promulgated by our culture, and fear is in our religious teachings. Is there any hope that we can move beyond it so we can live more of our lives in love? Yes!

Love has told us it is a power so great that it can pick us up and throw us across the room. It can melt a tumor, soften a heart, and erase the memories that hardened it. It is the power that pushes and pulls the essence of the child into being in spite of great odds. It heals, it nourishes, and it is green and growing. No matter how hard our emotional lives have been, most of us have touched love's power or we would not have survived our trauma. Love is an unlimited resource ready to be harnessed. It cuts through fear. To do so, however, requires moving from a "not safe to trust" to a "safe to trust" posture. It is that experience precisely that heals the heart.

BASIC TRUST
When we come to the end of all of the light we know and must step into the darkness of the unknown, we must believe that we will find something firm to stand on or that we will be taught to fly.

—Author unknown

There is a fundamental condition whose presence or absence has more to say about our ability to love than anything else. This something is what is known as *Basic Trust*. Basic Trust is not your ordinary psychological sense of trust. It is far greater and subtler. It is implicit, unquestioned, unformulated! By understanding its presence we can see why, for some people, surrendering to love seems relatively easy and for others it is a lot more difficult. Those who have it do not question Basic Trust; they probably don't even question its existence. When they see others without it they wonder why they are having difficulties. This sense of trust says that everything is as it should be even when life is painful and uncertain, love seems missing, or someone you love has betrayed you. It says that there is a divine order and a presence that sustains you, that the universe is fundamentally good, trustworthy, and loving and wishes you the best. Or, at the very least, it means you no harm. Basic Trust says that what happens is the best that can happen in the moment, given the circumstances of the human condition.

When Basic Trust is deep, we wear our hearts on our sleeves and walk confidently into life and love relationships. It is so much a part of our fabric that we do not give it a second thought. It just is! It's not based on a person, event, or situation, so nothing can disrupt it. When you're in Basic Trust you know deep in your bones that you are okay and that you will be taken care of no matter what happens. There is an unspoken confidence that if you have plunked yourself into a love relationship, you will have what you need to deal with whatever comes along.

Having Basic Trust allows you to accept yourself and others as and where they are, without personalizing their behavior. You stop trying to change them, grasping onto them, or manipulating them to give you what you need. Living in Basic Trust, you are free to explore potential love relationships without fear of rejection. Life is a smorgasbord of people, experiences, and exciting, energizing risk-taking. If life or love hurts you, you can feel the pain of it and yet remain resilient. With Basic Trust you put out effort in your love relationships, you suffer, and yet you are not attached to outcomes or the suffering. You do your part and let go.

When our relationships do not feel safe, we need to create communities of choice, which is what Perry and Lisa had to do to feel safe enough to bring forth that which they feared. Though our relationships are the most likely places to reenact our fear-based dramas, paradoxically, they can also be the places where we heal our hearts. To do so, however, we must create an atmosphere of absolute safety. Feeling safe was the very first task we had as a developing human being. When we were children we trusted ourselves to know what we needed by responding to our inner sensing, then to effectively alert the world that the need was present. When the response was warm and loving we felt great and began trusting others and life itself.

THE HOLDING ENVIRONMENT

We must have had some experiences of Basic Trust or we would not be as willing as we are to continue reaching out to people. It always amazes me that in spite of the awful betrayals we suffer, we continue to seek to know Love's Way. How much Basic Trust we have or how frequently we act from that place in our love life depends on our formative years. We started out with Basic Trust. To continue trusting, our initial "holding" environment (as described by D. W. Winnicott, an important figure in the British objects relation school) needs to be one we feel safe in as our "core seed," or unique self, unfolds. While our mother is central to this holding environment, that environment includes all of our early life experiences: the condition of our mother's womb, the demeanor of the people who greeted us at birth and those who held us as infants, the general feel of the physical world we were dropped into, the safety of the places we first explored, the amount and type of stimulus we received, and the relationships in our family. Our early container included everything: physical, psychological, emotional, mental, spiritual. If our world was in order and we were held in a supportive and loving manner, we felt safe, protected, secure, and loved. We were in a state of attunement or bliss, and we did not and do not question trust. We are prepared for love and loving.

Perhaps we can see physical holding as a metaphor for the more universal holding we experience in Basic Trust. Infants love to be held by Father or Mother. They take delight in feeling the warmth of the parent's body, the support of the arms, and the beating of the heart, which reminds them of the womb. In fact, they need holding—with love—to thrive physically as well as emotionally. Anyone can touch or hold a baby, but it is the child who experiences love in the holding that develops a sense of Basic Trust so necessary to adult love relationships. D. W. Winnicott puts it this way:

> It should be noted that mothers who have it in them to provide good-enough care can be enabled to do a better job by being cared for themselves in a way that acknowledges the essential nature of the task. Mothers who do not have it in them to provide good-enough care cannot be made good enough by mere instruction.
>
> Holding includes especially the physical holding of the infant, which is a form of loving. It is perhaps the only way in which a mother can show the infant her love. There are those who can hold an infant and those who cannot; the latter quickly produce in the infant a sense of insecurity, and distressed crying.[7]

Adults who lacked physical and emotional bonding experiences as children are in desperate need of caring communities to give them what they lacked as children so they can pass on caring experiences to their children, friends, and partners.

But what happens if, like Perry, our first experiences with those who hold us are shocking, chaotic, or hostile to us? First and foremost, our innocence is shattered; Basic Trust is gone. We now realize that what we had we can no longer take for granted. If these disruptions come only now and then, we can forget about them and get back to trusting the world and the universe that holds us. We can return to the state of nonchalance and continue our individuation process. That process allows us to grow in our capacity for mature human loving. We learn what it means to merge and hold our uniqueness at the same time. We develop from the inside out into the world naturally. Our soul flourishes. But if the disruptions continue or come to dominate our relations with our parents, fear and apprehension ensure that distrust will replace the sense of Basic Trust in reality that our souls know.

Our bodies begin tensing as we try to become our own holding container. We will look for ways to adapt to the world. We will learn to manipulate others to keep them around. We lose contact with our unique souls. The ego will falsify itself and construct a story that is filled with drama to keep others around. Yet a longing for this ecstatic state that we have known remains a part of us. We bring this to all of our love relationships. We long to be recognized, to be understood, to be held and supported. Beyond physical, emotional, and mental support, we seek a safe place where our souls and spirits can thrive and the heart can relax long enough to let love enter.

The challenge we have in our love relationships is to become aware that there are holes in our Basic Trust that we are projecting onto others. We want loving intimacy and fear it. As we allow ourselves to own this, we begin the healing process. This will not be easy, since most likely we have a history of painful trauma and betrayals of all sorts that tend to shift our attention from healing to suspicion about trust: "It is not safe to trust." "The world is a mess." "Love is a joke, some New Age crap." "I do not want to get hurt again." We must not deny the inner buzzing of these emotionally charged ideas. The story line has elements of truth. As we learn to sort out the truth from the fiction, we begin to live in Basic Trust again. We begin to say, "Yes, there is corruption, evil, pain in life; but there are also synchronicities, lessons, goodness."

"We can heal from pain." "There are safe people who will support me." "I have what it takes to deal with this." "I am not alone." Acknowledging the holes in our holding environment and the beliefs that sustain them is a step to reclaiming Basic Trust and ourselves.

As you change to more supportive expressions and live them, you invite a supportive response from the world. And each time there is a loving response, you remember Basic Trust. Basic Trust builds, and you begin to live in it. Your body relaxes, your ego decides to risk again. *Love naturally dwells there.* Each time you confront a fear and learn you survived it, you get closer to your fundamental nature.

To build Basic Trust:

- Know that the universe runs on Basic Trust: everything is as it should be.
- Realize that Love's Way depends on your living in Basic Trust.
- Know what a person who lives in Basic Trust looks like.
- Recognize that in the human condition we most likely experienced traumas that resulted in distrust taking over.
- Realize that distrust and fear go hand in hand. Fear is in the body as well as in the mind.
- Heal your traumas—or know that you are probably projecting your fear onto others.
- Know that you will probably deny your fear or resist change.
- Work to become a safe person: someone who lives in Basic Trust.
- Look for others who are safe.
- Become a safe container so that others can open their hearts to you.

We can create environments in our human relationships that are contemporary holding containers that allow us to be real. When we do so, healing will occur. Love is always present in the healing process, in the form of kindness, compassion, tenderness, caring. We do not need to remember all of the traumas or injuries. We do not need to dredge up painful memories. It is enough to recognize the immobilized fear in our bodies, examine the story lines that keep us tense, trust that the universe will not abandon us as we now examine and release the pain and look for families of choice that feel safe. What we need are places where our bodies and hearts can relax once again. There will be times in our primary love relationships when our loved ones are not available to us because of their woundedness. We must be wise enough to have communities to support us as we support them and let them do what they need to do to heal.

HUMAN TRUST

Basic Trust is a universal trust. There is another trust: psychological or human trust, a down-to-earth sort of trust that we encounter every day. In many respects the two sorts of trust are related. As we have been learning, we once had Basic Trust, and it was in our early human relationships that we were let down and began feeling fragmented, confused, traumatized, and uncertain. And now it is in our human relationships that we are being asked to heal Basic Trust so we can open to that enormous power of love. "How can I possibly do that when people disappoint me every day?" "Who can I trust?" "How can I know if a person is trustworthy?" "Who is safe?" Good questions.

We do not want to continue reenacting old experiences, and yet we are likely to be in relationships where, through our own body memories, need for arousal, projections, or selections, we find ourselves repeating history. The stories I hear each day graphically demonstrate how adult relationships hover like unseen ghosts in the shadow of childhood trauma no matter what category the trauma falls into. This proves that there is more to love than sexual attraction, romance, and compatibility.

Mature love is not shackled by childhood fears; it is laced with moments of profound intimacy based on trusting that the other will be there for us in ways that feel solid and nourishing. Our ultimate goal is to be so self-contained that we can live in love no matter what anyone else does. But because we were hurt in moments of trusting intimacy in the past and we want to heal those wounds, it is essential to develop human trust right now. To entrust ourselves to another and to be safe for others' trust, five qualities must be present:

1. Acceptance (unconditional positive regard): I may not agree with you or like the way you do or say things, but my love for who you are is unwavering.
2. Openness: I will take risks with you and share who I am, what I feel, what I think, and what I do in ways that respect you and me.
3. Reliability: You can count on my being there. My support for you will be strong and nourishing.
4. Congruence: I will work to make my words and actions match, and when they do not I will acknowledge it to myself and you and work to grow beyond the incongruence.
5. Integrity: I will honor my word to you. If I fail you or me I will own it and make amends.

Imagine being raised in such an atmosphere of trust. Is it hard to conceive? Well, it is not too late to develop these qualities as the result of a conscious decision. If we do not become a safe person—and I mean safe, not perfect—our chances for experiencing love may well be limited to our quiet moments of meditation. We are meant to be in relationship, and relationships are the place where either the shit hits the fan or it becomes fertilizer for some new form of life. It is in our love relationships that we will have the greatest opportunities to undo trauma history as well as to redo it.

As human organisms, we cannot escape the effects of trauma. But we can heal and even transform the traumas that we carry forward into life and love. The question is, Do we want to experience more love or not? If we do, we will have to admit to truths we have kept hidden and emotions we have squelched. Like Perry, we must create a sense of safety within ourselves and then with others in order to do so. Our hearts will not open unless we feel safe. Getting to that experience of safety and maintaining it is the greatest challenge our love relationships have.

We are all guilty of fear-based attempts to control our love lives at times. We must learn how to accept our relationships' limitations and not attempt to control them. We must step out of the illusions that we have created or that have been instilled in us.

EXTREME LOVE:
  LOVE BEYOND ADDICTION

Given the trauma factor in life, we both desire and fear intimacy. Basic Trust, once a given, is no longer there. Our ability to feel safe enough to trust others is limited. It is all a matter of degree. Most relationships fluctuate between the two—desire and fear— for the many reasons already stated and that we are yet to learn more about. When love eludes us, we opt for melodrama that ensures survival and a warped sense of connection. Sometimes the drama blows up in our faces. We continue to reenact dramatic scenes in our love relationships in our attempt to gain closure on old pain. But we learn that closure and healing old wounds does not automatically happen. Unconscious to what is driving us, we enter new love with good intentions. Deep inside we understand there is a way of being that we know we are entitled to. We somehow naturally grasp Love's Way. We hear it calling us in the distance; we search for the beloved, the soul mate, and the perfect connection.

Like Cynthia and John in the upcoming story, we announce: "Ah, we found it." Soon we may discover that good intentions are not enough. Believing we deserve love is not enough. In spite of ourselves we tumble into hurt, disappointment, or betrayal. Worse yet, we do the betraying and disappointing and we hurt others. We become confused as the safe feeling of new love disappears. The many faces of fear show up. But there is also love.

We know the divorce rate is over 50 percent. That rate is even higher among recovering sex addicts. Cynthia and John could easily have become another statistic. If they had listened to family, friends, and society, they would be a statistic. After all, he had completed the most outrageous betrayal: a string of sexual affairs in their home starting shortly after their wedding. When this became public news, Cynthia was devastated. She wondered if the wound would ever heal. In spite of the violation of trust and the shock, their story established that there is something bigger going on that can get us through the jagged times. Theirs is a story of extreme love. Love's Way demands that at these times we call on the knowledge embedded in body, ego, soul, and spirit. It compels us to go to the heart and look for answers. There is a multidimensional lover within each of us who can help build bridges and see the situation from the widest scope. It is the only hope.

Cynthia and John looked at this event as something bigger than both of them. They believed they were teachers to each other, that their souls understood the reason this was happening even though the physical and emotional pain ran deep and longed for relief. They had spiritual wisdom and spiritual mentors who listened and guided them without judging. They knew that if they stuck with the pain they would someday understand why it happened. They did not know if the wound and the rupture it created could be mended, but they were willing to honor their commitment to each other. Each went into the little story of the ego, not to dig out the past but to understand how they got there. And sticking with the Bigger Story of the soul, they did their best to stay in the now. Everything would be revealed to them in time, they believed. Determined not to bypass anything, they felt it all: shock, shame, anguish, rage, and fear.

Sometimes they stayed together out of fear. Mostly though, they dug deep inside for the faint recollection of love. They did not overlook anything. They acknowledged the trauma. John actively worked on his recovery program. Both did individual work that helped them identify emotional patterns and beliefs they had learned. They acknowledged how they had put their souls to sleep early in the marriage. And, most important, they owned that there were things they had needed to talk about before they married and had been too afraid to do so. They had both feared that if they'd spoken the truth the other would leave. Subtle resentment and distance evolved slowly over time. Given their histories, given their own emotional dishonesty, the blowup seemed the only option. Fear led them to their lowest point. And facing the fear would get them out. The irony is that their fear of rejection led to rejection.

HER STORY

Being older and having been married before, I was confident about my decision to remarry at the age of forty-nine. I had acquired an independent lifestyle, owning my own business for nearly twenty years, never having had any children, and supporting myself financially. I was assured that this must be true love for me to consider teaming up with this man. I had come to a point in my life when I didn't need marriage, nor was I particularly looking for it. Until I met John.

He was a minister and spiritual counselor. We originally met through a mutual friend when John was living on the East Coast and I was living in the Midwest. We began a long-distance relationship, arranging to get together as often as time would permit. Eventually he made the decision to move to be with me. He had recently been divorced, so he moved into my life with minimal baggage—or so I thought. He did have a son and daughter, although he seldom spoke of them. His son and daughter were living with his ex-wife in another part of the States.

We dated for a year before we made the decision to get married. Loving him was better than I had imagined. He was respectful, trustworthy, and loving in return. His reputation was stellar. People came long distances to speak with him. Most of his clients were women.

Only twice did his son and daughter come to visit. At a junior high age, they were going through lots of growing pains. I found their visits torturous and upsetting, and I was grateful they only lasted a week or so. Between visits, John would talk to his son and daughter once a week. Otherwise there was little or no conversation about the children. Often I would forget about them totally, not even considering that if we were to marry I would then become a stepmother.

But I did. One week before we were married the children's mother died and they came to live with us. John never asked if it was okay, and I was too afraid to tell him I was not prepared for this unexpected role. If I told him how I truly felt, surely he would choose them over me, I imagined.

A few months after we were married, I noticed John pulling away from me. He didn't share the story of how he'd spent his day anymore. He didn't seem interested in me sexually and sex was rote. The issues about his son and daughter were preoccupying him, I assumed. I wanted the children out of our lives. In my mind, everything had been fine until the children showed up. Little did I realize it was our emotional dishonesty and a sexual addiction that were responsible for our distance.

In the meantime, John's consulting career flourished and grew. He had become affiliated with a small church as a part-time minister. Everyone loved him, and I was proud to see how he had established himself in this area. I truly loved this man. If only his son and daughter weren't here. . . .

Three years after we married, John sat me down and told me that during one of his appointments with a female client, he had touched her inappropriately. It had only happened once, it didn't mean anything to him, it wasn't a big deal. In my wildest imagination I couldn't think of anything he could have told me that would have shocked me more. I felt devastated.

This couldn't be the man I had married. This couldn't be true. But she was reporting him to the church and he was going to have to resign his position. He told me because he had to or someone else would have. His justifications were many: It had happened only once, he'd lost control for just five minutes, and she didn't mean anything to him.

I insisted on seeing a marriage counselor. I could make no logical sense of why, at this particular moment in time, after only three years of marriage, he would drop his boundaries. He was doing his counseling in our home, which added to the hurt and sense of betrayal I felt. I wasn't sure I could ever forgive such an indiscretion. He risked his marriage, his business, and whatever connection he had to his son and daughter. Yet he seemed almost stoic about it. He insisted again and again and reassured me on many occasions that there had just been this one woman. He couldn't understand why I was so hurt. He reiterated many times that he wanted to be married to me and that he loved me above all else. What more could I want?

I spent an entire year trying to put this in place. I never did. I finally reached a point of forgiveness and a need to move on. John continued to move forward in his counseling career. Most people didn't know why he resigned his position at the church. But during the next year, I watched him lose weight, withdraw, and spiral into some kind of depression. I was convinced that it was the home situation that was causing his pain. Then one night I realized that he hadn't slept at all. He came into our bedroom about 6:00 A.M. and woke me up.

He admitted to me then that there had been one other woman. "Are there others?" I asked. Absolutely not, he reassured me. So now there were two women.

He spent a torturous day facing the reality of his behavior and another night went by when he didn't sleep. The next morning as we were attempting to eat breakfast together he said to me, "There were others." And then I watched this gentle, sensitive, caring man that I had married a few years prior, describe to me what had been going on in our house. I heard our worlds crash that day in the kitchen. Yet as the crashing was happening, I could now make sense of what I'd been struggling with the past year. This wasn't about one woman, this wasn't about me, and this wasn't about our marriage. I didn't know exactly what it was about, but I knew it was big.

Another day and night passed. We were both in a state of shock. My threat of leaving seemed empty. This was beyond our marriage vows. It was beyond my logical mind. I had to sit there and ask myself if I truly loved him. And, if so, could I stay? By the grace of God, I knew then and there that I did and I would. Telling him that I loved him, that I would stay and help him heal, not only came from a deep place within me, it meant he would have to be big enough to love himself and receive what I had to give. I wondered if the roles were reversed if I could be big enough to forgive myself and receive love. I might have said, "I spare you the pain, I don't deserve your love," and left.

John became proactive immediately. There were times when I didn't trust him—I wondered about all the meetings he went to at night. But I also knew there was nothing I could do except take care of myself. If he acted out again, he did. I watched his shame turn to sorrow. I saw him relive his own nightmare. I heard him tell me about insights he had in some of his counseling sessions or groups. I watched him dig in the garden as I watched him dig into his childhood trauma. I listened to him realize how long he'd been acting out—his behavior was in place long before he knew me. If he could recover, then I could, too. His road was steeper than mine.

More than a year has passed since the unraveling of his life and mine. We still argue over his son and daughter. But his inner work has been consistent and strong. He is still slowly recovering, but he reassures me by his behavior. From time to time, I see glimpses of the man that I married, only better. There are still moments when the betrayal is real all over again. When I hate what he did. When I hate him. When I wish I had made another decision about the marriage. But watching him face his demons unwaveringly and bravely, I live with the hope that our relationship will become deeper and more real than it ever was. I live with the hope that John and I can begin our marriage—which feels like it has been delayed these past six years.

Cynthia and John's relationship was, as we say, "saved." And it was transformed in the process. But Cynthia did a lot more than just support John in his recovery from sexual addiction. She looked deeply into her own life and reframed her own story:

Wondering what I could learn from this trauma, I started to look at me. I saw a pattern of self-righteous indignation. My setup was to expect perfection, judge, and leave. His was to say, I am bad and I deserve your leaving. Determined not to end up in a predictable melodrama, I dug deep into me. Growing up in a small family, I realize now that I experienced no true emotional intimacy at all. Our commitment to one another, such as it was, was always unspoken and conditional. We all had to "earn" the love we got. Getting and maintaining approval was the most important element in our family. Also, it was not uncommon to talk about the other family members to outsiders, discussing matters that I now realize should only have been discussed among the four of us. Nevertheless, I saw my parents remain faithful to one another, perhaps out of a sense of duty, certainly not out of joy. Emotional deceit was everywhere.

As I began to explore my own way of being in relationship, I naturally gravitated toward the same experiences I had in my family of origin—a joyless, passionless, immobilizing, yet determined commitment to another person and children. This inevitably resulted in a lack of respect for myself. Relationship after relationship had to play out before I could consider doing things differently. With John, I was resolved to take a new approach.

I believe that it was only because of this change in my perspective about what a committed relationship should look like that I could deal with a spouse struggling with a sexual addiction. It was supremely important to maintain respect between us, yet have a healthy way to discuss what was happening to our relationship without having to involve outsiders. Although initially my joy and passion for the relationship were shaken—not to mention my commitment to it—I knew the importance of this matter of respect to both of us. I also remembered that I didn't have to approve of his behavior to love him. He didn't have to "earn" my love.

The hardest part is rebuilding trust and capturing the safe feeling I once had. But being brutally honest with each other, as scary as it is, is helping to restore the trust. We talk about everything now and without defensiveness. We even identified why we stayed in denial for five years and see how our dishonesty blew up in our faces. Listening to each other's pain and story is, oddly enough, creating a feeling of safety. I experience more love and that love is getting me through a very difficult time.

As we have slowly crawled over the addiction hurdle, I'm proud to say that my determination to instill respect has enabled me to separate John from his behavior most of the time. Although this doesn't excuse his acting out in our home and during our marriage, I can still honor him with the respect and love of a committed relationship. And this to me seems to be what love is about—loving no matter what.

HIS STORY

I do not need to retell my story. Cynthia gave it to you. I am almost fifty and recovering from sexual addiction, a term I had no knowledge of seventeen months ago, yet it is something I have struggled with, denied, cursed, secretly lusted after, lied about, desired, manipulated, and fed for over thirty years. Now, after a year and a half of honestly looking into myself, I can be grateful for the lessons. There are still times, however, dark and seemingly endless times, when shame, remorse, sadness, pain, and regret just about bury me. Those are the moments when I fall into my brokenness and define myself through what I compulsively did with the protective shield of denial. My life of illusion nearly killed me.

I met Cynthia seven years ago. The first time we were together alone, one of those magic moments occurred when time stands still and one knows that fate is at work. Our souls touched. I knew I had been looking for her forever. Just before our marriage, my first wife died of cancer and suddenly my son and daughter were back in the picture. Being afraid that Cynthia might not want to be with me, rather than to risk asking how she felt about it, I announced that my children were going to live with us. After we married my teenage son and daughter moved in. We were a family, or so I pretended for five years. Any discomfort was rationalized or buried.

To sum up my childhood, I was a pleaser from day one. I loved my parents and was the star in the family. My father pushed me into athletics. Inside I was insecure and afraid. I hated playing sports. But I could not say what was going on inside of me. I learned how to do "perfectly nice," and I smiled whenever I felt angry. Yet I felt emotionally dead and looked for ways to excite my body and life. Sex was it. Remembering my mother's shock and shaming when I had an erection as a child, I believed I had to keep sex a secret. Didn't everyone play the emotional dishonesty game? Overall, I had a good childhood, I would have told you. There was no physical or sexual abuse. My parents got along okay and even did the perfunctory hello and good-bye kiss. But I have come to realize how subtle emotional trauma or neglect can be.

In my family of origin we never talked about anything personal, so I carried on the family tradition and never talked about the struggles of a stepfamily. I was afraid to ask or listen to Cynthia about how she truly felt, because in my mind she might leave. I also avoided talking with the children. I loved Cynthia and I loved my children. I was in the middle and couldn't (didn't know how to) talk to anyone or ask for help. The tension and pressure built. I kept it inside.

Unconsciously I only knew one way of making it feel better. My addiction began to surface, and I began secretly seeking women who would admire me, confide in me, and yes, I knew how to manipulate loneliness and spiritual seeking into sexual encounters. What was so unbelievable to me is that I was with a person I deeply loved and intended to be with forever, and yet I was seeking sexual experiences with others. That was incongruous.

When exposed, I was in shame knee deep. How Cynthia could forgive me I do not know. She did. Somehow she found compassion and strength to use the pain to look deep into herself and be strong while I disassembled my career, my public persona, my denial, my defenses, and myself. Though trust was shattered, neither of us bailed out. For the first time in my life I was ready to heal even though a big part of me wanted to run away. Instead, I dug deep into myself to find out what was behind all of this. There had to be something. I knew I was basically good, but I did not trust my own goodness.

The greatest challenge is trust. I broke Cynthia's heart. I damaged our spiritual connection, and I am feverishly working to restore what was lost. I am doing a lot of self-restoration work so I can feel safe with me. If I can't trust me, I can't expect others to trust me. I had a lot more trauma than I realized, and I see how it all fits together. This is in no way an excuse. But as I understand the connection, it is easier to live the life I want—personal integrity. I not only needed to stop my compulsive behavior, I had to pull the trauma out of me. My body, so uptight, my people pleasing so entrenched, I now understand the power of sexual release.

Looking back over the last eighteen months, I am aware that there was a presence in my life and in the life of my relationship with Cynthia that was always present and that guided the situation in a way that was healing and compassionate. That ever-present force was love. True and honest love. Not the type of love I was most familiar with, where I needed to be admired and had to please in order to feel important and special, but a love that always directed events and situations in a way that worked out for the highest good for all. Whenever the situation looked hopeless to me, whenever I wanted to run and hide, whenever there was seemingly no way out but to end our marriage, this presence gently flowed in. I also can see now, in retrospect, that it flowed the strongest when I gave up trying to control the outcome.

The power of this newly discovered love (which was always there) continues to guide me toward deeper intimacy with both Cynthia and my children. To think that I was substituting temporary and compulsive sexual rushes for deep and loving intimacy still disturbs me. I still carry some fear at times when I reveal my hidden inner self, but my experience recently continues to be that love penetrates into that fear and allows it to fade away. When I am present without fear, I experience the love in my cells and in the depth of my heart. I know that Cynthia loves me and that I love her. I know that she is not going to leave me, and that our relationship is built on the solid ground of honesty, caring, and mutual respect. Those were just words to me before. Now they are real experiences, gifts of love.

I am learning that love never depletes or uses anything or anyone up. When love is present, everyone grows and is fueled. There are no secrets or separations. Love doesn't hurt. In the short term it does require me to face and feel some pain (pain of my creation), but as I learn to trust I know that what follows the pain is the intimacy that I always wanted. In intimacy, my soul reveals itself to me. I remember who I am, and I believe that Cynthia and I will grow together. One big insight is that when I was acting out sexually, I had to leave my heart outside the door. My heart was reserved for Cynthia. Now, I always check in with my heart to see if what I am doing has real honest heart in it. If not, I know I am trying to deceive myself.

Damaged by the inevitable traumas of growing up, battered by cultural messages that glorify promiscuity, hedonism, and total independence, this couple decided nonetheless to stay together, stay committed, and reach for a deeper and deeper understanding of love's mysteries. They are true followers of Love's Way in this imperfect world.

Now let's hear what Love has assigned to our body, ego, soul, and spirit so just maybe we can do what Cynthia and John have managed to do. We will look at the body in love first.

Memo

To: Body

From: Love

Re: Your assignment

You are a miracle of life. You contain the matter and circuitry that will keep you alive. You will play an important role in human love relationships. Without you, body, there is no place for ego, soul, or spirit to live here on earth. You are the foundation, and you must take care of yourself so I may enter.

Your task is to physically ground heaven on earth in your love relationships, using the special intelligence given to you. You have been endowed with physical energy that will allow for the experiences of sensuality and sexuality and the ability to bond with others. These will be essential to human loving. It is a powerful energy that must be creatively used. It can be used to heal yourself and others. If it is stopped you will get sick or you will explode and hurt yourself and others with words or actions.

You have been created in a moment of sexual union and will remain a sexual being all of your life. That is a special gift that will give you much pleasure. You have the characteristics of a specific gender, and that will present opportunities and challenges. You have what is necessary to create other bodies through sexual union. Though you are similar to other bodies, you are unique and you must respect the differences of others.

As a biological entity, you have basic survival needs that must be met or you will die. You will do whatever is necessary to get those needs met, and you will put those goals ahead of the interests of ego, soul, and spirit if you need to. You have been given the gift of pain to let you know a need is present, and though you may not like discomfort, you must listen to it. It is your job to cry out for attention. You are a creature of habit and will be conditioned very easily. This will be both good news and bad news as it pertains to your love life.

Like other animals, you have been given an inner signal that will alert you to danger. It is called fear. You must listen to it and take care of yourself, as there is both pleasure and danger on earth. You will go into an automatic fight, flight, or freeze mode. You must let this sensation run its course and return to an agile state. This is because, though you have a neocortex with which to think, you also contain the primal brain that has long been necessary to survival on earth.

You will have the desire to bond with the hearts of others. You learned of that in the womb. When you bonded with your mother's heart you felt safe and relaxed; you will look for this feeling with others. When it is not there you will feel unsafe.

You have been given five senses with which you are to enjoy your life on earth: taste, sight, hearing, smell, and touch. They will bring you great pleasure. In relationships, these senses will contribute to your physical attractions and aversions to others. You have bones, muscles, and an elaborate nervous system that allow you to do many things. You can cuddle, dance, make love, and hold hands. You have been given hundreds of neurochemicals that let you feel aroused when you need to be. There are other chemicals that will help you develop a rich fantasy life and let you know when your need has been satisfied. These will be delightful aspects of your humanity that tell you that sex, love, and romance can be lifelong pleasures.

You are the storage container for all of the experiences you will have in your relationships. You have neurological memory. Many of these memories will be forgotten by the conscious mind but will continue to direct your life. This memory will contain the ego decisions and beliefs, attitudes, and how-tos. Your brain has a neocortex, which gives it capacities beyond that of other life forms.

You have been given a heart. Your heart is the portal of entry for me. Keep it healthy. Protect it but do not put up barriers so thick that no one can experience me. If your heart is closed or tense, I cannot enter. If it is unprotected it will get hurt. Your heart has been given an intelligence all its own, and your task is to discover that intelligence and use it in all of your relationships. When you do, you will be amazed at what you can do and what you can become.

Be forewarned. Life and love will betray you. Given earth conditions, it can be no other way. You will experience more than one trauma, and when you do you will begin to hold your breath and recoil. These instinctual responses just happen. You will be encouraged to deny the normal reaction and the trauma. When you do not release the trauma you will experience a hyperarousal-depression cycle. You will then naturally look for other ways to release—violence, drama, addictions, depression, and compulsive behaviors.

At times your ego and spirit may ignore or try to limit you. They will have adapted to get your needs met, and your life energy will be bound inside. You will feel agitated. Your soul, though it wants to be your ally, may dig deep into the tasty pleasures of the senses and dwell there. You, yourself, may become so infatuated with your pleasure planes that you will become addicted to your own neurochemicals. When you do, you will forget about me.

You may engage with other bodies frozen in fear or depression. You will recognize them when your body wants to bond and they cannot. Sometimes others will hurt you with touch or use you to please their senses. If others do not touch you in good ways you are likely to reject physical closeness or distrust others.

Over time your heart will feel as though it is injured and will have an ache. Because it is a muscle it will even tighten. When these common human experiences happen, it will be difficult for you to receive me and put me into your relationships. Sometimes you will wonder if you can experience me at all. But do not despair. There are ways for you to mobilize yourself and live and love gracefully. There are ways to bring me into your heart.

It starts with understanding the gifts you have been given and reclaiming them for the good of all. When you do, you will experience the marriage of sexuality, sensuality, and nurturing impulses and bring them to your relationships for a vibrant physical love life. You must also discover and listen to the ego, soul, and spirit. Each of you has an important place in Love's Way. In fact, you will discover that you cannot *not* be in relationship with them. Together you will know me in a way that far exceeds your physical experience alone. Then you will know how immeasurable I truly am.

Good luck.

CHAPTER THREE

The Body in Love

◼ ◼ ◼

> The body is not a frozen sculpture.
> It is a river of information—a flowing organism
> Empowered by millions of years of intelligence.
> —Deepak Chopra, *Journey into Healing*

Our body may give us trouble, but it should not be looked at as a troublemaker. Sensuality, touch, attraction, and sex—phenomena of the body—are not meant to be dirty words but to help us achieve and appreciate a vibrant physical love life. Love's Way has shown us what a wonderful gift it is. Though love is not about putting the perfected body on display for consumption, a vibrant body plays a big part in our love relationships. Our brain contains hundreds of chemicals we are only beginning to understand, chemicals that help us enjoy our own and another's body. In addition to all of these, we have four million pain-sensitive structures and five hundred thousand touch detectors. If we feel too tired or depressed to love, we only need remind ourselves that we have enough atomic energy in our bodies to destroy a city and rebuild it.[1] Your heart is strong, pulsating hour after hour, day and night. It brings love in and it puts it out. The body is the material temple that houses us in totality and can enrich life and love. The body is the physical doorway to our relationships and has an intelligence of its own. With our body we can fight for love and we can fly from love. We reenact dramatic and traumatic events. We have instincts to be hunter and gatherer. We have neurological pathways with grooves leading to intimacy or disdain. The heart quickens at the sight of a loved one, or sometimes shows no remorse or feeling at all. The body squats at the toilet, performs sex, savors a scrumptious meal. We have incoming sensory information and outgoing messages to the autonomic nervous system that controls the involuntary mechanics of the body. Our palms get sweaty, our pulse races, and our blood pressure increases to let us know what effect another has on us. We want to reach out and a disabling terror stops us. Someone strokes our forehead and we crave more.

In fact, the more we are touched, the more responsive our neurons become. Neuropsychologist James Prescott's cross-cultural studies indicate that societies that gave the greatest amount of physical affection to their infants were characterized by less crime and violence. He also discovered that the beneficial effects of physical affection in infancy could be negated by the repression of physical pleasure later in life.

There's no question about it: a healthy, energetically alive body is necessary for the giving and receiving of love. We often do not pay attention to our body until it is sick, out of condition, numbed out, or engaging in a compulsive habit. Valuing its intricacies is one of the ways to love. We can walk, we can talk, we can hug, we can cry, we can make love. We can dance and sing, ride the winds with our five hundred muscles, two hundred bones, seven miles of nerve fiber, while our hearts pump blood through sixty thousand miles of veins, arteries, and tubing. We must own it and take good care of it. We must share it in ways that honor those we say we love: ourselves, our children, our partners, our family, and our friends.

THE BIOLOGY OF LOVE

Love itself has a physical place of residence in our organism. Antonio Damasio, a neurologist at the University of Iowa College of Medicine, researched a man who, after brain surgery to remove a tumor, had no feelings at all. The operation successfully removed the tumor, but the man failed in his personal relationships. He divorced his family, took up with a prostitute, and acted irresponsibly without feeling anything at all. He had no concern or bewilderment. Using magnetic resonance imaging to peek into the patient's brain, Damasio located damage at the locus of emotions. Presented with a barrage of emotionally charged pictures and sensual experiences, he had no response. Pleasure was indistinguishable from pain. His ability to know and share love was disabled.[2]

If we aren't disabled in this way, biology provides us naturally with the three sensations of pleasure—arousal, fantasy, and satiation—as a way to experience life to its maximum. These three planes are controlled by hundreds of brain chemicals that we are only beginning to understand. Without these chemicals we would not have the ability to appreciate our own human nature and the earthly gifts. PEA, for example, is a neurochemical that produces *arousal* states; it keeps us alert and motivates us to action. Discomfort states —including pain—are also identified by the presence of neurochemicals and help us identify our normal human needs so we seek *satiation*. Chemically controlled feelings of satiation then tell us we have had enough and—ideally—we stop and experience a feeling of physical balance. Eating until we are full is a good example. Still other chemicals are necessary to a rich *fantasy* life. We luxuriate in a future of pleasing options. We revel in a piece of art and feel great passion as we write a song. The biochemistry of this self-induced trance state allows us to deeply experience a sunset or envision our beloved.

Contentment, creative passion, fear, sexual excitation—each has a neurological analogue. Though these chemicals are meant to enhance our love life, we can become dependent on these "feel good" chemicals and try to self-medicate our ills with them. We are neurochemically vulnerable. Some people self-medicate with arousal and exhilaration chemicals and look for anything that is dangerous, risky, or stimulating: compulsive gambling, secret affairs, driving at high speeds, stimulant drugs, melodrama, and sex. Others crave the sensation of ecstasy and opt for a rich fantasy life and drown themselves in mystical preoccupation, romantic affairs, psychedelic drugs, romance novels, obsessing about love, and sex. Still others feel "too much" and want a numbing-out experience. They call on the opiates of the mind that kill the pain and reduce anxiety. People seeking sedation stimulate endorphins by compulsive food, alcohol or opiate drug use, compulsive "hanging on" to others, and sex.

All addictions summon the chemicals that produce the sensations of arousal, fantasy, and satiation, whether the vehicle of transport is a substance or a process. Any activity that evokes these three sensations brings alterations to the brain chemistry and holds addictive potential. Sex is the only experience that evokes all three of these pleasure planes at once and has, according to Harvey B. Milkman and Stanley Sunderwirth, the potential to be the pièce de résistance among life experiences.[3]

It is easy to see, then, how we can delude ourselves and make sex a drug of choice. Perhaps the obsession with sex is simply an admission that spirit is missing from our lives and that we know something greater is available and want to experience it. Unless we get the order right—spirit first—sex will never help us to know love in the context of sacred sexual intimacy.

BODY, EGO, AND TRAUMA

Though we have an ego that accounts for a big part of our psychological makeup, we also need to understand the interplay between the ego and the body, especially as it pertains to our traumas. There is an intricate balance between body and ego in love (we'll discuss it in greater detail later). If parental love does not emerge as a binding force, the experience of love doesn't emerge in the child, either. How we give and receive love is determined early on. Trauma is interference. Without a well-integrated ego, soulful living, and spiritual compassion, the body can and does resort to primal instincts, and, without outside help, ruthlessness and fear prevail.

A powerful example of this was reported in a study conducted in the 1970s by Colin Turnbull, who spent two years with the Ik, a small hunter-gatherer tribe in a remote region of Uganda. Anticipating the usual cooperation and other virtues found in hunter-gatherer communities, Turnbull was shocked to find just the opposite. Pushed into barren living arrangements and subsequent drought and starvation, the Ik had become hostile, selfish, and mean in just three generations. They seemed to have abandoned love to focus on survival. Every second was used to look for meals. "On one occasion," Turnbull writes, "I saw two youths on a ridge . . . masturbating each other. It showed some degree of conviviality, but not much, for there was no affection in their mutuality; each was gazing in a different direction, looking for signs of food."[4] There was no loyalty to family. Turnbull witnessed a mother setting down her baby and leaving it in the wild. Later, she was actually thrilled that it had been carried off by a leopard that was later tracked, killed, and cooked. Survival mode was everything.

The body is meant to be the vehicle of physical bonding with others, and it can do so more easily when survival needs are met. Abraham Maslow was pretty astute when, explaining his hierarchy of human needs, he said that our physical survival needs precede our needs for security, belonging, self-esteem, and self-actualizing. (There are important political consequences of this truth: to promote love in the world we must see that the abundance of earth's natural resources are shared with every child so that he or she can grow into a physical human being who knows the pleasures of receiving and giving love.)

THE BIOLOGY OF ATTRACTION

Physical attraction, the spark for romantic love, was originally grounded in the physical needs of the species as well. Love may be a many-splendored thing to romanticists, awe and mystery to philosophers, shaped by individual history according to psychology, yet biology and anthropology say it may simply be hormones and genetics guided by Stone Age rules set to guarantee survival of the species. For more than twenty thousand years, say researchers, men have been drawn to a magical proportion of hip to waist that has been seen as "sexy." Fat around the hips and a narrowing waist suggested a good estrogen level and fertility. When food was less predictable, fat on the hips could get a pregnant woman through her third trimester and the period of nursing. For some reason, the heart-shaped face with wide eyes and narrowly sculpted chin was important to the male's historical mating pattern. Why not go after the mate that has the best chance to have our offspring and ensure that our genes get passed on?

The female, valuing her ability to pass on genes and spending a good portion of her life in pregnancy, wanted a strong and healthy male. Outer signs of high testosterone and disease-fighting potential could be seen in a strong jaw, symmetrical features, and muscle mass. Love was no more than a mating game. Males showed off their assets, flaunting a strong immune system and sexual prowess: "I have what it takes to be a good mate" was their message. Women openly exhibited full hips and breasts and a small waist; the message was "I am available to bear your genetic offspring."

The biology of attraction did not stop there. Partners could sniff each other out. The female was most attracted to the scent of males distinct from her, ensuring genetic diversity and preventing inbreeding. Beyond smell, odorless chemicals—pheromones—helped determine who was the right mate. Flirtation with the eyes and body, gestures of the come-on, sent biological signals to the desired mate. Primal courtship intensified as both sexes scanned the potential mate for clues that suggested mutual availability and safety. Approach or rebuff could be seen in the body. A shoulder shrug, a tilted head—each had a different meaning. Our ancestors could identify danger and knew that safety guaranteed the future of their genes.

Even conflicts in love relationships are healthy from a biological perspective. British psychiatrist John Bowlby's research explains why. As animals we all have impulses and urges that may not be compatible or in sync with another, such as fight, flight, and freeze and the sexual approach. In the prey/predator world of nature, an armistice must happen when animals are ready to mate, and certain instincts must be quelled. In the dance of many bird species, the male feels conflicted between attack and sexual advance and the female between flirtation and flight. Are we humans much different? Conflicts in relationships are inevitable, given that we operate in a body and have a psychological history that models it. *How* we mediate conflict in love, romance, and family matters is more important than what we are conflicted about. And sometimes our less evolved creature cousins do a better job of it. They seem to know the dance.

We're thousands of years removed from the survival imperatives of our ancestors. We do not *need* to procreate. In fact many choose not to have genetic offspring. There are same-sex relationships. Yet we continue to focus on image and ownership and the chemistry of love. Plastic surgery is geared at the biological ideal: full breasts, a sculpted chin, and all the rest. We are crazed in our search for youth, the perfect body, the right diet, and vitamin supplements so we can physically attract or keep our object of love. Stone Age–style gymnastics continue to control us. From singles bars to sitcoms, we see woman-as-exhibitionist coyly seducing the male, getting hooked on the biochemical high as she sits exposing her breasts and thighs and watching the males in return get high looking at her. Or the male, muscles pumped up with steroids in his skin-tight T-shirt, cruising the bar looking for the one who will feed his biological appetite for the night. Intimacy has been reduced to "having sex," and sex to ego feeding. In this respect, we may actually be less idealistic than our biology. Biology wants us to continue the species and enjoy our sexuality, not egotistically feed our sensual appetites at the expense of others and higher values.

Love is not a predetermined set of biochemical responses. It is not the act of sex, though it has a sexual component. Indeed, everything in the universe is sexual—male and female, yin and yang. The first experience you had was sexual. You were created a male or female in a moment of sexual union. Some of the most powerful experiences relate to the meaning and beauty of sex. Sex can be a sacred form of connecting, or it can be an egoist's attempt at self-fulfillment.

In cultures where sexuality is not considered sacred, the spirit of the relationship cannot be present. Communion—sacred intimacy—is missing. Many indigenous cultures understood this, and ancient rituals to bring spirit into the relationship deepened the experience of sexuality. Sexual intimacy was not merely about feeding the senses or a power trip, it was about experiencing a power only spirit could give. As Sobonfu Somé, a West African teacher, so eloquently says in *The Spirit of Intimacy:* "When people recognize that they are spirit in human body and that other people are spirits, they begin to understand that our bodies are sacred and that sexuality is far more than a means of pleasure; it is a sacred act. They look at other people differently, seeing the body not as a source of physical attraction but as a shrine."[5]

Modern civilization seems to have lost this knowledge. Demoting the body from its ancient status as a sacred temple has resulted in more desperation, shame, obsession, and sexual addiction. Though many are in denial about this, we are learning that sex can be a powerful addiction. We are surrounded by symptoms of sexual addiction and refuse to recognize them. Until we do, we may not realize love. Some information is frightening.

In 1991, according to Patrick Carnes, over forty million American adults were sexually abused as children. In addition we have learned that one out of ten men have committed date rape and children are now being exposed to pornography at age six and a half. With the advancement of communication technology we can bring spirit into our love life or keep it out. While many individuals find comfort and connection on-line, others are there to fuel a biological habit and become turbocharged with on-line sexual compulsivity or addiction. In August 1999, 31 percent of on-line visits were to adult Web sites. Though most visitors to these sites are recreational users, many are not. The effect of cybersex on love relationships is just hitting us. A recent survey of couples in which one partner is a cybersex user found that cybersex was a major contributing factor to separation and divorce. Of the couples surveyed, 68 percent had lost interest in relational sex. Where is physical intimacy that includes heart in cybersex? As one recovering sex addict has said, "The only way I could feed my pornography habit was to keep my heart outside the door."[6] I would like to think that we have evolved as a species, that we live not only in primal urges but also in the wisdom of the heart.

THE BIOLOGY OF EMOTIONAL BONDING

Beyond the biochemistry of love is the issue of emotional bonding. Emotions seem to be the bane of our existence. We feel too much! We feel not enough! Emotional intelligence is the hot theme. Why do we need emotions, anyway? And how did they evolve? Again, let us take a closer look at our history. The need to be close to other people—the yearning to be special to someone—is so deeply ingrained that it may be considered biological.

According to anthropologist Helen Fisher, emotional bonding evolved early in our history when the female of our species lost her period of heat and her ovulation became hidden. If the male was attracted to her to guarantee his genetic ancestry, he now had to spend more time with her to guarantee he would be there when she was fertile. It was one thing to woo her with mating rituals; it was another to keep her from other predatory males who found her attractive. Now that her period of ovulation was no longer clearly signaled, the paired couple had sex more frequently to ensure genetic heritage. It seemed inevitable that attachment and bonding would occur.

Women began to bear more children and needed more physical and emotional support from their men. Women and men began exchanging favors, dividing labor, and tightening the relational "knot." Mating went beyond creating offspring. She wanted someone who was a good hunter, who would protect her and her offspring, and guarantee her well-being and that of her children. Eventually, emotional bonding went beyond mere functional ties to sexual partners and genetic offspring. Both began rewarding what pleasured and served them. Babies began to bond with their fathers. Friendship and primitive expressions of caring were established. Personal relationships and the family unit, with all of its complex rules, developed. With these rules came more intense emotions that would both preserve and complicate life. The desire to share, to protect, to nurture, to feel affection, and to live in organic harmony were perhaps among the first expressions of love. And, given the human condition, other emotions emerged as well. These have been considered the curse of humanity. With partnerships and sexual bonding came jealousy, fear, possessiveness, guilt, and vengefulness.

Perhaps wanting to protect his genetic heritage, the male became jealous and possessive. Because a female and her offspring might die without her mate, the first fear of abandonment appeared. Like other primitive fears and habits, many strongly emotional behaviors governing relationships have stayed with us even though we may not need them. We still flirt; we still feel infatuated at the onset of a love relationship, allegiance during it, and sorrow when it fades. We feel guilty if we have been promiscuous and jealous and vengeful when we have been betrayed. Men still worry about their wives being unfaithful; women still worry about being deserted. We no longer need to bond to guarantee sex or keep our young or ourselves alive, yet we continue to do so. To be human is to desire closeness with others.

Like other emotional patterns from the past, our primal brains still bring out emotions and correspondent behaviors that were necessary for survival. Fear of falling, fear of heights, fear of enclosed places, fear of the dark, and fear of being alone—these primal fears still haunt and limit our love relationships. If you look at these fears metaphorically, they all speak to love. In order to know the quality of love we are capable of, we must transcend or transform these fears so we are free to fall into that all-knowing abyss, love, and become willing to climb to love's heights, surrender to its possibilities, and walk into the caves and dark mysteries of love's soul. If we do not do so, we let our biology limit our possibility as a member of the human species.

THE BIOLOGY OF PARENTAL LOVE

Of course, romantic love isn't the only kind of love that has filled important needs for humans as a species. Bowlby, borrowing from the work of animal behaviorists Konrad Lorenz and Harry Harlow and their work with infant birds and monkeys, sets parental love in an evolutionary setting in his "attachment theory." Most animal infants form a passionate attachment to their primary caregivers, usually their mothers. When separated from their caregivers, infants become anxious and then depressed. Biologically this makes perfect sense; in the wild an infant animal is vulnerable and could easily become food for a predator or die of hunger.

Even the human child instinctively knows that if a caregiver does not respond it will die, so it will cry harder to be recognized. If it is not responded to, the baby begins to shut down physically and go into a suppressed state. We can only tolerate so much pain before the adrenals are alerted and we begin to shut down, numb out. In worst-case scenarios, if left unattended, a baby will give up and die.

I can attest to this firsthand. Working as a therapist for a community mental health agency many years ago, I was sent to a home where physical neglect of a child had been reported. There I encountered a depressed mother with marital problems and five other young children. In her depressed state she had refused to bond with her newborn infant. Now six months old, he was found in a crib in a small dark room that was really a large closet. She had refused to hold him and gave him only minimal care. A bottle lay propped up near him. At six months he was refusing to eat and weighed only six pounds. He was lifeless and unresponsive. Another therapist and I rushed him to a hospital where he was put on intravenous feeding. He died within twenty-four hours. Had he lived, he would have been permanently retarded, according to the tending physician.

This behavior contributes to the psychological premise that most relationship illness is a result of inadequate bonding or broken attachments. Studies show that even one caring adult in a child's life can make a difference in a child's ability to form intimate bonding experiences as an adult. Ideally a child needs someone who is a protector, cheerleader, admirer, and nurturer all rolled into one.

As Bowlby points out: "The standard responses to loss of loved persons are always urges first to recover them and then to scold them. If however, the urges to recover and scold are automatic responses built into the organism, it follows that they will come into action in response to *any* and *every* loss without discriminating between those that are really retrievable and those . . . that are not."[7] There are biological reasons that we cling to others or attempt to reproach them even when some enlightened part of us knows that doing so makes no sense at all and wants to do otherwise. Often when a loved one dies, a relationship ends, or a child moves into adulthood, we feel grief and find ourselves irrationally reproaching the dead and those who have a right to be leaving.

Because of our inability to care for ourselves when very young, attachments are strongest in childhood. As adults we still need safe people and communities to provide tender care and respond to our physical and emotional needs. If we have grown up in a "safe container," have had good bonding experiences, as an adult we will look for those people who cope well in life, are strong and confident, and for whom bonding comes easy. The sweet calm and peacefulness of physical intimacy triggers oxytocin, the "cuddle chemical," and endorphins, the opiates of the mind that give us the relaxed body we need to keep our hearts open. Though some may prefer the rush of PEA, the body's arousal drug, we must remember that the rush wears down the body, including the heart. It is no easy task to keep our biochemistry in line with love's best interests.

If we are selecting our companions to provide drama more than sweet calm, we'd best examine our early bonding experiences with our caretakers. A love-thwarted child may spend a lifetime searching for that safe, secure relationship where it's safe to share her heart, but she will miss cues because of her trauma history and will end up isolated and alone, even in the company of a companion. A child devoid of early affection and bonding feels anxious, clings, and does not take many chances to explore love's possibilities. Childhood experiences trigger and distort the love relationships we later engage in—if we're able to engage meaningfully in love at all. Almost every relationship problem is a love disorder problem. This is not because love itself is the problem, but because love has been lost or denied, twisted and distorted, perverted or betrayed. Perhaps we are all a bit love disabled, veterans of an invisible war we did not even know we were in.

BONDING AND CHEMICAL LOVE

The hormone oxytocin, which is released in response to physical touch, probably first flows when a mother holds and rocks her infant. Bathed in rhythmic and chemical beatitude, both mother and child experience the ecstasy of connection. They do not need to think about how or why to love. Everything is as it should be. The sun is shining, the ground feels solid underneath, and the heart-drum beats. (It should come as no surprise that the drum is found in nearly every culture on earth. Perhaps it is unconsciously reminding us of this powerful first experience that resonated throughout our hearts and then grounded us in both sacred and secular realms.)

Unlike other hormones, oxytocin can be stimulated by both physical and emotional cues. A certain look, a smile, a gesture, a richly woven fantasy or memory may be enough to hormonally stimulate the smooth muscles and sensitize the nerves. A chemical symbiosis occurs between people. In the mother-child relationship, the mother secretes more oxytocin as she hears her infant cry out. Her milk flow increases, and as the baby nurses, there is a hormonal outpouring that compels her to lovingly nuzzle and adore her child. In nursing, the mother's uterus contracts, and with those contractions her bleeding stops and her muscles are pulled back into shape. It is a mutually beneficial arrangement. Mother and baby are in love.

Oxytocin is as important in our adult love life as it is in mother love. It encourages cuddling and caressing between partners and increases the pleasure of lovemaking. As in infant bonding, such closeness produces more hormones, and this process produces an even stronger desire to be close. It is essential that a person be psychologically free to give and receive. It has been said that it takes four years of strong, intimate connection for our bodies to move from the romantic chemical high to the more calming pleasures of oxytocin with which intense and loving intimacy occurs. The hormonal outpouring, in addition to more universal love urges, may help explain our physical yearning to be close, to touch, to embrace after lovemaking, to bond heart to heart. When our hearts and bodies are calm, safe, and sensual, love has an easier entryway into our life.

In the human realm, our biochemistry interrelates with ego, soul, and spirit in unique and mysterious ways. But not everyone's heart is open. A person with a closed heart may opt, when the biochemical high wanes, to leave a relationship and look for another rush of intoxicating feelings. Seeking sexual highs without the loving connection not only leads to sexual addiction, loneliness in the presence of others, and destructive relationships, it causes the production of large amounts of the stimulant epinephrine. Frequent biochemical highs generate feelings of restlessness, irritability, fatigue, and stress, all of which ultimately cause a breakdown of the immune system. Chronic anxiety and depression follow, leading to further disengagement from life and love. Then, feeling desperate, we begin the addictive love cycle once again, attempting to self-medicate our ills. This "chemical love" is exhausting. Our bodies and hearts are imploring us to love well and to enjoy loving physical connections, not run from them.

CHARLIE'S STORY: THE BODY IN RECOVERY
We have often disgraced the body by our compelling need to serve an image and our overindulgence in bad habits and addictions. We eat too much or too little, and usually the wrong foods. We care too much about how we look or about pleasuring the senses. We have ignored the body, or it has been shut down via trauma, neglect, or the memory of a parental injunction: "Do not feel" or "Do not be sexual." "Don't touch" are words some little children hear more often than "I love you." We carry these same

patterns into our adult lives. The irony is that if we neglect or shut down the body, and if we lack physical intimacy and gentle touch, we are more likely to seek hyperarousal experiences or to numb out with food, mind-deadening TV, alcohol, and other drugs.

Sensual pleasure is important. Taking care of the body is important. Loving touch and sex are important. When an individual or couple are recovering from the trauma of sexual betrayal—rape, sexual addiction, or incest—they have the challenge of learning to love and share their bodies in good ways. Often they want to punish the body for its out-of-control behavior or to go into body anorexia. Afraid to be sensual, afraid to be sexual, afraid to be close, they need to examine their history and look at how and when they shut down or why they pursue hyperarousal activities. Then they must reclaim the body, forgive it, love it, and walk back into a full-blown sensual love life that starts with the self. Charlie's story addresses the way a person shuts down and shows how this leads to trouble. It also shows how to come alive again.

Charlie came from what looked like a normal family. His parents tended to his basic needs and treated him as special. He thought his childhood was pretty good. He liked to please his parents, smiled a lot, and got good grades. He could not understand why he had become a sex addict. As he told his story, he began to solve the puzzle. When he was not yet five he broke his leg and had to be hospitalized. He was in excruciating pain. He was told in many ways "not to let it get to him." He remembers using his little mind to leave his body or numb the pain out. That was a strategy that made sense then. In fact, it was quite clever. He accomplished what a hypnotherapist is paid to do. The problem is that he never came out of the self-imposed trance. He never quite thawed out.

There were also very clear rules about touch in Charlie's family: they did not show open affection, kiss, or hug. In fact, they didn't touch at all. Charlie remembered when he had his first erection. Scared, he called his mom into the room to ask her to explain what was happening. She responded with shock and walked out of the room. He felt utter shame and shut down even more. Expressing anger was forbidden, too, and fear was never talked about.

By age nineteen he was shut down big time. Sexual excitation and living on the edge of drama became his way to feel alive. He became a star athlete. The adrenaline rush of performance also made him feel alive. From there he went on to become a star in his profession, as well. Until he came to grips with his sexual acting out, he may not have realized how shut down he was. He was a massage therapist. But because he was so shut down sexually and had so many prohibitions against intimacy, the rush of feelings he felt when giving a massage became addictive. They began to serve his self-importance and his need to feel alive.

In the process of Charlie's fall and recovery he realized just how shut down his body really was. He lived in his head. His actions kept saying, Please help me feel. He even lacked the full sensation of hunger. He had been chronically underweight. Like many other recovering addicts or victims, he wanted to punish his body. He withdrew sexually from his wife, he stopped giving her massages, and he neglected his self-care. As he discovered the underlying reasons for the shutdown and began mobilizing the energy in his body, he gradually began to feel energy surges. He gained the twenty pounds he had always hoped for, he joined an athletic club and began working out, he took up biking and gardening, and, to the surprise of his wife, he signed up for a dance class.

His biggest challenge was to develop the capacity for a sacred sexual intimacy. He started slowly. First he needed to enjoy sensual pleasures for himself and get back into his body. Sensual pleasures with safety were his first steps: preparing and savoring gourmet meals, receiving caring massages, tai chi classes, visiting art museums, gardening, listening to music. Gradually he began to share these with his wife. Sensual intimacy began with hand holding, gentle kisses, gentle touch. There was no expectation of sexual performance. The couple agreed that it was important that they get to know each other's bodies and move slowly into sexuality. The biggest challenge for them was to bond heart to heart. Yet they knew they needed to be comfortable with that to get beyond the trauma present and past as well as to conquer the inner rules they had about physical intimacy. Their assignment was to embrace with hearts touching, then to slowly open the heart and feel the other's heartbeat.

When Charlie was finally able to do this, he said:

I felt this profound warmth and tenderness throughout my body that extended then beyond me to my wife. I had this full sensation in my heart and I noticed a moist glaze in my eyes. I felt her and myself in ways I had never felt her or myself before. I knew we were getting close to healing the wound and feeling safe with each other again. In all of my sexual escapades, I never felt this. I felt excited, I felt aroused, and I felt like reaching out and merging with her without sexual movement. I really felt the urge to nurture her in ways I had never done before. It is good to have my body back again. And, not only do I experience more aliveness, pleasure, and intimacy, I actually see more vividly. Colors are vibrant, my vision has improved, I taste my food, and I hear the quality of her voice. I feel her skin.

Beyond all that I feel feelings I was terrified of—anger and fear—and they no longer terrify me. It is undeniable—we are housed in a material body and that body plays a very big role in the way we express love in our relationships and whether what we express is love at all.

THE BIOLOGY OF TRAUMA

Beyond the mechanistic, reductionistic view of life, there exists a sensing, feeling, knowing, living organism. This living body, a condition we share with all sentient beings, informs us of our innate capacity to heal from the effects of trauma.
—Peter Levine, *Waking the Tiger*

Though we can generate fear in our imaginations, the fear associated with trauma is quite different. We can't glaze it over or solve it with denial. Science has shown us that repressed fear secretes hormones into our bloodstream that can wreak havoc in our immune system.[8] Psychobiology knows that feelings are energy, and if they are not expressed, that energy will eventually implode and create illness or explode in rageful outbursts.[9] We recoil when we sense danger. We relax when we feel safe. This all happens naturally; all animals do it. Our hair bristles, our hearts beat faster, we hold our breath, and our bodies put us on alert in anticipation of danger. In our animal nature we have the instinctual knowledge that something bad is about to happen—not unlike dogs that anticipate their owners' impending seizures hours in advance.

We are, in the most primal terms, on the lookout for the predator. We are an unusual species, we humans, as we have become both prey and predator. In our relationships we enact sadomasochistic melodramas, enrolling one partner as the victim, the other as the one who torments. Unlike other members of the animal species, we seem to stay in this hypervigilant, recoiled state long after it has served us, imprisoning ourselves in grids of fear.

Not all fear is illusionary, and to understand this let us look at the evolution of our brain. A popular theory of the brain is Paul MacLean's triune brain model, which says that we have three integral systems in one: the reptilian brain (instinctual), the mammalian or limbic brain (emotional), and the human brain or neocortex (rational). According to trauma expert Peter Levine, a threatened human is not unlike his reptilian and mammalian relatives. When we feel threatened, our biology instinctively reacts with a primary fight, flight, or freeze response that is not under our conscious control, even though we would like it to be. The important point is that the physiological response is involuntary. All three of these responses are physiologically adaptive.

We humans are more familiar with the fight-or-flight mechanism and less familiar with the freeze response because of the cultural interpretations we have given to it. Modern cultures tend to judge this instinctive surrender as a sign of pure cowardice. Physiologists refer to the freeze mode as the *immobility response*. Nature has two good reasons for such a response: playing possum may guarantee survival, and entering this "frozen" state eliminates the experience of pain should our predator get us. We fear death and thus resist the immobility response because of its deathlike quality. Our human rational brains become confused and override our instinctive healing mechanisms. What results is that our bodies—including our hearts—can literally become frozen in fear.

According to Levine: "Traumatic symptoms are not caused by the 'triggering' event itself. They stem from the frozen residue of energy that has not been resolved and discharged: this residue remains trapped in the nervous system where it can wreak havoc on our bodies and spirits. . . . This residual energy does not simply go away. It persists in the body, and often forces the formation of a wide variety of symptoms, e.g., anxiety, depression, and psychosomatic and behavioral problems."[10] Unresolved trauma trapped in the body generates unresolved trauma in our human love relationships. As adults we may not even be aware of our childhood trauma or the impact of our adult traumas, yet we enact them over and over, attempting to get a new ending. We cannot bypass our wounds; we must heal them by being sensitive to our primal instincts as well as our more highly evolved capacities. Our wounds are in our bodies! And they must be released.

LINDSAY'S STORY

I felt in awe of what I was witnessing. Lori, propped by pillows, gently yet firmly held Lindsay, another group member, in her arms and stroked her hair. Lindsay's body had naturally found a position where it could feel Lori's heartbeat. There was a quietness that allowed the senses to be filled with the subtle sounds of the wind brushing against the leaves. Outside, birds chirped their delicate and welcoming songs. Through the open window of the group room, waves could be heard sounding against the rocky beach. Lindsay was somewhere else, at another time, at another age. In fact, she felt as though she had just been born and was experiencing a bonding she had so long ago missed. She was in a state of absolute bliss. Her fully relaxed body and smile confirmed her experience.

Lindsay had come to the group with the universal questions: "Why do we have certain attractions?" "Why do we both want and fear loving intimacy?" "Why are my relationships so melodramatic?" In this group session she had come in feeling a distinct pain in her heart and a feeling in her body she identified as terror. She was exploring a new relationship and recognized familiar sensations and feelings. "It is terrifying" were words she used to describe the possibility that this person might not accept her. She was already either sensing or imagining that this was happening as she monitored every nuance of his gestures and his words. "I want to run before that happens again. Should I?" She continued talking and at one point, in all sincerity, asked, "What do I need to do to be wanted?" Struck by her question, I asked her where it came from. She proceeded to tell her story to me and the other group members.

> I have never felt wanted. Perhaps it goes back to before birth. I was an unwanted child. My parents were forced to marry because of me. My mother told me she cried for days before and after my birth and became very depressed. She gave up a promising career. My father was not there for her at the birth, he was off doing his thing. He was not in love with my mother. They lived a miserable existence for twenty-three years and finally ended it. My father told me he suffered each day of his relationship for those twenty-three years.
>
> I tried to become the perfect child. My dad loved beautiful women, and I worked to look like he wanted. I knew how to act coy and seductive. I believed that if I acted the right way and dressed the right way I would be wanted. But the truth is that I have never felt wanted, and I'm fearful that I am attracting men who only reinforce that. Though I do not want to admit to this, I also believe I am terrified of being close, so I deliberately sabotage those who have good potential. I get out before they don't want me. It may be no coincidence that my job involves international consulting and most of the men I fall passionately in love with live miles away.

As she spoke she sunk into a bed of pillows, took a deep breath, and followed the sensations in her body. Listening to her body, she moved into a fetal position. She continued her story. "My mother tried to abort me on her own, and several times." She shivered as she imagined the cold metal poking at her. The shivers changed to a noticeable tremble.

Taking a deep breath she began deep, deep sobbing, not unlike the cries of a newborn. Her heart sobs released the pain in her heart that had been with her for days, perhaps years. The group waited. Exhausted, she finally asked for someone to hold her. That's where Lori stepped in and became the good mother.

Feeling safe, Lindsay fully collapsed into the experience. She had the sensation of being wanted. A caring community was there to support her. With an open body and mind she could hear and take in the greetings: "I am so glad you were born." "You don't have to look a certain way, act a certain way, dress a certain way, think a certain way to be loved." "You are a beautiful child." "You came through your parents, and you are not of them."

What Lindsay discovered was that her body had a memory that equated closeness with death—her mother had tried to abort her. But she also knew what all babies physiologically know: that separation from Mother meant death. She was in a double bind that continued to be reenacted in her adult relationships: wanting love and fearing love. Until now she had not realized how her romantic and sexual drama not only ensured repetition of her initial betrayal, it also had the potential of becoming an addiction. Though there is no guarantee that this experience will be the end of her terror, it has been my experience that if we are able to release feelings circling the betrayal *and* create a different, more positive story line, we change.

Relaxing her body, Lindsay relaxed her heart. Viewing the past from the present allowed her to recreate the future. She could see the past as one incident behind her. She might not stop her body's reaction but she now has a consciousness about why she chose the men she did. She could stop looking for men that fit her history. With time, and with new bonding experiences, her love life can change.

THE BIOLOGY OF SAFETY

What allowed Lindsay and others in the stories you have heard to access and mobilize the fear still lingering in the body? In the human condition that "what" is a rare commodity called the experience of *safety*. Our parents, families, and communities were supposed to have provided us with the feeling of safety. They often did not. Lindsay and the others were wise enough to create communities of choice in which they felt safe enough to collapse into the fear that kept them from the full expression of love. The safe feeling is biological as well as emotional. It is called homeostasis.

As important as the reframing of these experiences was, just as important was the bodily sensation of safety she experienced in the session. A vignette of safety is now a neurological memory she can call upon; it joins the dramatic, fear-based vignettes she has been repeating over and over. When we feel safe, our hearts remain open. There are real reasons for that. Contrary to the tension we feel when we're afraid, when we're safe our bodies feel a sense of warmth, organismic zest, and fluid musculature. Our sphincters are mobile, neither tense nor too relaxed.[11] And it all just seems to happen.

I do not know if it is humanly possible to live in sustained love, yet that is precisely what we seem called to do. I do not know about you, but I do not see a whole lot of love around. About 90 percent of what I see is nonlove or love's illusion. What I do see is desire for love, judgment about love, caution about love, and a lot of wound-up, uptight bodies trying to get some release.

There are reasons our bodies are uptight. Any time you felt a violation of trust you felt betrayed and abandoned. If the wound is deep enough, your body shifts to an alarm state. It never feels safe. Your guard is up and your body scans for the next hit. You block the fear, sadness, and anger—all pain of the betrayal. But as if that were not enough, you discover that you have bonded with the betrayer. You want to think of bonding as a good thing, the kind that releases oxytocin. It may not be. It can be a highly addictive attachment to a person who hurt you. And you keep seeking it in one form or another. You continue to need a stimulated system to dull the pain or hold back the pain. You go to relationships for drama, high risk, crisis, high stress, and living on the edge, and you use these like a drug. And then when the hyperarousal gets to be too much for the system you need to relax and cool down, but the relationship won't let you. You are up and you are down. Sometimes being in a relationship is like gambling. When you are about to give up on it, you get a few quarters and stay in hoping for the jackpot. Tense with anticipation, you keep playing.

There is a significant correlation to love addiction and trauma. On the one hand, a person like Lindsay wants release from the original trauma, and, on the other, she keeps going for more of the same. Intensity is misconstrued as intimacy. We learn the games. Countless investigative studies show that fear can intensify human attachment. Traumatic incidents in a relationship increase the attachment bond. The brain is altered. When we're in jeopardy our defenses kick in. Adrenaline flows. The electrochemical reactions between synapses in the brain speed up. We are full speed ahead and then we crash. Two factors are important: how intensely and how long we were traumatized.[12] What this suggests is that for some people, sex, love, and romance need to be supercharged and highly dramatic in order for them to experience attachment.

TRAUMA AND DRAMA

Drama in our love life is more than biochemical. The heart plays a part as well. Numerous experiments show that the messages the heart sends to the brain affect it all—what we perceive, how we process what we perceive, the feelings surrounding the event, and how we behave.[13] If the rhythm patterns of the heart were chronically dystonic as a child, as they are in a trauma, we find such events familiar and even desirable. We become comfortably miserable. It is what we know. It is as though we are addicted to the drama, the chaos, and the pain. Edie is a classic example.

Edie came in surprised to find herself in a state of anxiety. She and her husband were getting along well, she said. He was actually honoring the contract he made to stop his outbursts of rage. They had a heated argument, and he did not become aggressive. Instead of feeling better, she had a panic attack. Both her body and psyche were poised for the usual attack and remained in anticipatory mode, wondering when the "boom" would fall. She recognized: "I liked it when he would attack because then I knew it was over with and I could then relax—for a while. I do not trust him. I am waiting for the hit. My father was a raging alcoholic. Even though I hated his outbursts, they were predictable. Once out—I could relax."

It is no surprise that she chose a man who so easily fit her first experience with love. We each have a heart story that is worth looking at. These unconscious physical memories affect our choices, perceptions, and reactions. On a body level Edie seemed to need inescapable pain to jar her into a view of what she was doing to herself. She did. She had an affair and made sure her jealous and rageful husband would learn about it.

Fortunately both she and her husband caught on to the drama and saw the roles they played. They are working to find a new definition of love that includes self-love, forgiveness, compassion, safety, and gratitude.

We must be aware of the part the body plays in our love relationships, look for repetitive patterns, remove ourselves from toxic and dramatic relationships, create safety, get oodles of good bonding, and be comfortable with it. Unless we do, love will come and love will go. We are forced to live in the illusion.

All animals go on alert when they do not feel safe. They sense an imminent danger and automatically go into a defensive posture. We humans, remember, contain the reptilian and mammalian brains as well as the neocortex, and though we can learn techniques to take us to higher states of consciousness where we can experience love profoundly, our animal nature will not leave us— at least not yet. Have you ever experienced total safety in a human relationship, where the level of trust was so complete that you were able to surrender yourself completely? More important, do you feel totally safe with yourself? If not, do something about it.

As biological creatures, we cannot escape the effects of trauma. But we can heal and even transform the traumas that we carry forward into life and love. The question is still: Do we want to experience more love? If we do, we will have to admit to truths we have kept hidden and emotions we have squelched. Like Charlie, Lindsay, and Edie, we must create a sense of safety within ourselves and then with others in order to do so. Our hearts will not open unless we feel safe. Getting to that experience of safety and maintaining it is the greatest challenge our love relationships have. To do that we need the full cooperation of our ego, our soul, and our spirit.

Sometimes we need to get the ego involved before we are ready to heal trauma trapped in our body and move on to core heart feelings of care and gratitude. The ego, too, has a story that gets etched in stone. But the ego can look at its story and change the ending. The ego's assignment is the topic of the next chapter.

But before we move on, here is a recipe worth paying attention to:

Recipe for a Vibrant Physical Love Life

- Find others who value and are comfortable with their bodies.
- Treat your body as sacred.
- Listen to your body.
- Be sure sensual pleasure is not only allowed but also plentiful.

- Be open to a high level of physical intimacy: hand-holding, hugging, and kissing.
- Nurture and protect.
- Bond heart to heart.
- Work to have an agile, fluid, graceful body.
- Give and receive body massage.
- Trust in instinct; communicate nonverbally.
- Express your reaction to trauma spontaneously.
- Live life with gusto.
- Acknowledge discomfort and pain and use it to tell others what you need.
- Pay attention to repetitive habits and stop or change those that limit or negate you and love.
- Work to be free of addiction and compulsive habits.
- Get comfortable with giving and receiving from others.
- Create a safe holding environment.
- Become a person others can trust.
- Fill your environment with items that please the senses: art, music, flowers, color, and good food.
- Develop a strong connection to nature and spend time there.
- Use your personal energy to touch and heal others.
- Be in charge of who gets to touch you.
- Develop rituals that help ground you and your relationships.
- Create safe boundaries.
- Laugh a lot and cry a lot.
- Don't be afraid to dance.
- Have a pet.
- Let only those who are safe into your space.
- Stand tall and walk with confidence.
- "Be" serenity.
- Show concern for the well-being of the other.
- Demonstrate comfort expressing personal power.
- Provide lots of oxytocin and endorphin activities (cuddles and comfort).
- Share your heart any way you can.
- Be playful, creative, stimulating, and energetic.
- Keep your mind active and growing: exchange ideas.

- Smile, smile, smile.
- If you have cravings, let them be for intimacy, warmth, and empathy.
- Stop worrying and wonder.
- Stroke, stroke, stroke all that you like about others and yourself.
- Look in the mirror each day and remind yourself what a precious life form you are.

MEDITATION FOR THE BODY IN LOVE
In appreciation for the body and all that it provides you and your love relationships, try this simple meditation. First take a deep breath and relax. As you read the words slowly and thoughtfully, take the words in. Then work to make your life congruent with the words.

I am in awe of my body's intricate intelligence. I will do my part to care for it in loving ways. I give thanks for its vibrancy, beauty, health, sensuality, and the many pleasures it provides me in life and love relationships. I will do my part to keep it safe and not use or abuse it. I will free it of pent-up fear and other emotions.

Memo

To: Ego

From: Love

Re: Your Assignment

You have a big job ahead of you. In navigating this mundane life you tend to take over and put love relationships out of balance. Do not misunderstand me. You are not bad. You have many gifts that are needed to live Love's Way. In fact, you are so emotionally tender that when you are hurt or betrayed, you try to protect the pure essence of soul by writing a story. You have a close relationship with your body and its trauma. Though you write a story for self-protection, you must not get lost in it and forget who you are and begin stuffing the life energy and gifts given to you. You are to keep your heart open even though it will be broken on many occasions. You are to be an emotionally intelligent lover.

You have been provided with a rich emotional life. You are to value these feelings because while you are on earth they will be talking to you. They will tell you what it is you need in your emotional development to grow into a full and caring human being. They will help you to *bond* to others in good ways. These feelings will provide the current your physical heart needs to bring me, Love, into life. You may be mocked for what it is you feel. Some feelings you will not like and you will try to stop. You must never deny an emotion, but you must take care in how it is expressed. You must never hurt anyone with your emotions or become too attached to them.

You do not operate on emotions alone. You will be given a mind that will develop over time, help you assess what it is you need, and create a map to get your needs met. You will have a psychic box that will contain a recording of all life events. These will direct how you feel, think, and behave and who you invite into your love life. You will be given a voice, a means to tell others what you need and want, how you are separate from them, and what you do well.

You will be given parent figures who are to nurture and protect you, make the world safe, and teach you how to do that for yourself. They may not be good at it because they, too, have been traumatized. If they are successful, you will know how to be a "good mother" and a "valiant father" to yourself and others. They are to teach you values and how to be a good human citizen. You will be given a family, and that family will have the responsibility of teaching you how to navigate life and love relationships. Your family is to model for you what it means to be a woman, what it means to be a man. It is to show you how to express love and power in ways that do not harm you or others. You may get confusing messages about all of this. But know that there are lessons to be learned even in the confusion. Every relationship is a teacher to you, no matter what it presents, no matter how it may betray you.

You will belong to a larger community of people, too, who will have specific and important roles, and they are to help you find yours. They may teach you that some roles are more important than others, but they are not. Each has a place of importance in the bigger picture. When you grow up, you will leave your family and create the life that is unique to you. You will have many love relationships, not just one. In those relationships you must always remember who you are and not be afraid to show me to others. You must also listen to others and see and hear how they are different from you. You must respect those differences You must become a person you and others can trust. Trust is the most important human experience. It is where you will feel safe in bringing me —Love—forth.

But be forewarned. You will be greatly challenged. Other egos will try to control you. You will be misled. Since most of what you learn comes from outside sources, you must sort out your psychic box carefully and see that what remains aligns with me and does not interfere with your many birthrights: freedom to be who you are, creativity, spontaneous expression, and emotional intimacy.

There is an emotion called fear that many people get lost in. It is different from your physical fear. It is learned. When you believe your fear you begin to forget who you are and begin to live in the *illusion* of love. Fear will have many names. Fear will be known as hate, jealousy, anxiety, depression, loneliness, shame, procrastination, suspicion, and more. These things will create moods and emotional pain. You will take on the fear. To relieve the pain you will forget yourself and succumb to many diversions. You will hurt yourself and others. You will get sick and desperately look for life and love. You will become lazy and forget about me. You will get lost in the material world and think of it as more important than it is, and your life will be filled with drama.

But do not give up. You have everything you need to overcome fear and bring me forth. Though you have been influenced by others' opinions, values, and how-tos, you will have written your own story. When the story lines hurt too much, you can stop and change the lines.

Good luck.

CHAPTER FOUR

The Ego in Love

◼ ◼ ◼

When I was little I was sick once, and I wanted something, only I didn't know what it was. My father sat by my bed and talked to me.

"I want," I said.

"I know, Twink."

"What do I want?"

"Everything, Twink."

"Can I have it?"

"Yes."

"When?"

"Just as soon as you are better."

"Right now?"

"In a little while."

"Tomorrow?"

"Tomorrow for sure."

"What will everything be?"

"You, Twink. You'll get yourself back the minute you're better. You'll forget you ever lost yourself. And that will be everything."

"Is that all? Just me?"

"Yes, Twink. That's all there is."

"But I always got me, Papa."

"Except now, because you are sick. Because when anybody is sick, he loses himself—you want all kinds of things—everything—but what you really want is always yourself, because if

115

you've got love, that's all there is—yourself and love, and I
love you, Twink."

—William Saroyan, *Mama I Love You*

That we are more than the chemistry of love should be clear by
now. Love's Way has another perspective on love relationships—
that is, through the lens of the ego.

This little word *ego* can suggest many things. In philosophy
ego often refers to the entire human, body and mind. In psychology *ego* points to specific energy structures filled with composites
of life experiences, conscious and unconscious. In pop culture it is
usually a put-down: people who are "in their ego" are selfish and
conceited.

For our purposes, let's look at the ego simply as the material
and emotional human being, the entity that takes us through earth
life. It is our emotional, mental, and behavioral doorway to life
experiences. Sometimes referred to as mind, we must understand
that this mind is not only rational, but is also run by emotional beliefs buried deep inside of us. For our love relationships to succeed we need a well-integrated ego. Earth life is linear, and ego
knows how to "do linear" very well. It organizes, plans, and sets
goals. It figures out what we need and goes searching for ways to
get it.

Needs are those things that are important to our survival as
physical, emotional, mental, and spiritual beings. If we need food
we get food. If we need life-affirming recognition we go after it. If
we need to belong we figure out how to belong. If we need to pass
an exam we study. If we need a spiritual life we discipline ourselves to live it. If we have a broken heart we look for supportive
friends to help nurture us.

The ego also helps us identify and get what we want. Wants
are different from needs. We can get along without wants, but
they enhance life and make life enjoyable. The catch is to know
and get what we want without trampling other people or getting
lost in the pursuit and compromising higher values.

You and I are never without ego. It is the part of you that for
some reason decided you needed this book and found the time to
be reading it now. It is the part of you that is looking for ways to
do your love relationships better. It is the part of you that is deter-

mined to change your story lines when you see yourself repeating negative patterns. Though it is important not to get lost in the kind of black-and-white thinking the ego specializes in, it does have its place. It is efficient. The ego helps us navigate the mundane world and is responsible for our emotional life. It is through our ego life that in our many and varied roles we get to experience appreciation, care, safety, tough love, nurturing, dedication, boundaries, personal power, and self-esteem. And all of these are essential to our love relationships.

The ego has the capacity to help us become whole human beings, but it can cause us trouble, too. Intended to live harmoniously with our body, soul, and spirit, it often overloads our boat, and we sink. We get consumed by our ego life and lose our way.

Following Love's Way means keeping our original assignment from Love in mind and noting where we get off track. The ego's task is to be an emotionally intelligent lover by staying awake to who we really are, separate from others, and keeping our heart open even though we have been hurt or betrayed. Ego easily gets conditioned and goes to sleep. (In fact, it has been said that 99 percent of who we are is not in our conscious awareness.) In that conditioning we may come to believe that we do not deserve love or that it has to be earned. We may even have decided to close down our heart and pretend to love. Whatever it is, it is important that we look at the glut and clutter of emotional beliefs, outdated opinions, and how-tos our egos have accumulated over the years and do our housekeeping. When we do, it will be clear why we are having so many problems in our love relationships. On an ego level, everything that is happening and not happening in our love life makes perfect sense. We have a story, a little story designed by the ego. It is much like the story of Pandora's box.

PANDORA'S BOX

In Greek mythology Pandora was a beautiful woman sent by the gods to earth to avenge the theft of fire from heaven by Prometheus. She brought with her a box; when she opened it, all human ills were released into the world. Hope alone remained. According to another version of the story, she brought blessings in her box, of which all but hope vanished.

We, too, have a Pandora's box—it's our ego, and its contents are a secret. The greatest lie we can tell ourselves is that we know who we are. Oh, it is true that we think we know who we are, and most of us believe we are honestly disclosing our true identity to those around us, but the truth is that to do so is quite impossible. Hidden deep in the recesses of our ego mind is a cauldron of life experiences that contribute to who we say we are and the temperament of our love relationships. Some fear this Pandora's box and refuse to go anywhere near it. Within it lie the unknown secrets, the forgotten memories, the buried traumas, the unmet needs, and the magical beliefs and myths that dominate our tragic love stories.

Each life event is there in that psychic box, whether we want it to be or not, and it contributes to those things we say and do that we promised ourselves we would never say or do. We react out of the blue. We see a stranger and feel like running, not having a clue as to why. We want love and we push it away when it is right there in front of our eyes. Often we feel an inner war going on. One part of us wants one thing and another part of us wants something else. We compromise, we lie, and we cheat. We wallow in shame or rationalize our outrageous and self-defeating behaviors. Our drama escalates. We try to stop and we cannot. We strike out at others and we get depressed. We try to buoy ourselves up by taking actions—pleasing others, looking good, buying a new car. We get so caught up in our life of illusion that we do not know who we are.

Everyone is living out a melodrama, like it or not. It goes along with the human territory. We have an ego, and that ego has us in its grip. We live in a body, and that body records events in its nervous system. Our human nature has biological needs that must be met or it dies. Using all of our senses we explore and then adapt to a limited world to ensure that our needs are met. Certainly many of the adaptations are healthy. We eat three meals a day, we get to school on time, we stop at red lights. We become good citizens. Such adaptations make life flow easier and guarantee safe communities.

But there are other adaptations made by our egos that are toxic. They are the ones that begin limiting us. The grown-ups in our lives did not tell us overtly to give up our rights and even our very selves, but we intuitively knew what the rules for living in the world were and what it meant to disobey. And so we gave the grown-ups our spontaneity, our creativity, our thoughts, our feelings, our self-esteem and self-worth, our capacity for loving intimacy—to name just a few of our birthrights.

And from this we began writing an ego story that would define for us how we would live and how we would love. We learned our lines and we kept repeating them. We got so good at them that we soon fell asleep to who we really were. Our authentic selves got buried. The question is, Can we ever find ourselves in the rubble? And why is it even necessary?

Knowing our story does not mean dwelling in, blaming, or conjuring up the past. Often my clients say: "I do not want to go into the past. I've been there, done that—and it's behind me! Put it to rest." It's a reasonable wish, yet when clients tell me this I always suspect that their problem is related to some reenactment of the past. In other words, for them the past is not the past at all; *it is right here now, in this moment,* and it's the filter through which the person is relating to me and everyone else.

To get to love, we must know the ego's story and sort out what is real and what is fiction, what supports our health and the health of our love relationships and what does not. Shit does not just happen. Our muck usually has a story behind it. We cannot experience the full spectrum of love unless we are real and present, living in the now. Being real in this way is not a "mind thing." It is not being what I *think* I am, it is being *who* I really am.

There is great delight in knowing who I am. Suffering comes from the not knowing. Though the ego is here to be in the service of love, it often entraps us. Implicit in the human condition and thus in ego is a fundamental distrust and the development of a false sense of self to deal with this distrust. Distrust is the enemy that keeps us from experiencing emotional intimacy, the greatest gift the ego has to offer.

We are pregnant with possibility. Our true nature lies buried beneath the ego's learned habits, traits, quirks, beliefs, and fears.

WHY WE NEED TO KNOW OUR STORY
Knowing our personal story is crucial in changing it. If we do not do so we spend our lives focused outward, constantly reenacting our drama and ceaselessly searching for the right "someone" to

fit it. We get stuck in a repeating hologram of the past, struggling to change the other person to fit our drama, when the only person we can change or have a right to change is ourself. We need to know our story so we can see what is keeping us from being emotionally intelligent lovers.

Though our story is often difficult to know because much of it has seeped underground to the unconscious mind, it is essential to opening our hearts, seeing the wounds that need healing, and returning to the innocence and beauty of the soul. As we do so, we not only nourish the life within us, but also the lives of those with whom we share our love. To begin, we need to know how and why our stories were created in the first place.

THE LIFE SCRIPT
To be born again is to take the responsibility for being the father and mother of my own values.

—Sam Keen

It has been said in innumerable ways that we are the creators of our own realities, that our outer experiences are only reflections of our inner states. We have in our life what we intend to have, and what we don't have, the theory goes, we don't really want. Some will deny this truth, to avoid guilt or personal responsibility. Frankly, I find this to be good news. Knowing that I am in charge of me gives me a vantage point. I no longer need to look outside of myself for a sense of wholeness. I no longer need to have others change in order for me to be content. I no longer need to control my love life.

This statement does not negate the fact that we are all related and what you do or don't do affects me as well. What it means is that in exploring our little story we discover what we began to believe because Mom was depressed or unavailable, what we decided when Dad was a rageaholic or absent. Those are the story lines we created, and we now get to change. The problem is that the story lines have gone underground, and we often don't know that until we get into trouble in our relationships or notice that we have repeated a pattern one too many times.

Not only do we have story lines—beliefs that unconsciously run our love lives—but they often came about in a moment of trauma, when something we legitimately needed was not there. Nancy told her mother that Uncle Tom was sexually abusing her, and Mom did not respond. Nancy concluded that being abused was normal and she was not worth listening to. When sexually abused as an adult she kept it to herself. She kept picking out abusive men with the hope that one day one of them would stop the abuse, apologize, and tell her she didn't deserve it. The relationship would give to her what Mom and Uncle Tom did not, and she would live happily ever after. We are unaware that we are running around with holes in our psyches, unfinished gestalts hoping to get what we did not get as children.

Most relationships are in trouble because the need-clouded self insists that it is incomplete and searches for a someone or a something to make it feel happy. This self forms an emotional attachment to a love object, to a habit, to a thought, or to a favorite bad feeling.

How do we come to feel incomplete? To answer, we need to understand our ego development. The seed potential of our wholeness resides within the child part of our personality. This child identifies needs, wants, and feelings. It requires a responsive environment that affirms its rights and teaches it how to live in cooperation. This ego child never leaves us and can be stopped only by death itself. Often, however, it is depressed, suppressed, or made unimportant. Secretly it still runs our life. It chooses our partners and even our careers.

The ego not only records life traumas; it also designs beliefs and comes to conclusions about those traumas. It thinks in black and white and can easily personalize life events: "This always happens to me"; "I'll never get what I need"; "I disappoint people." Once willing to trust itself, others, and life, it closed down only after it got burned. It is not rational; it surveys life intuitively. It has a logic all of its own, and it attracts people and events to fit that logic or, when such attractions are lacking, creates scenarios to fit the logic.

Most important, it is that ego child who determines our most important decisions or who pulls the plug even when a more enlightened part of us wants something else. It is essential to understanding the ego stories that we take seriously the important life events the child in us has felt good, bad, or indifferent about. It is through these experiences that we decide about love, power, men, women, and life. As adults, we can and must illuminate and heal the injuries the child has suffered. We must examine closely the beliefs it sustains and change those that keep us from what we say we want in our love life. Many of our beliefs have come to us through generations of men and women and will resist change.

The stories presented help us see how easily we lost touch with a deeper identity. The stories also show the psychological power we had as children to make decisions. Though the options available were limited, even then we did have choices. Those choices become adaptations, a way of life that at best provides us with banality, an ordinariness. To belong we overadapt, and little by little we give up pieces of ourself: our spontaneity, our creativity, our autonomy and our capacity for intimacy. From time to time we make contact with this void, the boring, empty quality of our love life.

In order to claim who we are, we must first discover who we have become. It has been suggested that the majority of our time is spent operating blindly out of a life plan. To quote psychiatrist Eric Berne, who referred to our ego story as a "life script":

> Each person decides in early childhood how he will live and how he will die, and that plan which he carries in his head wherever he goes is called a Script. His trivial behavior may be decided by reason but his important decisions are already made: what kind of person he will marry, how many children he will have, what kind of bed he will die in and who will be there when he does. It may not be what he wants, but it is what he wants to be.
>
> Scripts are artificial systems that limit spontaneous and creative human aspirations. Transactional Analysts did not start out with the idea that human life plans are constructed like myths and fairy tales. They simply observed that childhood decisions, rather than grown-up planning, seemed to determine the individual's ultimate destiny.[1]

The mystic says: "You have abandoned yourself to your false personality. You have a veil of illusion." Sigmund Freud refers to the repetition compulsion. Carl Jung invokes archetypes and the persona. Archetypes, the collective thoughts and emotions of humanity, provide us with models of what we are and what we hope to become. Though intended to serve us as legitimate soul aspects, archetypes often get stuck in a role we decide upon as we write our little story. The "good mother" becomes a depressed martyr; the "valiant father" turns into an unfeeling macho man. Later we find the role is not serving us. Alfred Adler said, "If I know the goal of a person, I know in a general way what will happen." R. D. Laing used the word *injunction* for strong parental programming. The idea that myths, legends, and fairy tales pattern lives and dreams was recognized by Otto Rank and is eloquently presented in Joseph Campbell's *The Hero with a Thousand Faces*. Each of these thinkers, in his own way, was helping us to see our way to living a unique story, a story that belongs to us. We decide which character in the story we want to be, and it will be the one our family wants us to play.

Originally, our scripts were not bad. We even enjoyed the many roles we got to play. Our scripts were designed to protect the real self from perceived or imagined danger. They became the outer shell that covered the vulnerable seed; we trusted that there would be a time of ripening when we could escape. This life plan, or script, however, became our way of life. It began to provide a sense of comfort and grounding. A composite of our early life experiences, it became the frame of reference through which we began to view the world. We were in the play and we were a player. In order not to be lonely, we drew in other players. The drama went on and on and on. As unique as our fingerprints, our drama became the mosaic through which we interpreted the world, and we believed others viewed life from this perspective, too.

Think of the drama we concocted as the protective outer shell of a seed. Initially the seed greatly benefits from this protection. People couldn't hurt us as much; we could hide our vulnerability. In some odd way we felt safe and life was predictable. We had the illusion of control. We adapt to the world, not with the intent of dishonesty, but because we know of no other way to care for ourselves. If Mother rewards Johnny for lying to the bill collectors, he learns to be dishonest. When Sally is given attention by being coy with Dad, she becomes a seductress. When we're children our ego will do whatever is needed to feel safe, to get attention, to have predictability, and to keep people around.

When our love relationships in adulthood display repetitive patterns, words, and choices that feel hurtful and abusive, it signals to us that we are not the captains of our own ship. Some unknown within us is the driving force. We can certainly recognize such behavior patterns even though we often don't understand the motivating force behind them. But we can come to terms with our drama, as one couple did.

SANDY AND JACK'S STORY

I sat there watching them. As many times as I had heard stories like theirs before, I still felt deep sorrow and compassion for the couple sitting before me. I could see the repetitious legacies, the fears, trauma, and lack of emotional bonding they had experienced as children being reenacted right there and then. My knowing it could not stop the pain evident in their sullen bodies and dejected expressions. My hope was that they could see how they each got there and not repeat an awful history, and could instead let this be fertilizer for their growth.

They both struggled to maintain composure as they spoke of the awful pain they each felt. Sandy spoke first:

> I hate you for tapping the phone, invading my privacy. Yet, in listening to myself, I live in self-disgust. I am a hopeless love addict. I relapsed big time. I disgust even me. Hearing myself made me sick. I am better than that. My children deserve a mother they can be proud of. I do not know if I should hate you or thank you.

Jack spoke next:

> It was wrong, I know. Something inside of me said I could not trust you. Thinking of living with your affair again tortured me. In the past I would have exploded. Instead I am sick and tired. We were doing so well. Now that I heard your conversation with him I don't know if I will ever be able to trust you again. I feel used, second-best. I want to be your soul mate.

I encouraged them to be present to the pain and not run from it or shift to blame and shame. "Hear each other from your heart, if you can," I said. Jack continued:

I wonder if we ever really loved each other. Though I say I fell madly in love with you, I wonder if I know what love is. It has been one up-and-down melodrama since the beginning. I saw a pretty woman in need of being rescued from an abusive man, and being a hero sparked something in me. I could rescue and take care of you. I really tried to be what I thought you needed. I could never satisfy you, and I just kept trying. When I couldn't get your acceptance, I thought I could control you. Fights and making up, fights and making up. Our whole marriage has been that way. It was almost like a rush. I don't want it any more. I need to find myself now. I want to get away from it all—work, you, this pain. Only I can't run from myself. I know I have problems, but I did what I knew.

Accustomed to rageful outbursts, his tears were a shock to himself and to her.

What a mess. How in the world did we get here?

Sandy went on to say:

I don't know, but I don't want to ever get back here. I've never felt this much pain before in my life, not even when I was raped. What I know is that something big happened, and I realize how my insecurities possess me to look for love in a man. I feared you. I saw you as having more power than me, so I used manipulation to get my needs met. I've been terrified of being alone. I was afraid to talk to you and afraid to love you. I've been living in a fairy tale—like a seventeen-year-old and I'm forty-five. I need to find security inside. I never want to hurt you, me, or our children like this again.

Jack responded:

It may be too late. There may be too much damage to ever feel safe together.

Not ready to leave, not ready to trust, they each needed to journey with themselves for a while. In the meantime they agreed to safety guidelines that would encourage healing instead of the painful drama they were so familiar with. Would this be yet another melodramatic payoff with a predictable ending that would reinforce their histories? Could they get beyond the nostalgia and hurts of the past? Could they stop living in the future with dread or impossible expectations?

Or could they see the possible kingdom at the bottom of the abyss? There were signs of hope. Though they had hurt each other deeply, they were not personalizing it. For the first time they examined themselves and began owning bits of their parts in the problem. They were beginning to understand that they had intuitively picked each other to fit their stories.

As we neared the end of the session I saw two fragile children uncomfortably clothed in adult roles. The world, their families, their children expected them to have the answers, to do it right, and "right" meant "perfectly." Living in the ego's illusions, they might not have the courage to see the moment as an opportunity to reclaim their possibility.

Sandy and Jack had lost basic trust long before they met each other. They all but forgot love's assignment. Jack was the firstborn son in an alcoholic family. He never had emotional contact with his father, and he kept his mother and younger sister out of harm's way, clear of Dad's rageful outbursts. He gave up on having closeness and affection. Emotional intimacy was outlawed. Like most adult children, he wanted to keep life predictable for the sake of his security.

Later that would translate into control, rigid thinking, having a handle on everything and everyone. He knew people would disappoint him; they always had. He gained acceptance by his gregarious and entertaining demeanor. Underneath the charming and rugged exterior was a frightened and angry man whose fear and anger were the products of trauma. But now, unhealthy adaptations to that trauma and erroneous belief systems were running interference in his love life. Sandy fit his story like a glove. They were made for each other. But not in heaven.

What about Sandy? The only girl in her family, she was led to believe she did not have power, worth, or beauty. Her story was not unlike many of the fairy tales that I am sure were read to her. A jealous mother berated her at a very young age for dressing up and looking pretty. Dad, once close to her, moved away when she began developing into a sexual woman. Thanks to physical abuse at the hands of older brothers, she entered adolescence confused about herself and boys. Naive and ill informed, she did the best she could. Like other adolescent girls, she relied on image and looks for acceptance. She was a magnet for sexual perpetrators. Then came the rape, and what little self-esteem she had was all but gone by the time she met her first husband and the father of her first child. It did not take long for her to become a battered wife. Enter Jack, our hero.

With enough maturity and insight these two will make it. There may well be too much damage to salvage their relationship, but they can individually grow beyond their learned limitations and dig deep to find their real selves. Though they had a hard time understanding it, they were encouraged to get back to the state of Basic Trust that had been ripped away from them as children. This is not easy. It means believing in their own goodness and the goodness of the universe to support them through this rough time. It means completely surrendering to what is happening even though that is bound to bring up every fear tucked away in Pandora's box. It means doing their part and trusting in a positive outcome without knowing what the outcome will be.

Next they need to trust themselves; to become people of integrity who can hold one another through difficult times. As Jack and Sandy get to the source of their heartbreak and heal it they will begin to travel Love's Way again. Back on track, they will stop looking for love or attempting to control their love life. Emotional intimacy that feels good may return. They may even discover the words of Rumi to be true: "Love annihilates all your faults and defects."

AWAKENING TO OUR ILLUSIONS
The beginning of love is to let those we love to be perfectly themselves, and not to twist them to fit our own image.
—Thomas Merton

It is true, and sad, that we often don't realize how alienated we have become unless, like Sandy and Jack, we are faced with some major life event that comes crashing in on us and says "Stop!"

What Jack and Sandy experienced is not a gift in any conventional sense. And yet, there is a gift in it for them if they want it: the opportunity to get real and become emotionally honest; the chance to contemplate the meaning of life and death, and, most important, to live Love's Way and from there look at the quality of their relationships. The challenge, as always, is to do so in a world where most people believe they are choosing rather than reacting from a life plan that they previously created, a plan now recorded in their unconscious minds.

Our ego story contains not only our most immediate psychological influences, but also years of historical references that contribute to the misunderstanding of love and power. It is generational. It is in our bones. Sooner or later, all of us must confront our part in the messes in our relationships and decide how we can change in order to contribute to the greater whole. Each of us must examine our state of unconsciousness and see how it affects the relationships we draw into our life, the habitual patterns we are repeating.

This is what Michelle had the courage to do. Severely depressed when she first came to therapy, she wanted answers as to why, once again, she was feeling abandoned by another lover. In spite of all the relationship books she had read and all she knew, it seemed as though something inside of her insisted on running amok. As you read her story you will understand why there are no surprises in these matters.

MICHELLE'S STORY

My earliest memory is of being stuck in a playpen and longing for the mother lying on the couch to notice me. She did not, so I flew away for the first time. Leaving my body was the only way out of a room filled with dense darkness. Not even the curtains were to be opened.

When I was old enough to tie my shoes I would go outside alone. I wanted love so badly that I would go and hug a tree and say, "I love you." This became my haven. I craved love. When I was able to read I went through the Bible and underlined every love word in it. There were a lot of underlined words, but that didn't fill the loneliness I felt. Sometimes I knew love when I was with my tree and when I saw the word in the Bible.

Love did not seem to be in human relationships. It was elsewhere.

My experience of relationship was one of depressing, painful silence, gut-wrenching fighting, threats of abandonment, constant tension, unspoken secrets, obligations, entrapment, and joyless existence. My response was terror. I recoiled, turned silent, and the light in my eyes dimmed. I could feel an ache in my heart, even then. I learned to suppress not only my joyful curiosity and happiness, but also my right to be close, for fear of bothering my depressed mother.

With Mother paying no attention, I looked to my dad for love. Maybe I could earn it. I put on a good-girl face whenever I saw him. Sometimes it worked, though I never knew when it would. To assure the timing would be right, I made sure my plastic smile was always there. It became my trademark. I became male-dependent at a very young age.

I developed some very sick beliefs. Men were absent and got to do what they wanted. Women were victims and chased men away. I was not visible. I would have to do life on my own. And as for power, only the loud and angry ones had it. I would have to disappear or perform to get my needs met. As for relationships, they were about distance or fighting. Love was just a confusing word. My story lines were set in stone by age seven.

My world of escape expanded into an abnormally rich fantasy life. I created places in my head where I could go. I could be Peter Pan, flying out of the window to Never-Never-Land, or the princess whisked away by a fairy godmother. Soon I took this nighttime fantasy with me into the daylight hours, to the point where I truly believed I could fly. I spent a lot of time out of my body.

When I was Cinderella, a handsome prince carried me away from my painful existence. Having a man take me away from the pain and suffering was what I hoped for someday. In the meantime I focused on being a good girl at home and at school.

As I entered puberty, my craving for love and affection intensified. Now I had body feelings to add to the drama. My fantasy life came down to earth as I obsessed about boys, particularly bad boys. My need to excel in academics in grade school now gave way to proving myself the most desirable and the most popular girl in high school. Being popular was what mattered now. I wanted to be the prom and homecoming queen. I wanted to be chosen for sports in gym class. Though I achieved my goals, inside I felt depressed, unloved, and unpopular.

My cravings persisted into adulthood. Looking for someone to fix the wounds of childhood, I sought out men. I chose men who reenacted my childhood. Craving love, I got pain instead. I became involved with violent men, men who were distant physically and emotionally and who had themselves been victims of abuse as children. I didn't learn of their stories until it was too late. I don't know if it would have mattered. It seemed that we were unconsciously drawn to each other as though fate had us in mind to play out a particular drama.

I continued in my rich fantasy world of magical deliverance, believing that another love would appear and make me whole. I married, had a daughter, and discovered I was married to a tyrant who enjoyed physically abusing me. I was getting glimpses of my repetitious pattern and decided to run for my life. Thereafter I tried to stay away from "bad boys" and dated men I was not deeply in love with. That is until I met Cliff. I really thought I'd found my soul mate. He was in recovery and he was in therapy. Maybe he would be the one to heal my wounds and provide the love I had been looking for. I was now forty years of age and still looking elsewhere for love.

I had for an entire lifetime been attached to being rescued by either a knight in shining armor, a handsome prince, Superman, a rich handsome man, or a charming man who would fulfill my dreams and complete my other half. This most recent relationship was certain to be it. He told me he loved me in the first week we were dating. That should have been my clue. We fantasized about our shared life together. We shared a dream of marriage, living and working together, sharing our spiritual life. He was intrigued by my sense of magic and wonder and connected with me in a mystical way. He wanted entire honesty and disclosure. Then his sexual addiction led him to another woman. I was devastated.

The relationship ended painfully. No more, I said. I need to look at me and my patterns and choices. I need to find love inside of me. It was time to face my psychological addiction and dependency.

Even after he was off with the other woman I'd get cards telling me he loved me and telling me that our time together had been a "magical year." I had not seen the compulsion in him. I began to understand how I fed his compulsive need to be a fantasy fulfiller, to give a woman what she wanted.

He fit my life story exactly. I thought I needed him to have wonder in my life, to have a spiritual, magical existence. This experience jolted me right into therapy, where I realized that he had not
given me a sense of wonder, dreaming, creativity, and mystery—I
already possessed them. They were my gifts of life. Yet these gifts
had become mere coping mechanisms to help me live in an abusive world. Now I could choose how to use them. I want to use
my fantasy creatively and not get lost in escapism. I want to trust
my intuition to call attention to abuse and discounting of my feelings when I see them happening.

It's time for me to claim the gifts of my soul. I have wonder,
magic, passion, mystery, dreams, and creativity. I will not give
them away, nor can anyone take them from me. I will carry them
with me always. I can let go, take life moment by each magic moment, believe in the synchronicity of life, and more quickly see
the lessons I am to learn.

I am processing this loss of "us." Along with letting go of the
pain and obsession, I am grieving the loss of some wonderful and
sacred moments. I am sure that the love that I felt for Cliff had validity. It was a great teacher. I would do it all again. There was no
waste. I called him in to teach me something and I think I'm getting the lesson. I am changing right before my very eyes. I'm in
pain, and that is a part of life and love.

I never thought I would be saying all of this. But I know that as
I grow and heal I will see more of what the experience has to
teach me. Right now I'm too raw. I'm not only living through the
grief of loss, but in the process I'm reliving the grief and loss of
my childhood. I am trying to see the roots of my behavior patterns in order to move beyond them, to understand how and why
I took flights of fantasy.

Some days I feel all alone in suffering the breakup. I can feel
the dull ache of my heart mending. Often I am aware of my broken heart healing, especially when I go within, see God within
me, and am still. And then I know what I need to know. My heart
knows. My body knows. My soul and spirit know, too.

When I get in touch with myself by going within and am able
to let go of unhealthy behavior patterns and unhealthy situations
and people, I am authentic. This letting go allows something beautiful, powerful, and healthy to show up in my love life. I have had

moments of profound love. When I'm there I am grateful for the people and experiences that created such pain in growth.

AUTONOMY

In understanding her story and changing the lines on an emotional and mental level, Michelle herself changed. She claimed the ego's birthright: autonomy. *Within autonomy lies the power, the right, and the responsibility to self-govern. Within autonomy is the return to emotional honesty that allows for profound and loving intimacy.* Though she still has "down" days, Michelle has a psychological freedom she did not have before. She understands the roadway into her patterns, and she has established a roadway out. She gave up beliefs that were outdated. She saw how a young child would easily conclude what little Michelle concluded, given the experiences she had, and would look elsewhere to get emotional needs met. There was truth in what she experienced, after all. She developed compassion for the little girl inside her and promised to care for her in ways she had not done before.

She also learned that this kind of healing is not a theoretical concept. The child with emotional needs holds energy in her psyche that can be owned and put into life in good ways. Embracing the symptom instead of scorning it helped to speed up her process. She replaced fear with appreciation and tenderness—two ways the ego can show us Love's Way. To ego, love illusion is always a search to get something we needed to get in our development and did not. How can we fault ourself? Michelle is grown-up now and can know what she did not know before and bring love to her healing.

Recognizing our drama in the here and now seems essential to moving out of our denial and into autonomy where love can more easily flow. Our challenge is to spend more time in a life of autonomy, our original destiny. That reality is our birthright. In actuality, the autonomous self should not have to be identified and reinforced. Since we have been asleep for so long and the grooves of our early influences run so deep, we initially lack trust in ourselves. And since most of our transactions are invitations to repeat our story, we slip from time to time, even under the best of circumstances.

When we are real, the sense of our worth and that of others and the world at large is not based on conditions. We are accountable to self and others. We maintain a position of emotional equality. We experience a renewed passion for living and respond to primal urges. We are spontaneous. Our intuition is heightened as we open to the world. Creativity works through us and we live in the present moment. We recognize that the past and present are all really one. We look back only long enough to reclaim parts of ourselves lost in early development.

The autonomous self opens the door to love. It is important to spend the time that's needed learning about our story and how it protected us as we separate from the past. Our foothold can be a bit uncertain, and we need time to get comfortable with our vulnerable state.

We must integrate such changes into our mind, our nerves, into the very body we live in. After all, we do live in a human body; some say it takes six months to incorporate a change so that each cell is in tune with the change. In addition, we often find present relationships changing, some outdated friendships ending, and new friendships beginning. We are working toward a well-integrated ego that will allow for heightened states of loving intimacy. Often, this starts with an inner struggle. That struggle, however, later becomes a dance. The dance occurs when we allow ourselves to be in our story just long enough to experience ourselves changing. Now we have moved to the Bigger Story where the soul reigns. The soul is home. We notice we have become wiser and have brought in an observer self who keenly watches and nonjudgmentally calls us to attention as we do our relationships. Spirit is there, too. In autonomy, we have developed the internal man and woman, the "good mother" and "valiant father" we've been looking for in others.

CHANGING OUR STORY: THE PAIN AND THE JOY

All does not run smoothly in this wonderful process, however. As we begin to change our stories, doubt and resistance appear. It's as though we want to make one last test of the old scripts. "Am I sure I want to go ahead with this?" "How do I know my new story will be any better?" "I haven't had it so bad, have I?" "My life was predictable before; what can I count on now?" "Will anyone be there for me after the transition?"

Sometimes we feel as though we are being crucified, arms outstretched and pulled in opposite directions. Resistance is only doing its job. *Whatever we are asking the ego to give up is what it designed for us in childhood to keep us safe and give meaning to our life.* Thank it; talk to it and educate it; be patient. Soon it will join you, and as it does, healthy aloneness replaces loneliness, and periods of solitude come to be felt as freedom. This is a time of "falling in love"—and all by yourself. It may be one of those stellar times when you really do know that love is everywhere.

Once we have owned our story and consciously made a shift to reclaiming our authenticity, life is never the same. A life of autonomy feels right. It calls us forward to the best aspects of our humanness. We may spend considerable time in the search for identity, focused on knowing ourselves, experiencing great insight, developing an inner parent, and being more concerned with self than others. But this is both temporary and necessary to our relationships and our self. When we consider that this is nothing less than destiny, opening the heart to experiencing more love, we can see that it is worth the time and effort required.

Before long there is still another shift. We take fewer trips into the past to find ourselves. We are living more in the now and are surer of our footing. Whether or not we are responding from our story becomes irrelevant; we know we will learn from any experience we have.

We notice a change in our focus: gradually we move from "I versus you" to "we." We take what we learn and walk more fully into our relationships, choices, and life decisions. We are *aware.* We are amazed when we realize that *we are more like we were and more different than we ever dreamed possible.* And we know what those words mean.

We ask simple and deep questions, just as we did in childhood: "If I'm so little and the stars are so bright, big, and far away, why do I feel so important?" "Why do I feel like the stars are my friends?" We begin seeing plants, bugs, snakes, birds, clouds, people, land, and lakes in a new way.

At the same time, we begin feeling a double bind. We are at

once more connected to, and more alienated from, life. We take more care about what we say and to whom we say it. Living in love, we may not like all that we see, yet we are called to live with it and love it all. The authenticity of our heart has spoken.

Autonomy, we discover, is not anarchy, antidependence, or doing what we want when we want to do it. Autonomy is not an excuse to fight or grab for a privileged place with power plays. Nor is it a justification for self-gratification, greed, collecting more possessions, or staying out of relationships.

Autonomy comes to mean the freedom to be who I am as I am, to know what my truth is, to know what feelings in a relationship belong to me as opposed to what I believe others want me to feel. It requires taking responsibility for my actions and the ensuing consequences of those actions. It requires living my life in ways least harmful to others, life, and myself. It is ethical. Autonomy becomes the discovery of my essential nature, which was separated from me as I got lost in the little story. It is the ownership of the bruised and neglected inner child who feared love and intimacy and developed a misguided sense of power. It means developing the inner woman/man, the inner father/mother who can care for the child within me and guide it into trusting itself, others, and life again. And it means absolute emotional honesty. That honesty becomes an opening to a deeper understanding of falling in love.

And yet autonomy is not a stopping place. It is not *the* answer or *the* end. To our goal-oriented minds, it may seem that once we achieve autonomy our ordinary love relationship problems will fall aside. Our relationships will be easier, and there will be less pain. Not so. Because we are honest, what we learn instead is that in our love life *what is easy isn't always honoring, and honoring isn't always easy.* And once we are awake to love and realness, once we are out of our sickness, there can be no going back to the blame, shame, control, or addictions of our old drama without taking full responsibility for these behaviors. Slips, yes. Excuses, no.

This step in humility, this acceptance of our life of illusion, presents a paradox. As we own the powerlessness of what we have learned, we are free to fully experience the creative energy that helps us see ourselves anew: "I am less who I thought I was and yet more than I dreamed possible." We continue in search of who we are born to be and discover what we are here to do in this life. We begin following our bliss. We begin unveiling the multi-dimensional lover in us.

As people discover their realness, they develop well-integrated personalities. They speak more frequently of God, destiny, world concerns, moral values, and meaning. They more frequently experience warm, close, supportive relationships that are capable of deep love. They exude a confidence that draws others to them in good ways.

Focused solely on autonomy, however, a person can remain narcissistic. Had each of us received everything we needed in just the way we needed it as children, we would be autonomous as we left our family of origin near age eighteen. So what, we should ask ourselves, is beyond getting real? Is knowing our own story an end in itself? Is personal authenticity all there is?

Remember that everyone has a little story. None of us had all of our needs met in childhood in an orderly way. That is impossible. Our parents, being human, failed us at times. Their failures will only remain our weaknesses when we blame them or demand from others what we failed to get in our developmental process. We all suffered trauma and not always at the hands of parents.

Keep in mind that on some level our drama is perceived by the ego as crucial to survival; thus it won't easily be given up. You will discover that there is always an element of truth to it.

Remember also that your story is as unique to you as your fingerprints. You can discover what purpose it serves; you can find what fears keep you from letting go to love. If you are unable to let go of fear, self-destructive relationships, self-defeating beliefs, hurtful behaviors, and limiting emotional responses, it's time to seek outside help.

Remember also that this is a process and will not happen overnight. But with clear intention and faith, you will get there. And "getting there" doesn't mean tying everything up in a perfect package. It simply means you will be able to understand why you say and do what you do, what is your stuff and what is not. That will allow you freedom to stop stressing out about love relationships and relax long enough to get to your heart and to harness that powerful resource, Love.

THE WAY OUT

Pandora left one thing in her box: Hope. Just as there is a way into the messes we make in our love lives, there is a way out. There is a road of self-discovery if we want to take the time. Many will not. But those who do will be the ones who "walk the point." First in the line of combat, they take the greatest risk and get the most hits. They are the warriors of the heart.

In my books *Is It Love or Is It Addiction?* and *Loving Me, Loving You,* I wrote about how I struggled in my own ego life and wished I had models and a roadmap to guide me. Since I did not, I reflected on my process and the process of my clients and discovered that there are seven stages that we go through to get back on track with the assignment Love gave to the ego. Clarifying the phases, knowing what leg of the journey I was on and where others were in their process, helped me immensely. I understood the meaning of the word *process* and that I could not be anywhere other than where I was, even though I didn't always like where I was. That was true for others, as well. And in my ego life I couldn't skip stages or jump ahead of myself even though someone wanted me to be elsewhere. Nor could others automatically be where I was even though I wished they could be. I learned that a person further ahead in the process had to develop patience while waiting for the other. A seven-year-old can know what it is like to be three because he has been there. But no matter how hard she tries, the three-year-old cannot be seven or understand what it is like to live as a seven-year-old. But, oh, how she wishes she could hurry up and get there.

Here are the stages we are each called by Love to go through:

- Denial
- Discomfort
- Confrontation
- Psychological Separation
- Resolution of Self
- Healthy Belonging
- Reaching Out

Denial

Here I remain unaware that I have fallen asleep. Given that I have joined the masses and learned my story well, I live in the world of great pretenders. I look around and notice that I am like the others, or if not, I have a predictable role that keeps being reinforced. My relationships have a semblance of predictability. It does not seem to matter that they are addictive, dependent, or immature. As I look around, my condition looks quite familiar. Besides, I have my roles, my compulsive habits, my addictions, and my illusionary life to keep me in denial. And I seem to be getting through life okay.

Discomfort

I begin moving out of denial when I feel inner rumblings of discontent. "What is this agitation I feel inside of me?" "Why is there not more love in my life?" "Why do I not feel safe?" "What is wrong with me?" "Do I love him?" "Do I love her?" Still in my little story and true to what has been modeled, I take care of the restlessness by looking outward. I move from one compulsive habit to another. I may self-medicate with addictive substances or relationships with people and things not good for me. But it works for a while. I take care of my agitation with affairs, pornography, overeating, having another child, or a spendy shopping trip. By now I have forgotten Love's assignment and cannot remember that the agitation is the energy of love waiting to be owned and expressed. So I watch what the masses do and move ahead or return to denial.

Confrontation

I'm getting ready for a good fight. This pain is too great; this relationship or being out of relationship is too painful. I cannot stand the death I feel inside of me. I want out. Now I'm ready to take the bull by the horns. The things I have repressed or denied start coming out, and others are hearing about it. Crisis and more melodrama are on the increase. There are words and more words. Sometimes in relationships too many words are spoken, the wrong kind. They hurt and injure. Sometimes there are ugly scenes, and I say and do things I never thought I would. I up the ante with power plays in desperate hope that the others will change and get me out of my self-imposed prison. I have a right to my rage and my judgment now. I may have been collecting it for years. Still in the old ego story, however, and true to what I have learned, I will focus on what others are doing or not doing and get them to change so I can have the life I deserve. I confront them now. And whoever is in the story today will get the accumulated venom of my history and maybe even Mother's and Father's and Grandpa's and Grandma's histories. "How dare you abandon me? How dare you not let me have my feelings and needs? How dare you try to control me?" I say, until I drop in exhaustion. When nothing changes I get a wake-up call: depression, illness, a threat of divorce, hidden shame, domestic abuse. I begin to get it. Maybe the answer is not in the other. Maybe it—the way to love—is inside of me. I can begin to see my patterns, my self-medicating, and my loss of self, and I'd better do something about it. If doing something about it is too painful, I can always go back to my comfort zone of denial for a while.

Psychological Separation

It is time to look into my ego story, my life script. I must disengage from others for a while. I realize I have been playing a role and I don't know who I really am, what thoughts are my thoughts, what feelings are my feelings, what actions are done for them or me. I'm confused. I can no longer deny the wreckage of my life and make others responsible. I must stop empowering and learn what is driving me. I'm not ready for emotional commitment because I have too many inner taboos in my psyche that prohibit it. Why do I say yes when I really want to say no? Why am I afraid to tell others what I really think? Why am I afraid to love? What do I believe about men, women, power, love, and relationships? These questions need answers. Given the space and time, my ego is happy to be recognized and have the opportunity to tell its story and get back its birthrights—autonomy, spontaneity, creativity, and the capacity for emotional bonding. I will examine decisions I've made and see if they hold any truth today. I may not have much to give other relationships right now as I go into the trenches and heal old wounds and traumas. But this is temporary. Already I feel myself changing.

Resolution of Self

I am beginning to integrate the old and the new. I get to marry me. I like who I am becoming. I like claiming my birthrights. I like having a rich emotional life and wants and needs. I trust myself in ways I never dreamed of. I try on the coat of many colors. Some demons show up that require taming. I get to play with them un-censored for a while. But resistance shows up questioning me for one last time. "What are you doing?" "Do you really know where you are going?" "Can you trust the process?" "I want to have more predictability." "How do you know it is better on the other side?" I play with the old and I play with the new. I feel pulled by others. But I have seen too much and I cannot go back. Love's Way is the only way, and I find it starts out with me. But I am getting bored with this self-attention. It's been good but I want to try my new skills and discoveries with others.

Healthy Belonging

I enter relationships now with more fervor and commitment. I recognize that while love still feels great in my one-on-one rela-tionship, there are many relationships waiting for it. Love is much more like a circle now that I am open. My heart is really beating and it does not shut off unless there is a good reason to hide it. I stand tall, walk straight, and project my power. Yet I am not afraid to say I feel vulnerable and I need your love and support. I understand that there are three entities in every relationship and that two halves do not make a whole. How-tos are easier to take in now that I've rid myself of the inner clutter that kept me on the edge of emotional intimacy. I can say good-bye to old outdated relationships without shame or blame. Sometimes I need to. I am also free to commit in ways I never dreamed possible. I can for-give, though I might not forget. I have boundaries, not walls, that let me breathe my energy in and out. I am green and growing. And I am a safe container for others. People know that and come to me.

Reaching Out

This stage is a big surprise. I started the process to stop feeling so much pain in love and life. I wanted to have more fulfilling love relationships and more personal happiness. But I was hit with a big insight. To get into and clean out my story for my happiness only is narcissistic. To do it with the goal of more fulfilling relationships might be codependent. The reason I needed to do the ego-level work was to open me to love. And since I am energy, as are others, relationships are but the fueling docks we need in life as a place to mutually refuel our tanks. When we do, we each can go out into the world and do what really matters: share our soul gifts with life and do our spiritual lessons. We get to splatter love all over the planet—in our work, in our creative activities, in our love relationships, in our families, communities, and the world at large. We get to love the earth, the air, the wind, and the sky. We are emotionally healthy and bring that health to everything and everyone we choose to. And since on an ego level we have limits, we will need to make good choices to keep the ego vibrant.

EMOTIONAL HONESTY

The big bonus in knowing our stories is a return to emotional honesty. When we are living our melodramas, whether aware of it or not, we are living a life of emotional deceit. We did not start out censoring our feelings. We put them out for the world to see. We soon learned that some feelings were not okay and others were. We smiled when we were sad. We expressed anger when we were really scared. We learned that we had to lie about what was going on. Without emotional honesty we cannot experience love in the form of emotional intimacy—the great gift ego has to offer.

Emotions have been cursed for years. Plato viewed them as wild, out-of-control horses that had to be reined in by the rational mind. Some religious theologies have equated emotions with sin and temptation. Mind and emotion were pitted against each other, with mind clearly given higher status. Fortunately we are moving away from mechanistic notions, learning about the interrelationship between mind and emotion, and seeing that emotions have intelligence, too.

"Emotional intelligence," according to author Daniel Goldman, not only exists but also is a marking of successful dealings with life. Though separate, the mind and emotions relate. Neurologist Antonio Damasio points out that patients who have damage in the area of the brain that integrates emotions and thinking are unable to function effectively.[2] The key is how harmonious the two are. Have you ever had a strong emotional reaction to someone and talked yourself out of it? Synchronizing these aspects is important to love relationships and our health. It's interesting to note that there are stronger neural connectors from emotions to thinking than vice versa. When we feel about something, we tend to remember it. Once experienced, an emotion can become a powerful director of future behavior and perceptions.

Many experiments now show us that the emotional messages the heart sends to the brain affect it all—what we perceive, how we process what we perceive, the feelings surrounding the event, and how we behave.[3] If the rhythm patterns of the heart were chronically emotionally negative as a child, we find those patterns familiar and even desirable. We become comfortably miserable. In our emotional deceit we manipulate to get our own favorite bad feelings, since the healthy emotional responses are not allowed. It is what we know. It is as though we are attached to the drama, the chaos, and the painful feelings. Some emotions we manipulate with are deemed positive: being happy and putting on the good-girl face like Michelle. Acting courageous like Jack.

If what I have been saying is confusing, I think I can understand why. There are three categories of feelings we need to be on the alert for, and being emotionally intelligent requires us to know the difference. Emotional pain is nature's way to tell us we are getting too much of something or not enough. But not all feelings are reactively legitimate. Feelings can be tricky. Physiologically we feel in response to survival needs and emotional needs. These are *reactive* feelings. I experience fear when someone lunges at me. I feel anger when I see a child abused. I feel sorrow when a love relationship ends. Our feelings make sense for the given situation; we feel it, figure out an action plan, or just plain react and let it go. We are not attached to it. A second feeling is what has been referred to as a *rubber band*. Sometimes we feel too much and overreact to a situation and do not understand why. This is because it is related to some feeling-laden event in the past that we never got closure on. I smell cigars on a man's breath and feel repulsion and do not know why. Later I remember that the uncle who molested me smoked cigars. A third category of feeling is called a *racket*. It is called that because we learn to manipulate the world with it. Usually reactive feelings were forbidden or disapproved of in our little stories. Since we cannot *not* feel—feelings are electrochemical reactions in the body—we find substitute feelings that are acceptable. And they help promote our story lines. Most feelings we have are rackets, and we collect them to justify the big depression, the divorce, the domestic abuse, the one last relapse into our addiction, the affair, or the "poor me" victim posture. Self-righteous anger, shame, inadequacy, loneliness—all have a history.

As humans we need to feel. Suppression is not the answer. Emotions are energy, and that energy stored up will implode or explode at some point. Emotions do not come with a morality. They can be used to heal and they can be used to harm. Though we must take care not to lose spontaneity and prescribe how feelings should be expressed, we must find ways to develop a saner emotional life. We must find ways to get to the higher emotions of the heart and live from there. Putting heart back into our most intimate relationships can help us be smart about the way we feel.

"Emotional intelligence," according to author Daniel Goldman, "implies the ability to self-regulate our moods, control our impulses, delay gratification, persist despite frustration, and motivate ourselves. It includes empathy for others and the buoyancy of hope."[4] Knowing our little story, emotional intelligence and a well-integrated ego go hand in hand. Knowing our stories and clearing out what is no longer useful promotes a well-integrated ego. A well-integrated ego has the ability to read emotions, distinguish between the three categories of emotions, think about emotions, and act on emotions. There is an infectious self-confidence, creative problem solving, and the ability to delay gratification when necessary. I feel sad, I think about why I am sad, I acknowledge the want or need, I give it a voice and let go. If the need or want is met, I feel relief. If not, I grieve my loss and get on with life.

This is very different from the less integrated ego, living in its little story where our emotional rackets contaminate the thinking process. Art, in grief because of a relationship breakup, started out with "child grief" filled with old "poor me" story lines. "I cannot stand this pain, it will kill me if I don't kill me first. I am such a loser." With encouragement I asked him to become an adult man with pain. As he spoke the words "I am a man in pain," his demeanor shifted. He legitimized the pain, looked at it as a necessary part of his grief, and let go of old story lines he had believed as a child.

A person with a well-integrated ego who uses emotions wisely has been referred to as well-adjusted, confident, dependable, responsible, mature, of fine character, a caring leader, cooperative, steady, predictable, trustworthy, potent, self-motivated, and having good follow-through. This implies that such a person had many of the psychological needs met growing up or called on surrogate parents or mentors to assist along the way. It is important for children to get their parenting from many sources, not just two. In talking to my own children as they approached teen years, I told them to take the things they liked from my modeling, throw away the rest, and find other men and women they admired and learn from them as well. I would not be offended. In fact it gave me a little room for error.

Emotional Intimacy and Our Story

The greatest gift the ego in love contributes is the experience of emotional intimacy. Many of the old reasons for staying in primary relationships are no longer there and yet we stay. We feel a deep ache in our heart when our partner is not there. We long for connection. Why? Intimate relationships ground us emotionally and remind us of our inevitable connection with and need for others. They are a place of belonging that helps us tackle life fearlessly. They are our safe havens on earth. When we're safe, we are willing to look at our story and hear another's. They are the places we give and receive love on the ego level.

True intimacy—sometimes called emotional bonding—is rare. In fact, the word *intimacy* is often misunderstood to imply physical or sexual connection, often illicit. The best definition I have come across so far is by Eric Berne, who says intimacy is *a profound exchange of feelings, thoughts and actions in the here and now.*[5]

It can be verbal or nonverbal. It is authentic and is a reflection of who I am with you in this eternal moment. I have no walls, no barriers; only the truth of who I am in this moment. I do not hide in the future or the past or in analyzing you. Intimacy is not chitchat, lamenting past events, or projecting "what-ifs" into the future.

Emotionally intelligent people are not afraid to say what they feel or why. They communicate without fearing the outcome. Though brave, they are not stupid; they take care in what they share and with whom. We learned earlier that sometimes it is not safe to be open, and we might choose not to share. An emotionally honest person, however, acknowledges inwardly what is going on and knows that not disclosing makes sense in that moment.

Because intimacy is happening now and requires us to be open, vulnerable, raw, and emotionally naked, we seldom experience it. In moments of intimacy one is undefended and absorbs the total experience into the psyche, good or bad. A bond is a natural result of any moment of real intimacy. Though intimacy can bring with it a state of euphoria, it can be present in moments of profound terror as well. Vietnam vets bonded in crises of pain and terror. A parent and child may bond in a moment of sexual abuse.

If our experience was positive, we will seek more of the same experience. If it was painful, we recoil in fear and design barriers made of psychological beliefs in an attempt to be safe: "Do not trust anyone, you will get hurt." "Love hurts." "I am unlovable." A child who reaches out for closeness and is pushed aside or is injured may decide to stop reaching out. Whenever we experienced violations of trust, we felt some level of emotional pain in our intimate encounter. Since I believe most of us, if not all of us, had violations of trust, we fear intimacy as well as crave it. Without a willingness to examine our experience and beliefs around intimacy, all of which are part of our little story, it is unlikely that we will get to experience the ecstatic intimate moments we crave.

In our ego story we find an emotional event, usually painful, and create a story in an attempt to make sense of it. Then the story begins to take on a life of its own. It is all a cover for our fear. As if one fear is not enough, we pile a psychological fear on top of the initial physical fear we felt at the moment of trauma. It is one

thing to fear intimacy because a brother molested us; it is another
to fear intimacy because of the meaning we gave to the incident.
Self-made meanings like "men are scary" or "I am shameful" add
insult to injury and keep our intimacy quotient low. But it becomes the story line we live out, and we unconsciously seek
people who fit it.

Most people will deny that they feel fear. They cover it up with
self-righteous indignation, defensiveness, numbing out, keeping
busy, addictions, compulsive habits, sleeping, putting on a false
front, attacking others, creating an "I am fearless" stance, or fos-
tering melodrama with biochemical highs and lows.

Most complaints in therapy come down to issues of emotional
honesty. As Audrey said: "I have been married over twenty years
and have four children with this man, and I do not know him." In
her response to his question "How much do you love me?" she
answered: "I can only love you as much as you will allow me to
know you. All I ask is that you would expand yourself more so I
will know you and in time can truly love who I know." She also
later admitted that she was not going to make the first move. She
wanted him to open up before she was going to risk being honest
and express love to him. It was just too scary to be the first one rejected. "I want certainty," she said. And then she laughed at what
she'd just said. There is no such thing as absolute certainty in the
human condition. Love relationships let us down. They become
boring. We experience disappointment. As Audrey went on to
say: "I want the prince, the hero, the 'happily ever after' promised
me. I am a good person—why shouldn't I have it, even after this
many years?"

Fear of intimacy is perhaps the ego's number one problem. No
how-to-do-relationships book will succeed if a person has not examined his or her story to discover what supports the fear of intimacy that dwells deep in the mind. Intimacy is the profound
expression of our identities, and when the ego is willing to open
up, all the other aspects of the self come along for the ride: body,
soul, and spirit. When that happens—and it requires a high level
of trust—love is as good as it can get in this lifetime.

What appears to be intimacy in most relationships is not. We
concoct or copy dramas we've learned in our families, read in romance novels, or seen on television or at the movies. Melodrama

is psychological gamesmanship that pulls in players, lives on the edge of a promise of intimacy, and then pulls the plug. Just as we are about to get the ultimate closeness that is guaranteed to heal the wounds of the past, we discover instead the old wounds being reopened. But the adrenaline is running high, the chemicals are flowing, and we know we are alive.

Is it any wonder that we become addicted to melodrama? Think of the benefits—biochemical aliveness, a cast of familiar characters, predictability, recognition, reinforcement of our story lines, and the payoff: repetitions of bad feelings we are familiar with. Melodrama gives the illusion of intimacy without all of that vulnerability stuff. We are up; we are down. We are the sulking victims. We feel excited, at least for a while. Melodrama can pull us up from a depression or get us out of boredom. It seems to have so many benefits, of which the biggest is avoidance of fear: fear that you might abandon me, fear that you might not like me, fear that you might betray me, fear that you might want too much of me, fear that you might hurt me. Because of the fears, Eric Berne said we are lucky to have three hours of sustained intimacy in our lifetime. The rest is drama. The irony is that drama ultimately brings about the very thing we fear.

WHAT'S YOUR BOTTOM LINE?

To love somebody is not just a strong feeling—it is a decision, it is a judgment, it is a promise.

—Charlotte Kasl

Though following Love's Way requires an ego that supports a rich emotional life, including caring intimacy, not many people come into therapy because their relationships are blissful. We have all experienced pain and abuse in our love relationships. We have already given the many reasons, and they can be found in our stories. Psychological fear is the culprit; it is distinctly different from physical fear. Our psychological fears come about because of trauma, yet they are the fear on top of the physical fear. They are generated by the decisions, conclusions, and self-promises we made at the time of trauma and have all but been forgotten. Then these fears get projected out onto others in abusive behaviors.

he questions, then, are, How do I know I am being emotionally abused and how much should I put up with before I draw the
line? When does a relationship have more disease than health?
The answer lies in *progression*. Is the insidious disease, like any
addiction, progressing? Does being emotionally honest result in
an escalation of hurtful or attacking behaviors? Is emotional
abuse followed by mental, physical, sexual, or spiritual injuries?
Too often when we speak up, the other will try to shut us up, calm
us down, or fix us, or will condescend, judge, analyze, attack, push
us away, or leave. Love's Way is to stay with the discomfort and
work through it without too much damage.

The ordinary bumps and scrapes, the growing pains of a relationship, are inevitable. We try to do it right and we make mistakes. We flounder. We try to put together a hundred-piece
relationship puzzle with only a handful of the pieces.

Abuse is something else. Abuse refers to any time we are hurt,
injured, molested, ripped off, raped, mistreated, violated, damaged, defamed, attacked, misused, prostituted, neglected, slan-
dered, oppressed, persecuted, victimized, minimized, maligned,
deceived, ditched, disregarded, forgotten, avoided, insulted, ex-
ploited, restricted, ignored, abandoned, betrayed, overlooked, nul-
lified, ill-treated, vilified, or belittled. Any of these behaviors imply
insensitivity at least and cruelty at worst. They are toxic and kill relationships. The end result is heartlessness and a broken heart.

When we experience these hurtful behaviors, we will feel an
emotional discomfort. Giving voice to our discomfort *is* intimacy.
It is using our emotions intelligently. It is using our pain to stop
hurtful behaviors. It is taking responsibility for setting our bottom line. Love's Way is one of care, concern, generosity, praise,
appreciation, attentiveness, giving, renewing, recognition, respect,
preservation, protection, praise, benefit, regard, kindness, consid-
eration, nurturing, shielding, sustaining, self-rule, honor, dignity,
commendation, admiration, safety, loyalty, dedication, *and* tough
love. When we have put out our bottom line and others continue
to abuse us emotionally, we must call a halt. If not, we enable
them to hurt us.

Love's Way insists that in our ego life we identify emotional
discounts, those occasions when something about us is reduced,
marked down, cheapened, or downgraded. Some aspect of who

we are, what we feel, what we need, what we think, and what we do is ignored, minimized, slighted, considered irresolvable, made unimportant, or made greater than it is. We know we are living out or have returned to our little story when we continue to let things happen. Once is an accident, twice is coincidence, and three times is an established pattern. If you do not "call" the discount on number three, you are being emotionally deceitful. You have tolerated too much.

Like Twink in the William Saroyan story that opened this chapter, we are all sick at times. We bring our sickness into our relationships. And when we are sick we want and we want all kinds of things. But what we really want is ourselves. Stepping in and out of our ego's story, we are amazed to discover that what we were looking for was there all along—our soul. In our souls lies the jewel of many facets. We discover innocence, beauty, pure heart, passion, purpose, and inner harmony. Discovering all of this, we begin to see others as they are, wounds and all. We nourish health in those we love and in ourselves. We create safety that encourages emotional honesty. We begin to live the Bigger Story, the story where the soul resides.

In healthy ego love, two people need to be more interested in the process than the content or the outcome. Committed to the evolution of the relationship, viewing it as alive, each person takes responsibility for the story lines, the traumatic histories they bring in and often recreate, good and bad. Unlike the usual marriage vows, which stress commitment as ownership, the vow for healthy ego love says, "I am committed to being and becoming the best, most honest me and to sharing that me with you in a way that honors us both." In this vow there is an assumption that, though knowing our ego's little story *explains* our out-of-line behaviors, it does not *excuse* them.

Here is a recipe for a vibrant, healthy ego love life:

- Find a handful of people willing to know their little stories and to be emotionally honest.
- Have a genuine interest in being with a partner and creating a bond of intimacy.
- Acknowledge the ego's life of illusion.
- Balance giving, receiving, and initiating.
- Seek to know the other's story.

- Understand that we have heart wounds and thus fear.
- Never play with the heart.
- Be powerfully committed to inner work.
- Know that people hurt others because of their hurts.
- Work to stop projecting stories onto others.
- Provide a place to work through old wounds openly.
- Allow for tension and discomfort.
- Be open to whatever comes along and deal with it.
- Give from a well-developed sense of self.
- Be alert to the inner trickster and to self-sabotage.
- Display ego strength by displaying your autonomy.
- Explore layers of false beliefs about love, relationships, men, and women.
- Step out of cultural and family stereotypes or story lines.
- Make conscious unmet developmental needs and openly tend to them.
- Be safe, solid, and attentive.
- Be organic, alive, changing, and moving.
- See emotions as the ego's intelligence.
- Say what you feel, what you think, and what you do.
- Set a bottom line for acceptable behaviors.
- Resolve conflict creatively.
- Live with imperfection.
- Help others search for the truth of who they are.
- Nurture and protect the intimate connection.
- Satisfy emotional needs.
- Allow for the raw edges to come out into the open.
- Fuse sex, love, and romance with heart.
- Let someone get to really know you.
- Offer friendship, bonding, grounding, healing, laughter, tenderness, acceptance, and assurance.
- Embody personal responsibility, integrity, commitment, discrimination, and predictability.
- Carry out bonding rituals.
- Have both fervor and calm.
- Tackle the material world of money, work, service, power, and sex.
- Accept emotional reactions without overindulgence.

- Understand that words, thoughts, and actions are energies.
- Be intentional and conscious.
- Be full of self-love and self-intimacy.
- Maintain clear boundaries.
- Acknowledge and accept that each relationship has three entities: an "I," a "you," and a "we."
- Provide a place to share happiness and suffering.
- Share power.
- Own both masculine and feminine energies.
- Accept likes and dislikes.
- View mistakes as lessons to be learned.
- See a relationship as an ongoing process.
- Have a high level of emotional intimacy.

MEDITATION FOR THE EGO IN LOVE

My ego is a wondrous gift. It provides me with a rich emotional life, the ability to nourish and protect myself, others, and life. With its ability to think and remember, it helps me to navigate in the material world. I will free it of the glut and clutter it may have accumulated over the years so it is free to bond in loving ways.

Memo

To: Soul

From: Love

Re: Your assignment

You are the bridge between spiritual love and human loving. You will understand both realms. Without you, relationships cannot know me. Your responsibility is to bring desire, passion, longing, zest, awe, and depth to earth-based love relationships. You are deeply acquainted with both pathos and ecstasy. The ego can get trapped in drama, romance, and sensuality, but you bring entirely new and fresh meanings to these words.

You can fire up the heart in ways no other aspect of the human can. You will be housed in a body, where you will have to share space with the ego. That will not be easy. The ego has a way of taking over as it gets lost in its little story. You will help the body see that addictions are but a window into the soul.

You are to live the Bigger Story. You understand that simply *living* the story is more important than any outcome the ego might be after. To you, life is an eternal now. You do not judge events or people, and you understand they are there to help you on your journey. To you a love relationship will be just that: a journey. You bring gratitude for life's awful experiences and can do a lot to help the ego get to forgiveness. You are to help the body and ego extricate themselves from their conditioning and get back to Basic Trust. And when you do so, the human heart will not only open, it will swell because it is so full of me. Heart and soul are meant to be united.

You will be mesmerized by the wonderful delights of human experience, but you must not get lost in them. Your task is to be initiated by the fires and storms in life and yet to love so completely that you can come closer and closer to understanding my power. It may feel like you are going to hell, and some days you may want to give up. On some days even the little story that the ego tells will look good as you retreat. Stay in the Bigger Story, experience it all, and watch yourself transform. Without you, life and love are shallow and will be driven by the body or ego. But body and ego aren't the only ones to watch out for. Spirit, with its lofty goals, may want to bog you down or tame or "improve" you. Don't let it. You're meant to be a bit wild and wet and dirty.

Love relationships will provide the betrayals, pathos, longings, and tortures you will need on your spiritual journey. You must turn this lead of your life into gold. You are the diamond in the rough; the spirit's inner child—remember that. You have many gifts and you must put them into life and love relationships. These gifts are unique to you and will enhance life on earth. Your task is to live those gifts no matter what traumas, injunctions, and limitations you encounter. You must stay with all of life and not get buried in its debris.

But be forewarned. Your assignment will not be easy. Your body is dense and forms habits easily. It reacts to reminders of past experiences. The ego, living in fear of others, will put you to sleep. It means you no harm. In fact, it designed its story to protect you from others' desire to own you. But it will forget all that and believe it is you. You must come through, using all the creative intuition you can muster.

When trauma surrounds you, you may want to leave the earth plane for sheer self-preservation. But you are meant to live on earth and must go back to join body and ego. I cannot be fully present if you are not there, too. I know that there is some danger in you, something called Dark Eros. Relishing all aspects of life, you're drawn to the dark as much as to the light. You are curious and mean no harm, but you can harm yourself and others if you stay in the murky places too long. You may feed the body's and ego's tendencies toward addiction and my way may well be forgotten. But do not despair. You are not alone. There's plenty of wisdom and guidance for you. Listen to spirit and follow its guidance at those times. Spirit will guide you with compassion and help you get back home to who you are and what you are while on earth. On those days you will experience ecstasy.

Good luck.

CHAPTER FIVE

The Soul in Love

◼ ◼ ◼

Finding our camel, our soul—the thing rejected and almost
forgotten puts something alive and real back at the center of us
and from the centered aliveness we connect with others. Love
follows, since now there is someone in us to love and be loved.
Our true connectedness with people, other beings, as well as
the universe begins to emerge.

—Denise Breton and Christopher Largent,
Love, Soul, and Freedom

BEYOND THE EGO'S STORY

There is a monster inside the boy
Mothered by a Celtic Witch
Cast ashore by a demon Viking.
It crawled through the blue eyes of innocence
to perch at the edge of heart
waiting,
watching for whispers
the soft flutter of a monarch's wing.

And so restless becomes the heart
who lives to hear a kindred beating.
Whose food is flesh
and water tears
The flame of a million candles
to light the poet's way.

The boy looks to the sky
and sees God in the clouds.
He feels the rise and fall
and the rise again.
The burst of possibility,
the swell of love against his chest
turns to pain.
His heart is twisted
gripped in the hand of the beast.
Fast falling and falling apart
it retreats
to beat small
silent
and alone.

What mercy affords our demons?
Do we wait a lifetime for repose
from these villains?
When ropes and chains bind our hopes
the screams of these thieves
like sirens over doves.
When truth becomes a kaleidoscope

Remember
the human heart does not die
before the angels call.
This stoic army of one
can rise against the devil
beat back the monster at its door.
The heart is pure
and will defeat the chaos
If it only believes that it can.
                    —Nina Watt

What we can hear in Nina Watt's poem is that there is another
way to experience life and love, one in which we touch total
agony as well as moments of ecstasy, pathos, and longing. This
way of experiencing goes much deeper than our ego story—our
life script—and is longer lasting. Perhaps this is why we don't

spend much time there. It is Hades as well as heaven. It is soulful loving.

There is a Bigger Story. As we travel on Love's Way we do not stop with identifying our worn-out patterns and feeling our warped sense of self. We open up to a self in hiding, a self that was being protected and feels safe enough now to openly live its story. It was always there in the background. It used its wit and cunning and plucked meaning out of our human story. It is glad to have breathing room because it is the truth of who we are. It is our soul.

To the soul, drama has an entirely different meaning than it does to the ego. So does romance, pain, and yearning. The soul does not recoil from these experiences or judge them. It devours them and makes them a part of itself. To the soul, love is a fiery force incarnate, a force that it is searching for in this earthly domain. The soul has a Bigger Story, a bigger agenda, or no agenda at all when it comes to love relationships. Love relationships are the fodder from which the soul can magically transform. The soul is immersed in the Bigger Story going on and views it as a mythical journey. The soul is Cinderella, the victim of an alcoholic stepmother, who in her pain and agony discovers her true destiny. There is no right or wrong. The soul does not shy away from heartbreak, divorce, and scandal; no, it savors the experiences.

To the soul, love was once home and it knew love well. It believed love would be found on earth. Jumping into the human story, however, it soon forgot most of what it knew about itself and love. Gradually, lost in ego, it looked outward more than inward. In the ego story, in our script, we lost contact not only with our soul but also with the fiery source of love. But a gnawing nostalgia remained.

Some deeper part of us remains rooted in that vague sense of loss and incompleteness that gets translated into desire and longing. This is the Bigger Story that all mythology speaks to, including the story of Cupid and Psyche.

A MYTH OF SOUL LOVE: CUPID AND PSYCHE

There was once a king who had three daughters. By far the fairest was Psyche, whose beauty was such that men traveled from afar to gaze upon her. They would even say that the goddess Venus could not compare with this mortal. So enchanted with Psyche were the mortals that they began neglecting Venus. The honors once given to Venus were now being given to a mere girl who would die. Upset by this travail, Venus called to her son Cupid, the beautiful winged youth known by some as Love. His arrows had no defense on earth or in heaven. "Use your power and make Psyche fall in love with the most vile monster on earth," Venus demanded.

No doubt he would have carried out the plan had he not but seen Psyche. So struck by her beauty was he that it was as though he had shot one of his arrows into his own heart. Speechless, he said nothing to his mother, who confidently believed the god of love had done as she had asked.

Strangely, Psyche did not fall in love with a vile man. Nor did any man fall in love with her. Time went on and Psyche's less attractive sisters married. Psyche sat alone in her sadness, only admired and never loved. Concerned, her father rushed to an oracle of the god Apollo and asked for his help in finding her a husband. Unknown to her father, Cupid had already spoken to the god Apollo and revealed his love for Psyche. The father was told that Psyche should be placed on the summit of a hill where her husband, a winged serpent stronger than the gods themselves, would come and make her his wife.

The lamenting Psyche was dressed in mourning clothes and sent to wait out her fate alone on the hill. She sat in the dark waiting for the unknown. She wept and trembled. A soft wind, Zephyr, came and lifted her and carried her gently to a soft, grassy meadow, fragrant with flowers. It was so peaceful there that she fell asleep. She awoke near a river, and on its banks was a beautiful mansion made of gold, silver, and precious stones. She could see no one but a voice told her that the palace was hers and invited her to enter. She could feel that her husband was there and that he was not a monster but the lover and husband she had longed for. She was right. But she could not see him, only feel him. Though not fully content, she was happy enough and time passed quickly.

One night her husband sensed danger to Psyche in the form of her two sisters. He made her promise not to return to the hill where, he was sure, they would seek her out, for it would bring sorrow to them both. She promised him she would not. But, saddened, she finally convinced her husband that she should go. He set one condition, that they not be allowed to see him. If they did, Psyche and he would be separated forever.

Zephyr brought the two sisters, who joyously reunited with Psyche. Seeing her life of abundance, however, the sisters soon became filled with envy. They questioned Psyche about her husband. They departed with gifts of jewels, but when they returned home, a jealous rage overcame them. They began to plot against her.

They returned once again, against the pleas of Cupid to Psyche that they not be allowed to do so. When the jealous sisters arrived they told Psyche that they knew that she had never laid eyes on her husband and convinced her that he indeed was the fearful serpent Apollo had warned her about.

Psyche let fear overtake the love she felt for her husband. Terror flooded her heart. She became suspicious about why he refused to show his face. Listening to her sisters, she plotted to see him and then kill him. Anguish set in. She loved him; she feared him. She would kill him; she would not. He was a monster; he was her husband. Her anguish began to consume her. In her growing distrust she decided that when he was sleeping she would do the forbidden and look at him and kill the fearsome monster she was sure he was.

That night she crept into his bedroom, lantern and knife in hand, and saw her husband for the first time. As she saw Cupid's delicate beauty, she wept. Rapture filled her heart. As she wept, the knife she intended to plunge into his heart fell from her hands. It knocked over the lamp and Cupid awakened. Shocked to see Psyche and her faithlessness, he fled. Psyche rushed after him as he gave voice to the words: "Love cannot live where there is no trust."

"The god of Love was my husband, and I, wretch that I am, could not keep faith with him," wailed Psyche. She decided to devote her life to searching for him. It did not matter if he had any love left for her, she would demonstrate her love for him. She had no idea where she would go or where the search would lead her.

Cupid returned to his mother to have his wound cared for. When he told her it was Psyche whom he had loved and who wounded him, Venus left Cupid and was determined to destroy Psyche.

Poor Psyche was miserable. She prayed to the gods for help, but they would not go against Venus for fear of her. With no hope left, she decided to approach Venus directly. What else could she do? She would sacrifice her life, become her servant. Venus delighted in this and convinced Psyche that no man would have her. She gave her the menial task of separating poppy seeds from millet and left. Staring at the heap of seeds, Psyche gave up. At this moment, the tiniest of creatures heard her plight and appeared. They sorted out the seeds and left Psyche hopeful. When Venus returned everything was in order. She was surprised and angry. She sent Psyche on yet another seemingly impossible venture. "Go to the river, find sheep with fleece of gold, and bring me their shining wool," she demanded.

Psyche did as she was told but despaired once more and prepared to drown herself. As she was about to end her life a little reed spoke to her, explaining how to get the Golden Fleece. Psyche followed the directions and brought back a great heap of golden fleece to Venus.

Angered, Venus sent Psyche on still another futile task. She was to get water from a black waterfall in Styx, the river of hate. Psyche knew this was a hopeless task, but she had begun to trust that a way out would be provided. She was not disappointed. An eagle, poised on great wings, took the flask and filled it with the black water to be brought to Venus.

Venus did not stop. She gave Psyche a box to carry to the underworld, where she was to encounter the goddess Proserpine and ask for some of her beauty to take back to Venus. Obedient as always, Psyche went to find the road to Hades. Through many obstacles Psyche succeeded and returned with the filled box.

The next trial came through her own vanity. Curious about the contents of the box and hoping it would contain a way to Cupid's heart, she opened it. She saw nothing in the box, but soon a languor overtook her and she fell asleep.

At this juncture, Cupid, the god of love himself, stepped forward. Healed of his wounds and still longing for Psyche, he could not remain imprisoned by his anger or his mother. He flew out the window and began searching for his wife. Finding her asleep by the palace, he wiped the sleep from her eyes and put it back into the box, pricked her with an arrow, and awakened her. He scolded her for letting her curiosity get the best of her and told her to quickly bring the box to his mother. In the meantime, Cupid went directly to Jupiter and said he did not want any more trouble. Jupiter, father of gods and men, assured him that all he asked would be granted. Jupiter announced to all, including Venus, that Cupid and Psyche were married and that he had bestowed immortality upon Psyche. Venus could not object to a goddess as a daughter-in-law.

So all came to a happy ending. Love (Cupid) was united with Soul—for that is what Psyche means—and that union could never be broken.

THE BIGGER STORY

Our Bigger Story, the soul's story of love, is something like the story of Cupid and Psyche. The soul, like a capricious child, is not afraid to take the journey of the heart. It views love as a sacred mystery, a magical, mythical journey full of hills and valleys, joy and sorrow, impossible tasks, experiences deemed good and evil by our egos. But to soul, there is no right or wrong or condemnation. What's important is that the lessons be fully learned. In our Bigger Story we can trust that out of the chaos and light will come a lesson, a new form of life.

From a soul perspective, our life scripts are more than parental injunctions, negating beliefs, adaptations to trauma, fear trapped in our bodies, or emotional incest with our caretakers. Loving "with all of my heart and all of my soul" has a meaning far beyond anything the triune brain can process. The Bigger Story is a mythological story, a realm of the deep and the mysterious. It calls on the lover's heart, which is not afraid to live in suspense, awe, mystery, and imagination.

A soulfully lived love relationship is organic, alive, and tenacious. It does not concern itself about the past and the future; it is always happening now. It has an immediacy that cannot be predicted or controlled. This is why most self-help books cannot teach us to generate a vital, organic soulful-love story. The ego says, "God, give me answers to love and make it now." "Make her love me and make it now." "I cannot stand this pain a minute longer, take it away now." Even when our brains tell us that change is an ongoing process, we often rage against that knowing. We want our fix now, our answer now, and we want those answers to transform our lives into complete and perfect packages—now. The soul is not so urgent.

This urgency for positive outcomes becomes a frenzied search through self-help books, seminars, and therapy groups. We must not give in to this ego frenzy or believe that, just because we understand our life script and our limiting programs or have newfound "how-to" knowledge of love, our love life will be perfect bliss. On the contrary, what we have learned is how difficult the human life is, how easy it is to lose ourselves, just how dense life can be. But we have also learned that we are more than ego. We have soul and depth of living. And when we live from soul, we have more openings of the heart, allowing more of the rare moments when we realize that love is everywhere—above us, below us, in us, and around us.

The soul is happy that our little ego took the time to look at itself and discard the glut and the clutter that did not belong to it. From the Bigger Story's standpoint, our ego's little story was only a false attempt to keep secret our soul's blueprint and to keep it out of harm's way. Now soul can have some breathing room. Soul does not condemn us for the mistakes we made. It accepts pathology in our relationships as gifts that helped to birth it. It can find magic in any situation if it is allowed to reign. It knows that our love stories speak more directly to our soul life, anyway. Soul digs the myth.

Soul reminds us that we must take care in learning about the problems and patterns of the ego, but not stop there. If we do, we defeat the purpose and get back into control and narcissistic self-gratification. The purpose of knowing our ego drama is to stop empowering it and viewing our love relationships from a distorted perspective. Not only is the melodramatic ego way to love a distorted road map, it does not allow the juice and the freedom the soul needs to explore all of life and love. Therapy and self-help books cannot and should not attempt to define the soul of a love relationship or try to "fix" it. Though we might have strong desire for a relationship to continue, for example, from a Bigger-Story perspective it may have served its purpose. And we may not know the purpose until some time later.

The heart, in the Bigger Story, allows things to disclose themselves and does not get caught up in the "what ifs" or the "if only" that the ego is so bent on agonizing over. Love is not a project or an end in itself. It is a mystery. Living from the Bigger Story, we are not focused on success or failure, how-tos, or rigid ideas of how to live and love. Instead we let our love relationships reveal themselves to us. We do not analyze but reflect. We see beyond the human dilemma and limited beliefs. We ponder deeper questions that have a much different flavor than the ego questions: they are more poignant and have more universal themes:

"What am I to learn from this betrayal?"
"What is this ache in my heart?"
"Where is this melancholy coming from?"
"I wonder why this person came into my life now?"
"How is this present situation challenging my soul?"
"What is it stirring up in me?"

This is a big shift from the narcissistic ego questions: "Why am I such a failure?" "Why can't she love me?" "How could I be so stupid?" When you have made this great change in your mode of questioning, you are living the Bigger Story.

As Thomas Moore said so clearly in *Soul Mates*, "Relationships have a way of rubbing our noses in the slime of life—an experience we would rather forgo, but one that offers an important exposure to our depths."[1] Everything in our love relationships is material for soul making: the good, the bad, and the ugly. Unlike the ego, soul does not shame us. It recognizes that relationships bring out the worst in us as well as our virtues. Unlike the ego, soul does not seek perfection, but rather depth of experience. Right is not a set path or a yellow brick road that leads to one destination. Right is allowing a love relationship to be an alive process, always unfolding before our very eyes, with a soul and a spirit of its own. The magic is in the taking of the detritus and decay we experience in our lives and love relationships and turning them into gold.

The bottom line is that the soul gets to the heart of the matter. It does not need solutions or resolutions. Living the Bigger Story, we are not looking to the other to make us feel good, repair a damaged childhood, or become our sugar daddy or surrogate

mother. We are not looking for the image partner that helps us fit
into society. We are not dwelling on the past nor are we blaming
it. We are beyond the learned definitions and the cultural formu-
las for love and have dug deep into the love story itself. As we
dig, we understand everyone's part in the story, including our
own. We can stay with the chaos until it presents its truth. Not
caught up in the reactive nature of a feeling, we explore and wonder why we feel the way we do. Instead of analyzing things to
death, we remain curious. And instead of driving ourselves crazy
with obsessive worry, we wonder what went wrong and when
the pain will end.

As we go through each of the stages that free us from our ego
constrictions and the body immobilizations that accompany
them, the soul is surrendering to each moment of each stage that
moves through us. Each stage has a particular relevance and
meaning. We do not control the process, we are moved by it. We
do not judge the scripts we wrote; we know that we wrote them
to feel safe and keep our ego satisfied. But now that we know better, we live the Bigger Story. We also know that the more work we
do on the mundane personality level, the more our soul will show
up in our love and life. The soul finds its way into our love life
and then decides what to do.

Though this seems paradoxical, the more detached we become
from our human drama and obsessive fantasy life, the richer our
drama and fantasy life become. We recognize that we are in ego
drama when we tell our stories three times and nothing changes.
We are stuck. If we are living from the Bigger Story, the story of
the soul, the experience nourishes us into a new form. We are different, and the lines of the story are changing. The fires of love
have initiated us.

Romantic love energizes the soul so that the soul becomes
playful, buoyant, and even gets to use its cunning. It knows that
every moment can be lived erotically. Passionate living is not reduced to sex or romantic love. Unlike compulsive sex, love, and
romance addiction, where the hunger is never satisfied, loving
from the Bigger Story creates no hunger because we are fully
present, heart and soul. We feel the power of love as we taste it,
touch it, smell it, and sense it all. Love and life seduce us.

SOUL IN THE SERVICE OF LIFE
If the soul could have known God without the world, the
world would never have been created.

—Meister Eckhart

When soul enters a love relationship, you can be sure that it will
take charge. We want it to! The purpose of psychological work,
giving up addictions, and tending to personal growth is to get the
covers off the soul. It has been waiting for this glorious day for a
long time.

Soul, the spirit's inner child, just plain wants to explore it all. I
think we all know what that experience is like. We want to taste
the stolen apple, roll in the mud, explore the forbidden.

MY STORY
Several years ago I went through a dark night of the soul. Deluged
with major events—the death of my father, Lyme disease, and
being stalked, to name just a few—I went and hid out in my
North Woods retreat to catch my breath. I sold my clinic and my
urban home, told friends and family of my need for solitude,
packed up, moved in with nature, and sank into myself. It was
both frightening and exhilarating to have so much time to myself.

I went to the nil point—the place of absolute nothingness that
we're all supposed to have the luxury of getting to at least once in
life. I let go of all roles and illusions and waited to see into what
form I would emerge. It was here that I really got clear on the difference between ego, soul, and spirit. And it was strictly by accident. I took time to meditate, to come from my heart and ask deep
questions and sit till the answer came to me. I captured my experiences in a journal. Recently, I came across the following journal
piece that I had nearly forgotten.

What has repeatedly been presenting itself to me in the months
of my chosen time of quiet are the words *soul* and *alchemy*.
Alchemy, the sacred art of change, is calling on me to turn the
lead in my life into something greater. What is also becoming
clear to me is that it is not only my body that needs rest and
healing, but my soul as well. To my surprise, I am also discovering that my soul and spirit have been in conflict. I never sepa-

rated them before and thought my spirit and ego were in battle. Not so.

The soul in me is the little girl who learned to tie her shoes at age three so she could get up before her parents had opened their eyes, watch the sun rise, feel the dew on her cheeks, and breathe in the deep earthy morning air. It was the little girl who explored and risked—took chances. She sat under the neighbors' porch and said deep forbidden words with her friends. It was the little girl who made dandelion ring bracelets and gave them to her mom as a gift from the heart. It was the young girl who wanted to check out the dark man in the doorway who enticed her and her sister with a dollar. Her mom and dad warned her of him, but she just wanted to see what a real pervert looked like. "He doesn't know I know about him and I just know I can peek and run before he even sees me."

It is the part of me that still wonders what it would have been like to walk into the dark doorway. It was the young girl that played hard, got in trouble for exploring beyond bounds, and yet knew it was right to explore and it was parental duty to set limits.

There was no regret. How can there be when one is listening to the soul? It is soul that understands depth of living, is earthbound, imaginative, creative, lustful, passionate, is drawn to both light and dark, loves to explore caves, feel mud oozing through her toes and when she does feels vibrantly alive. I have always been soulful and others have not always appreciated living soulfully—not when I was a child, and often not even now.

I am learning that I am good. Many experiences I have been judged for have been necessary for my soul's journey.

The spiritual part of me has been the teacher, the one focused on learning lessons, conscious living, transcendence, enlightenment, evolution. It is the part of me that is like the blade of grass pushing its way through the hard dirt in its quest for reaching the sun—always growing, becoming something greater. It too has been an important part of my life as I savor a quiet moment, feel the presence of Creator in all things, feel the great oneness I am a part of. It gives me purpose and meaning beyond the material. It is the part of me that loves others in spite of what they have done to me. It meditates, prays. It helps me live in my heart, and guides the soul. It keeps me growing. And it has been running the show for much of the time in recent years.

The inner conflict I am experiencing is this. The soul says to spirit: "I am tired, I want to rest. I want my grief, my sweet melancholy, quiet. I do not like people right now. They have been mean to me—cruel. Stop pushing me. You always want to learn lessons, find meaning and bliss and pass it on to others. It is my time. I have been gravely injured. Why, you hardly noticed how black-and-blue I am; your goals have been so heaven-bound. Come back to earth—look around, experience life, get to know me. If you deny me or drive me, the dark side looks pretty tempting. I need my sorrow, my passion, to find soul mates, to heal my wounds. I do not always want to be growing and learning lessons. I want experience!! Gut-wrenching, heartwarming, deep, evocative, timeless experience. I want my longings. I am not your ego. I am the real essence of who you are. I want the raw stuff of life, the moment, the void, and to play in it until the form emerges. Stop trying to transform me or enlighten me. I like the boiling, bubbling, churning and yearning!"

What could spirit say but "I hear you"?

"And besides," soul went on, "I am not too deep, I am deep. I am not bad; I am good and lustful. I am not too picky, I want Soul Mates. I am tired of the 'do not,' the empty talk, the soul-less people. I feel lonely when people's souls are not there or they use spirituality or religion or propriety to box or judge me. I must be allowed all of my experiences without judgment or impatience."

"Yes, I know you are good," says spirit, "and I know you will hear me if I need to call you to attention. I love you. Thank you for talking to me."

This conversation from my journal may seem a little wacky, but it was a major turning point in my life. Before this conversation I felt tired and confused and was dealing with my problems on a strictly ego level—so nothing worked. Reconnecting with my soul saved my life.

DARK EROS

Now it's time for a few words of caution. I've mentioned the heart's role in soulful loving, and it can't be overemphasized. The fact is that being in touch with soul alone is not the same as being in touch with love. The soul, too, lusts after earthly pleasures, and that powerful desire, by itself, can be dangerous. Soul without heart can and does injure. Soul needs heart savvy to experience real love. Heart *and* soul together are what make the process of life joyous and put us in touch with sacred wisdom. Heart and soul combined are what give us depth in our love relationships.

On the other hand, it won't do to be in denial about the power and attraction of heartless soul love, or Dark Eros. (In the addictions field we know how powerful denial is and how we can be consumed by the very thing we are in denial about.) The Eros of the Marquis de Sade and other cultivators of dark love holds a fascination because it is essentially *love of our desires* and those things that fulfill them. Love's shadow needs to be owned and recognized; if we are innocent or naive about these dark urges we will be used by them, taken over before we realize it.

We are selfish, we lust, we hoard power, we delight in another's misfortune. We watch gory movies, we enjoy erotica. We feel pleasure when the boss who fired us also gets fired; we get off on not giving to someone what we know they want from us. We open our heart to someone and then close it and feel triumphant. The high-minded may feel regret after behaving this way, but for many of us it feels good to linger in the shadowy feeling of heartlessness even for a moment—especially if the one we've hurt has caused us pain, too.

The parent-child relationship is prone to sadomasochism, which flourishes there because of the power differential between adults and children and the drama of submission and control that is played out in the family. Blocked urges from a parent's childhood as well as ego projections are common themes in child abuse. Yes, there is a little of the Marquis de Sade in all of our souls and we'd better recognize it.

Why is it that human beings can murder six million Jews, liquidate a third of the population of Cambodia, and annihilate thousands of Tibetans and not blink an eye? Why do we use innocent children in pornography? Why is so much entertainment geared at stimulating us with every imaginable possibility of sexual and moral perversion? Why do we kill and rape? Why is there greed?

We may well be reenacting our earlier traumas, listening to ego-level messages that justify cruelty: "They have it coming"; "It's payback time"; "I'm at war." Chances are, however, that we are letting darkly demonic forces in our soul take charge. We may be so depressed that we have to act out. Denial and repression of the dark forces may make them all the stronger when they flare up.

What's most likely of all, however, is that we have not yet done the work to open our hearts and bring love into our desires. Lustful living is important, but it needs a giant dose of heart and the heart's virtue to give it the name of love.

JOE'S STORY

Joe couldn't believe it was happening to him. Severely depressed, he sat in my office in a state of shock. His wife had a court injunction against him. He was considered dangerous and was not allowed to see his wife or child.

"It started out innocently enough," Joe said. "We both enjoyed it. It started out with playful spankings. They thrilled us both. But it did not stop there. I wanted more. I thought she did, too. It escalated from there to painfully humiliating sexual acts. I stopped for a while when she was pregnant. But the power and depth of desire took over, and I forced the issue soon after the birth of our baby. I would not hear her pleas and forced my will on her. I got off on my power as I chained her to the bed and inflicted more and more pain. It was as if the devil himself possessed me. She was a mother now and that came first to her. I would not stop and let her nurse the baby. He was crying for her and still I could not stop. She almost died, and it was as though I did not care.

"I was not raised this way. Is there hope for anyone like me? Have you ever heard of a story like mine before? Am I evil?"

"Yes, there is hope, and, yes, I have heard this story before. What is evil to you?" I asked.

"You know, am I one of those people of the lie? Am I run by devil urges? Am I possessed?"

Both Joe and his wife were active Christians and from the outside looked naive and innocent, a model couple. They had suppressed much of their sexual longing and curiosity for most of their lives. He felt totally stifled by a rigid Christian mother who was afraid of her own desires and urges and punished him severely for any hint of curiosity and soulful exuberance. A sinister smile would come to her face when she spanked him; he suspected that she was aroused by the punishment. He became a model son—and an angry child who turned to masturbating in secret and exploring a neighbor girl's body. He always led a secret life and always felt guilt and shame.

Like so many people who suppress the soul's desires and fantasies, he thought he could let them come out and remain there in a playful and harmless way. It didn't work. Once the pent-up energy was released it took over and became power, dominance, and violence.

Before I could answer Joe's painful question about himself, it was important to determine whether he was in therapy just to keep his wife or whether he wanted to understand himself and own his soul's misdirected longings. His answer to that question was the right one. He went into treatment and he and his wife agreed to come back together with a new understanding of how soul urges can vivify, excite, and animate, if they are ministered to by the heart.

Soul Wounds

> What lies behind us and what lies before us are tiny matters
> compared to what lies within us.
> —Ralph Waldo Emerson

We all have wounds of the heart. Some are so deep that they go beyond the trauma in our bodies and our psychological memories and are etched deep in the soul. They hurt incredibly. Some of these wounds are sexual. But the soul, living in Basic Trust, understands that everything is as it should be, even the most excruciating pain. We might not realize until a year down the road that the horrendous betrayal we suffered was exactly what was needed to shock us into reality and catapult us into the next stage of our journey.

The ending of a relationship with someone with whom we

have shared love means a total surrender; a kind of death, but also a profound soul initiation. When we approach such events from the Bigger Story, we remain in love. Accepting this death without blame, shame, or endless explanation creates a sacred alchemical moment. We find ourselves in a passageway to something new.

All endings contain the seed of a new beginning. Inside the soul is a stirring of the new seed that's been planted. We cannot see it, but we feel its presence. Living in Basic Trust, we patiently allow for quiet gestation time. With hurting heart still open, we affirm the words of Kahlil Gibran, "The deeper that sorrow carves into your being, the more joy you can contain."[2]

In the loss, we do not see ourselves as doomed or as failures. Our self-examination is based on a sense of curiosity and is very different from the self-deprecating messages put out by the ego. We ask soul questions: "I wonder what my soul can learn from this?" "Is my soul asking more of me in my love relationships?" "How can I grow to be a more adequate lover or friend?" Rather than defend, deny, or exult in our wounds, we learn to bring them to every love relationship and give them a place. After all, they are a part of our Bigger Story. They can become the heart and soul of a relationship. To be responsible for everything is to honor the mystery and give sacred meaning to our pain and injuries.

MELISSA AND NED'S STORY

She had to tell him. It was time. For more than a year she had agonized over her decision. Her obsessive mind would go over and over every affair he had or could have had. She compared her body to their bodies. After all, she had learned that beauty is what counts and that she was not beautiful enough. He even told her so in many different ways. "Why don't you grow your hair?" "Get in shape." Two weeks after they were married he started his affairs.

"They must have bigger breasts, fuller hips. They must be better lovers," she continued to tell herself. She had been driving herself crazy before she came for help. In therapy she learned about her story. She remembered trauma created by a disjointed family, an absent alcoholic mother, a beautiful older sister with whom she always compared herself, and a father who convinced her she was a helpless child. She never felt a sense of being enough, of belonging or fitting in. She was ruthlessly image-oriented in high school. And then she met him, the ideal mate. A jock: funny, charming, the center of attention. Was she ever lucky! He fit the fantasy. It was the story of Cinderella herself.

If the pain had not been so great she might never have looked into Pandora's box and risked her illusion of herself. The pain forced her to look. She pulled out the dirty laundry. Gradually she uncovered the truth. Slowly she began to polish the little jewel—the little girl who had been lost and had been looking for love for years. She listened to her personal story, she cleaned out what did not fit with what she knew to be true. And she saw her soul: innocence, raw beauty, love. Slowly, over a year, she threw out negating beliefs, faced traumatic memories, and spent quiet moments getting to know herself.

For a while she felt smug, grandiose, and better than her husband. Her own perversion showed its face. "He's the pitiful one," she bragged.

Slowly her bravado calmed down, and she got to the theme of the Bigger Story. She saw how two innocent, unaware people had come together believing they knew what love was. All they had been taught they tried, and all of it failed them. As she let herself feel this, she began to feel her heart. What she discovered there was sweet sorrow.

She recognized how naive she had been. She honored the wounds she had suffered. There was no longer blame or shame. Yet in her heart she could not cross over and retrieve the connection she knew was necessary to live with her estranged husband. Though she had found forgiveness she could not find desire.

Anguish filled her heart as she told him what neither had wanted to hear, that she must leave. Yet she did so with as much caring and grace as she could muster, behind the tears. "This is not about you or me. I have been searching deep inside and speak from my heart. I love you and I cannot live with your addiction."

He was devastated. The inevitable had come. Could he remember his story, in order to hear her from his heart? Would he rage, scream, and project his shame onto her, as he had done so many times before? Could he understand that though their relationship had begun as episodes in their little story, they had reached this point of truthfulness thanks to their souls, and they were now living the Bigger Story?

Loaded with the guilt of his affairs, he lashed out. "I screwed up everything. I'm a loser." His devastation deepened into sobbing as he touched his soul and released the pain. Nodding his head with understanding, the rage and shame metamorphosed. His soul was maturing before our eyes. Bringing heart and soul to his shame, it became remorse.

"Oh no, oh no," he mourned. It was an acceptance of what was.

There was more love present in the room at that moment than ever before. Perhaps their souls knew that it had taken courage to get where they were, to live every painful human step—the addiction, the psychological drama—and to finally reach a point where they could be real and present to each other. Perhaps they could even be grateful. Each had grown enormously. Each had recaptured innocence and self-respect.

That they could not bridge the gap between them was not a sign of love's failure, not in the Bigger Story. In the ego's terms they had failed, and perhaps in the eyes of their families and community, too. But to the soul all was as it should be. The soul will digest the experience and change. It knows no other way to be.

Love is eternal, but a human love relationship sometimes needs to end. The ego foundation was wobbly, or built in illusion. No matter; Melissa and Ned's souls will always love each other. A soul knows no ending, and it does not judge. It mourns. Grief and mourning are essential soul elements. If we deny these, we are in our egos or shifting prematurely into a state of spiritual detachment that's not authentic.

If Melissa and Ned keep their hearts open, they will love with more soul. As they love with more soul, they will keep their hearts open. And an open heart, we have learned, is a direct connection to that blazing energy, love. They will share love in other places.

SOUL LOSS

Some soul wounds are so deep and extensive, however, that they amount to the loss of soul; we are emptied of this magnificent energy almost entirely. Sometimes in a trauma our souls appear to leave us. In psychology, this is referred to as dissociation. When it happens we might feel empty, bored, numb, or depressed. Other symptoms are staying stuck after the loss of a loved one. In our love relationships we sometimes give pieces of our vitality to others. Whether it is with a friend, lover, parent, or boss, it is as if we say, "Here, take a piece of my soul, my essence, my power. Now will you accept me? Now will you love me?" Sometimes we hang onto another person's soul by grasping onto them with our thoughts and obsessive behaviors. Like vampires, we steal their vitality as they try to disengage from us.

To fix the soul loss we self-medicate any way we can. We may look to others to fill the void. We may get more caught up in our obsessions, addictions, and other compulsive behaviors. We might wander around, stealing other people's energy. And we may not even understand what we are doing or why. As one client said to me: "I took delight in pointing out my former boss's faults, as she had done with me. It helped me get through the aftermath of being unfairly fired. Then I realized that every time I talk about someone's faults I give away a piece of my self-esteem, my soul. She was winning. Letting go, I took back a piece of me."

Living and loving with soul requires that our souls be at home. If we are to live the Bigger Story we must *be* big. To be as big as we are, to be the hero and heroine of our life stories, we need to have our souls back. We need our power, our essence, our vitality, and our personal medicine.

It may not be enough to stop an addiction, leave a toxic relationship, reframe negating beliefs, or release panic from our body. If there is soul loss, deeper measures are called for: attention to dreams, deep reflection, rituals and ceremonies, deep massage work, body work, telling our story to a spiritual mentor, or soul retrieval. Shallow conversation and behavioral and cognitive therapies do not touch it.

With the seeming increase in violence and trauma in our lives, we must take this seriously and develop ways to both heal and protect soul. Our bodies and egos are not the only parts of us that must step out of the past. Our souls, though immersed in a present now, often stopped the clock in a traumatic moment and are stuck there. We must retrieve them. In our love relationships we have a responsibility to discover our vulnerabilities and protect ourselves in ways we could not as children. We can sense when someone is draining our energy and we need to move away or put up a barrier. If we get sick in a certain work environment we need to formally request changes or remove ourselves. Surrounding ourselves with soul friends, soul mentors, and soul mates is a must. Waiting for toxic people to change is not the answer. Standing up to abuse is.

We are not helpless victims. Even in the most terrible conditions we can hang onto our souls. Viktor Frankl is living proof. Sent to Auschwitz as a prisoner in World War II, he was stripped of everything—his beloved bride, his parents, and his profession as a psychiatrist. His name was replaced with a number. He later wrote about his experiences in *Man's Search for Meaning.* They could take everything but his soul. In the darkest of days he was still able to contemplate the love he felt for his wife and his soul's meaning.

"Soul loss is a spiritual illness that causes emotional and physical disease. Who takes care of the spirit when it gets sick?" asks Sandra Ingerman, author of *Soul Retrieval.*[3] In many cultures there are soul doctors, medicine men, or shamans, whose gift is to intercede with the spirit world and retrieve lost soul parts in sacred ceremonies. We have exorcists in Christian churches, and we have alternative medical practitioners who understand and work with energies. But even if we make use of such healers, the main responsibility for soul health resides with us: We need to welcome and keep our souls alive and well. You can be sure our souls are not going to stick around if we keep empowering other people, failing to maintain healthy boundaries, believing we are unlovable, not protecting ourselves from toxic shaming, and sucking in other people's projections. Soul needs a healthy body, a well-integrated ego, and a dazzling yet wise spirit.

We've said that the soul is the spirit's inner child. If the child is not home, spirit cannot enter. If pieces of the soul are not home we cannot really see the sunrise or sunset, really hear a poem, appreciate music, resonate to the earth's heartbeat, or bond with our lovers, family, and friends. We lack depth in our spiritual life. We will operate from ego and will need the more authoritative religious systems to keep us out of trouble. We may have a physical heart but no greater heart. We will be dead inside. (As I look around, I see too many blank stares and numb faces, too much quiet desperation, too many criminals without remorse and seemingly without conscience. This deadness may operate at the level of psychological trauma, but I think that in most cases it goes deeper.)

A SOUL RETRIEVAL JOURNEY: JACOB'S STORY

Jacob had completed drug dependency treatment and therapy and left an unfulfilling job and an abusive love relationship. In spite of his major life changes, he still lived on the edge of a depression that was pulling at him to self-medicate in old familiar ways: drama-filled love relationships, gambling, sex, alcohol, and drugs. Feeling that he was on slippery ground and not wanting to go backward, he reached out for help. "I feel like a part of me is missing. I don't have my vitality. Life is good, my attitude is right, and I have a spiritual life going for me. But sometimes lately I feel surreal and only partly alive. I should be feeling better," was his cry.

He sought a soul retrieval ceremony with a man trained in core shamanism. Here is what the practitioner said:

> While there are many ways a person heals soul and spirit through ordinary means, soul retrieval is a very specific healing ceremony intended for this purpose. At their request I journey to nonordinary reality in an altered state of consciousness on behalf of the person, to gather information and to retrieve lost or stolen soul parts should there be any. I do not do the work. Spirit does. I am only Spirit's vehicle in the ordinary world.
>
> At his request and with no idea what might be discovered, Jacob and I did such a ceremony. With the assistance of my spiritual helpers, I journeyed on his behalf to recover the lost parts of his soul.
>
> In that ceremony I was taken to various realms and specific scenes, none of which I had known about before. I encountered a young boy in third grade who had been shamed by a teacher for stumbling on a word as he read in front of classmates. Knowing no other way to get out of a shaming situation, his soul left his body. He never got back. I spoke with the

absent Jacob, telling him that the earthly Jacob needed him embodied. He agreed to come back.

Next, I was taken to a scene where a hysterical woman was grabbing onto Jacob. Feeling enraged and jealous, she clung to him. Only after a long conversation with her did I persuade her to let go. This soul part of Jacob was eager to return home.

The next encounter was more unusual. I was taken to a very dark, musty lower-world scene where I met an adult figure totally immersed in perversion and rather liking it. He had many friends assuring him that if he stayed he could have all the money, sex, and chemicals he wanted. "Why should I leave?" he asked. "Can Jacob offer me anything better than this? I don't want to return to anxiety, loneliness, and depression." All I could say was that without the vitality and desire this soul part possesses, Jacob would remain anxious and depressed. Jacob wanted this soulful self back and had done a lot of personal work to prepare for his homecoming. And if the underworld dweller did not like it, he could always return to the lower world of primal urges. It was his choice. I was only here to help. Curious by nature, this part of Jacob's soul agreed to return.

In the ceremony I described the scenes I went to in the journey and the parts that returned. Jacob had exact recall of the third grade scene. He also identified the woman as the one he had recently been in a relationship with. But he was disturbed by the third soul part, the "dark" Jacob, and he felt some shame.

"I thought the soul always aligned with the light," Jacob said with a dazed look.

"Not necessarily," I said to him. "The soul lives in dark and light and we honor it all as part of the journey. Soul is different from personality or spirit. It needs guidance. Without wise spiritual guidance, soul can get into some murky places and delight in being there.

"You have developed a spiritual practice that you did not have before, when your addictions were active. But you will need to provide more substantial soul food or this part might well leave and go back to feeding off dramatic love relationships and addictions. You must not judge or restrain it—just guide it wisely. It needs to be a vital part of your life. Your addictions held a lot of your energy. So did your relationship.

"For seven days ask yourself: 'Am I choosing to live in the light now?' If the answer is yes, there will be further work to do. You must dialogue with these parts of your soul, welcome them home, learn about the gifts they bring, and find out what they need if they are to stay home with you.

"The outcome of the ceremony is less significant than what you become through the experience. My part was easy. Now comes yours."

Not all of us need to see a shaman to retrieve our souls. Every day I need to call myself back home. Some days I need to do it more than once. Even then there are occasions when I find myself listening without hearing, praying without feeling, or living life insensitive to my surroundings. It hurts most when I am unable to feel the love of those closest to me. At those times I find a quiet space physically or in my mind, breathe deeply, pray, meditate, and call myself back home. Connected by the silver cord, soul may not be all that far away but needs a safe container to come back to and sometimes outside help to get home.

LOVE'S INITIATIONS
It is in love relationships that we are challenged or nurtured. The greatness of love stories is not in how perfect they can be, but what lessons they reveal to us. Living the Bigger Story means seeing love relationships as initiations into love's mystery. In that regard nothing about our love life is to be considered waste. Even the most awful experiences.

Linda, having experienced the ending of an important love relationship, stepped into a well of darkness. She encountered her fascination with death. Here is what she wrote in her journal.

You, darkness, are a gathering place, a place of dreams and nightmares, of knowledge yet to be conceived. You, darkness, have been feared, scorned, avoided, put on trial, blamed and yet remain dauntless. You come each day and with each breath. You believe you have a place of majesty. You are relentless as you challenge the light knowing that the light does not exist without you. You laugh, you smile, you smirk like a wicked parent to an innocent child.

Death, death, death. How necessary you are. Pain you bring; pain you say is the fertilizer of tomorrow's dreams. Birthing the new, you are within everything, so you do not exist in static form. You are but a place, a moment, a transition. Always I must be mindful of your presence as a blessing; as a part of cruel mystery.

As I experience you I shudder at the pain. I was you. I fought you. I hated you with passion. You cracked the illusionary world I lived in. This should not be, I screamed and screamed. What? Do I deserve to be without change, immortality?

When I die, I die. I face death as it is. I will take you on with the fullness of life. To greet the way of change. To say good-bye to my beloved that touched my body, housed my soul, let me touch life passionately, imperfectly, and deeply.

I can face death now. The pain of a broken heart dampened my normal senses and I got a glimpse of other realms. It pulled me out of my ego and told me I could feel tortured, change form, die, and be reborn.

It's no accident that Linda's deep thoughts and feelings about the death of her relationship read like poetry and myth. For the soul, myths provide the images and stories necessary to develop our wholeness. In them we value and explore all parts of the self. For hundreds of years fairy tales, myths, plays, and poetry filled with tragedy, romantic love, gods and goddesses, kings and queens, and lost boys and girls have spoken to the soul's yearning to come home. Something in all the great stories sparks the life in our soul. The stories have a psychic depth that is familiar. Though we walk through a life that is defined by externals, inner soul work helps us discover that the real journey is an inward one, filled with imaging, dreams, and reflections.

Religious historian Mircea Eliade, exploring ancient initiation rites, discovered that there were always three events necessary to usher the initiate into a totally different mode of being. First there was *torture* at the hands of the spirits; second, there was a *death* ritual; and third, there was a *resurrection* into a new form. In the process, the innocence and ignorance of the quester was transformed, and he or she was fired into a new and greater human being.[4]

Pain and suffering in love relationships dampen the ego long enough to give us glimpses of other realms where we can die and be reborn. Most spiritual traditions, too, speak to this process, whereby we discover the truth of our existence.

Alchemy, the sacred art of change, also posits three stages in the transformative process. *Nigredo* is the dark night of the soul. It is pathos, trauma, shattered dream, the wake-up call. *Albedo* is the period of whitening where we begin to see the jewel, the true reality of who we are, the soul. We experience moments of intuitive knowing and begin to understand what life is truly all about. *Rubedo*, with its intense reddening, purifies our human fixations and passions. It is the baptism of fire that ultimately frees us. We go from a tiny spark to a great flame. In matters of the heart, this is where we touch the electromagnets of love.

The alchemical vision says that unless the initial elements die, the Bigger Story cannot proceed and the soul remains entrapped in its limited human form, lost in its conditional and habitual existence. Yet alchemy does not create something out of nothing. It works on a base metal, improving and transforming it. In the soul-alchemy of love, our human story is the base metal that is eventually turned into gold. It is the black carbon that ultimately yields to the diamond, that allegorical symbol of love and marriage.

The late Joseph Campbell examined 240 of the world's greatest mythic stories and found that at their heart was a metaphorical journey that the hero or heroine was challenged to embark upon. Campbell became convinced that these tales were, at the deepest level, a guide for the hero and heroine within each soul—that this heroic journey played itself out in all of our (supposedly unheroic) lives, too. The heroic journey is a soul story, since the soul loves the messiness and complexity of stories and loves to encounter witches, sorcerers, vamps, and secret helpers, and in it we can recognize our own souls' itineraries through the fires of love.

There are seven phases of the great story we live, according to Campbell—The Call, Refusal of the Call, Gathering Allies,

Crossing the Threshold, Belly of the Whale, The Road of Adventure, and Great Revelation.[5]

The Call

First you hear the call. You may not understand, because of the circumstances, that the call is to a much bigger life than the one you know. Somehow you are being asked to leave the old and the familiar. The circumstances that have brought you here may not be pleasant. Your lover has left you. Your inner sexual addict jumps out at you. A trauma pops into your mind and you can't get it out. You question love. The unknown is calling you. It is in your face and will not go away. You slam the door, but the door keeps opening.

Refusal of the Call

You refuse the call any way you can.
"I don't have the time."
"The thought of it terrifies me."
"When I have enough money . . ."
"Not now, maybe later."
"After college, the wedding, the children, the divorce."
"After my parents die."
"Maybe then."
You immerse yourself in the children, the career, community service, and accumulating money and possessions. You self-medicate with compulsive habits, roles, and pretension. You have affairs, you drink too much. But the door keeps opening and you leave it open. The lure of love, the big love, is much larger than you, and you answer the call.

Gathering Allies

Moving into the unknown feels uncertain, sometimes treacherous. You have never been on this road before. Wild, daring, intense curiosity about the realms of the unknown bubbles up and keeps you going. Strangers show up, old friends come by. Strange synchronicities begin happening. Someone gives you an inspiring book. You bump into an old but much-needed mentor. You need all the help you can get, so you gather your allies. Mythic friends, talking dogs, nature spirits, or angels show up in dreams and visions. You are guided to the right group of helpers. You begin to feel safe and supported so you stay with the journey into the unknown. There is no turning back, and you understand that you are where you need to be even if you do not fully understand why.

Crossing the Threshold

With allies lined up, you step into the realm of amplified power. You are ready to face the monster. You leave the abusive relationship. You confront the scary marriage problem. You challenge the addict self. You step into bravery with a vengeance. You come face-to-face with the monster, who invites you back into your most primitive and reptilian behaviors. Perhaps it is a lover, a friend, a boss, a demeaning relationship—the monster screams as you move away and sticks its talons into you. It does not matter. You are being challenged to stay with the call or desert it. The monster wants you to be a co-monster and summons you to a duel. But you sharpen your wit and valor and get across the threshold. You do not abandon yourself. Ripping yourself free from its talons, you fight off the monster.

Belly of the Whale

You have crossed the threshold and entered into a new life. You are in the belly of the whale. This is unfamiliar territory. You have left the past and you do not know where you are or where you are going. The future is a mystery. Though unencumbered by the past, you are raw, too. The territory often appears dark and murky. Parts of yourself that were latent show up. Monsters you did not know existed come from deep within you. Anger, fear, primal urges, sexual passion, and naïveté come forth. The wild man and untamed woman inside emerge.

Archetypes burst forth, shattering ego illusions. In your excitement, you take the lid off pent-up instincts. Sometimes you even trample others. Vivid memories you do not want to deal with are a part of the package. Depression, fear, and uncertainty—you are required to face it all. It is the dark night of the soul.

In this uncontrolled metamorphosis you notice you are changing form and you cannot stop it. Exhausted, you wait.

The Road of Adventure

Spewed forth from the belly of the whale, you enter the unbounded, the open spaces. Having found soul, you bravely explore the unknown—the ocean, the desert, the cosmic spaces. You can live inside or outside of yourself. It doesn't matter. You have passed the tests and you are free to live and love with a passion, zest, and wild daring guided by deeper and more refined values. These values are not of the masses. They come from an undefined source that provides safe footing. You are renewed. You have found the beloved. Soul and spirit have united, and you once again know Basic Trust.

Great Revelation

You have arrived at the Emerald City, the realm where soul reigns. It is a universe of seeming myth and magic. You have tapped into the all-knowing abyss and felt the hand of love. You walk in several worlds at the same time. There are new challenges as you walk back into life and relationships. You are not the same, and only other heroes and heroines will understand this. You reflect to find answers.

"With what I know, how can I create a new story?"

"How can I love with caring detachment?"

"How do I orchestrate my several realities?"

All love stories are adventures that burn with a fiery passion that annihilates us and challenges us to a new life. If we are looking for a neat little story, then we should stay away from love. Love is an electromagnetic force ethereally, a pulsing heart emotionally, and luscious passion as far as the soul is concerned. When these are aligned, we feel movement that catapults us into a new reality. To attempt to control love is not unlike telling the sun to stop melting snow. Love does what it does. It moves the universe, and we are along for the ride.

SOULFUL LOVING

A soul mate is someone to whom we feel profoundly connected, as though the communicating and communing that take place between us were not the product of intentional efforts, but rather a divine grace.

—Thomas Moore, *Soul Mates*

The Soul selects her own Society—
Then—shuts the Door—
To her divine Majority
Present no more—
                    —Emily Dickinson

With the heart present, what does soulful loving look like? Actually, it has been everything we have been talking about. A soul mate comes in many shapes, not just one. It can be a cousin, a best friend, a daughter or son, a great-aunt, or even good old Mom or Dad. It can be a therapist, a spiritual mentor, a marriage partner, a lover, or a boss. Soul intimacy is rare and is not limited to one person. The person may come in your life for a short time only, but once you made the connection the spark of connection ignited something in you. You were changed in some way.

Soul luxuriates in attachments and yet yearns to be free. One can never cage the soul of another without causing harm. Our soul may be ready for a mountain climb when our soul mate would rather play in the muck for a while longer. Honoring the impulse of individual souls is part of soulful mating. The soul wants to be understood. "See me and hear me," it cries.

If we have soul in relationship, we can more easily put soul in everything we do. Life feels richer. Soul is what takes ordinary relating and elevates it to intimacy. Assuming that heart and compassionate wisdom is along for the ride, here are some ingredients for a relationship full of soul. Vary them according to which rare intimate relationship you are in.

A recipe for a vibrant and soulful love life:

- Find a handful of people who value soul.
- Love with everything you've got.
- Allow for the unknown.
- Expect everything.
- Expect nothing.
- Write letters, poetry, and songs.
- Sing, dance, and play hard.
- Touch, taste, and smell.
- Hang everything out to be seen.
- Never shame or blame.

- Love everything even if you do not like it.
- Live now.
- Accept everything in your love life as fuel for change.
- Feed your soul and the souls of others.
- Accept suffering but do not attach to it.
- Appreciate human folly.
- Deepen and enrich your imagination.
- Live in the mystery of relationship.
- Keep your feet on the ground as you reach for the sky.
- Take love to the edge of experience.
- Savor it all.
- Don't be afraid to step into the dark.
- Stay curious.
- Accept pain and longing.
- Go for depth of experience.
- Hope that you fall in love, and when you do, keep it alive.
- Live in a state of wonderment.
- Look in someone's eyes and really see them.
- Listen deeply.
- Feel it all.
- Don't be afraid to get dirty.
- Have deep conversations, even in silence.
- Go with your intuition.
- Look for the lessons in all things.
- Go to your heart for answers.
- Use your imagination.
- Wonder instead of worry.
- Enjoy the story you're in.
- See the preciousness of other souls.
- Give others their space.
- Look for synchronicities.
- Be real.
- Grieve and mourn when you have to.
- Don't get lost.
- Be passionate about your solitude.
- Leave incidental things alone.
- Never try to change anyone.
- Never hurt anyone with your desires and urges.

- Know that soulful love relationships are where ego dies and is reborn.

P.S.: I'm sure your soul has a few ideas of its own!

MEDITATION FOR THE SOUL IN LOVE
I am deeply grateful for my soul and its ability to fire up my life with passion, zest, curiosity, and longing. It allows me a depth of loving that bridges the sacred and secular worlds. I will guide and protect it and heal its wounds. I will not give it away.

Memo

To: Spirit

From: Love

Re: Your assignment

There is a reason I have left you till last. I wanted the others—body, ego, soul—to understand their part before I returned to you. And I say "return" because you and I know you never really left. You are pure energy that brings the great wisdom of the universe to the human love stories. You have been dwelling in the background all along, whether recognized or not. You are the energy that binds people and lets them know they are a community. You are life. You infuse the body and connect to ego and soul as well as the great cosmos. You are wise, compassionate, and detached. You are known by many names: higher self, the observer, energy. You blow spirit into every relationship that exists. You make a relationship sacred. Your purpose is to dwell in the hearts of women and men. In the heart is an intelligence that can elevate the mere human into a new species. You have a sixth sense and a quantum brain.

You must take me—Love—and use me like a laser to cut through deceit and pain. You are to help the ego stay detached so as not to personalize another's behavior. You are to help the soul live the Bigger Story and pull out its meaning. You will bring compassion to both the little and bigger stories. You will heal the body. You will dwell in all and everything and remind people that they are a part of one big universal story, the cosmic story. You help connect people and communities, even when they are separated in the time-space continuum.

I am an atomic powerhouse and it is your job to harness me, to put me into life and love relationships so humanity can once again dwell in the heart of God. You are to teach body, ego, and soul that I must be given with no thought of return. You show that I am a gift to be received and shared by all, and although humans will experience me in a love relationship, the relationship does not own me. You, spirit, understand that if someone refuses to receive me I do not go away. I cannot be destroyed. When you align with me, we are the Beloved that everyone seems to be in frantic search of.

You are to teach lovers that they are more than matter, that they must connect with both primal and more elevated levels of intelligence. You must help humans get out of the swamp and show them the top of the mountain. Yet you must let them dwell in both places. In fact, you must accompany them wherever they go. You must work with the soul and let it get a little dirty and, like a parent with a curious child, you must allow it freedom while keeping it safe.

But be forewarned. Your task will not be easy. Human life and love relationships are filled with hurt and pain, image and ownership; and the unhealthy ego will forget about you or give you a lowly place. Though you are meant to be the driver, you probably won't get much attention unless there is trouble. Then you will be called upon to intercede on the ego's behalf and help it know me.

You will not like it much on earth and you'll want to dwell on the mountaintop, away from everyday love relationships. But you must return to them and stay with them. Soul will give you a hard time by getting lost or ignoring you from time to time; you will have to work hard to get its attention. You have tendencies to be lofty and pedantic, especially if the ego says it owns you and tries to fit you into a box. If you ignore the body or the little story, thinking you are above it all, you will be humbled in a big way. You are not separate. You are in relationship with them all.

But do not despair. You have clear intention and faith that will be your saving grace. You are truth. You are conscience. You are light. You are happiness. You are compassion. You live in Basic Trust. And you have connection with the Divine. As you bring these to relationships, there is harmony.

Good luck.

CHAPTER SIX

The Spirit in Love

◻ ◻ ◻

> Intimacy . . . is a song of spirit inviting two people to come and
> share their spirit together. It is a song that no one can resist. We
> hear it while awake or sleeping, in community or alone. We
> cannot ignore it.
>
> —Sobonfu Somé, *The Spirit of Intimacy*

SOUL: DELIGHTS AND DANGERS

Putting soul into our love relationships gives them a deeper
meaning. With soul, love becomes playful and buoyant, and this
makes the hard parts of life bearable. Though some would have
us stop in the soul realm, when it comes to matters of human
heart, we dare not. We can easily get lost there. Glad to have permission to roam the earth unencumbered, the soul can forget its
loftier purpose, the creation of an exalted human who lives from
the higher emotions of the heart as well. Remember Psyche's curiosity? It well nigh banished her from Cupid forever. We know
what happens to uncontrolled fire.

Soul is neither good nor bad, but, as we've seen, it can become
engrossed in the darker side of Eros, from erotica to sadism.
Jungians warn that the archetypes—inner soul energies—like to
take over. We can go from not enough soul to way too much.
Disarmed and able to eat the forbidden fruit, we might keep eating until it poisons us. We might go for serenity and get lost in
sloth. We might go for passion and forget compassion. Wet, wild,
daring might forget about generosity, gratitude, luminosity, and
grace: gifts of the spirit.

Just as we get comfortable with soul in the unadulterated now, something inside jostles us. We are reminded that not only are we "being" our true self, we are becoming something very different from what we already are. We have been sent on a mission, and that mission is to bring heaven to earth. We are connected to the Divine. We must look up to the heavens *and* keep our feet on the ground. To walk in balance means to consider the seemingly disjunctive parts of ourselves—secular and sacred—and give each its rightful place. Our challenge is to make sacred the mundane by not only harmonizing our body, ego, and soul, but also giving it a dose of spirit as well. It is time to live the bigger picture of love's mystery and to fire it up with spirit intelligence. With spirit, love dwells in the cosmic story. If we do not comprehend this, our love relationships can get into serious trouble.

SPIRIT'S SHARE

Soul wants to *be* in the raw makings of life. Spirit, on the other hand, wants to climb the mountain and step out of the swamp of love's entanglements and pathos. It is always looking upward and onward, transforming and transcending. It is the oak tree in the seed that knows it will become an oak tree. It has a meaning and it means to fulfill it. Focused on the afterlife, cosmic issues, universal truths, justice, tranquillity, universal love, and devotion, it often removes itself from the human mass and the jungles of earthly experience and, solitary, ascends the mountain.

It does not want to be interfered with. It seeks awe, bliss, and altered states of consciousness. Removed from chaos, it can bask in the light. Sitting on the peak of the mountain, it can merge with the cosmos. It is divine light. It is the Beloved. A friend of the all-knowing abyss, it experiences a profound oneness, a state of bliss unencumbered by mortal living.

Up on the mountain the air is thin and pure, the flowers delicate. In this spirit realm, this altered state, I am higher than high and lighter than light. I am close to what most spiritual teachings aspire to—a transfigured, nonmaterial entity free of physical limitations. I am the universe. I am love.

It is spirit that brings more elevated love songs into the heart, too. When spirit enters, care, kindness, and thoughtfulness enter as well—qualities much needed in today's world.

Spirit refers to the life force in everything. It can enter any relationship and keep it organically moving. It helps people connect.
As Kabir said, "The river that flows in you also flows in me." It is
in spirit that we are one and can see our story in someone else's. It
is in this realm that we understand that we are all related and that
what we do or refrain from doing affects others. Though we may
grovel in the dirt for what seems to be too much of the time, we
are also sentient beings who live in the great cosmic web. We are
microcosms of the macrocosm. We are a universe in miniature.
We have within us something of the stars, the angels, the flowers,
and the sea—this is the truth that spirit knows and bestows. Ah,
but what gifts the spirit brings!

It is our spirit that brings wisdom and sacredness into our love
relationships. It provides a safe container and keeps love alive. It
heals the wounds of the heart. The world of spirit blazes with a
light that rapidly transforms what it touches.

THE LIMITS OF SPIRIT

Yet if we stay in this lofty, high-reaching, transcendent state,
spirit monopolizes life and bores the soul. Kicking soulful living
aside, our spirit imagines itself above human life, abstracting and
distancing itself, pure and uncontaminated. The haughty spirit
denigrates body and ego, too.[1] No, we cannot separate the spirit of
love from the soul of love. Nor should we try. Just because spirit
focuses upward does not mean that it is greater than our horizon-
tal living. Getting high on the union with the Divine can keep us
separate from our humanity. An attitude that is too exclusively
spiritual, too "heaven-bound," can blind us to real problems. In
our bliss we can forget that the earth is being destroyed, our children are being terrorized. We become numb to world suffering.

The spiritual message "Be in the world but not of the world"
does not mean heedlessness. It means wise detachment from the
illusions life presents. All true mystics have understood this difference. They brought love to earth and lived it! At times it was
extremely painful to do so. Christ was betrayed by his beloved
friend and he soulfully mourned. But he knew why he was on
earth and kept going directly toward impending crucifixion.
Great visionaries lived life fully and deeply even though they
knew what was ahead: Martin Luther King Jr., Gandhi, Chief

Joseph. Not one of them stopped loving. And their love was not sweet and syrupy. It was gargantuan and strong. It looked physical death straight in the eye.

Of course, removing ourselves from the heaviness of mortal living has its appeal. I have days when I want to feel "above it all" and go into solitary mode. I need time to commune with spirit world, to elevate my conscious thinking and choices, to experience the all-knowing abyss directly.

I'm not alone in this need. Thousands of people leave their families and follow this or that guru to enlightenment. Still others abandon mates, families, and communities to go in search of meaning. And while an ascetic life is a legitimate choice, it must be done with consciousness and with the desire to take part in a cosmic community. We must take care that dogma, discipline, and self-realization do not distract from dreams, intuitive knowing, and organic living and make us forget that the reason for the climb, the solitary journey, is to soulfully mate with the spirit world and bring a divinity to the human condition.

We seek enlightened experiences to bring a quality of meaning into our human relationships. We must walk our fiery, heart-based spirit into daily life. The quality of experience and loving should be enhanced by spirit, not demeaned by it. Moses went to the mountain, encountered a flaming bush, and came back with the Ten Commandments. These commandments were not intended to bind the body and soul into servitude, but to create a safety net so the people would thrive and celebrate life more fully. If we stay on the mountain or get lost in the blissful state, we are creating yet another human addiction.

Spiritual teachings that negate the soul life and put us in bondage will eventually inspire revolt—the soul can't be repressed for long. Your rebellious inner teenager, a saucy soul, will show up with melancholy yearnings, resentments, spite, and pettiness that often turn to compulsions, uncontrolled passions, greed, and addictions. To avoid such catastrophes, we are challenged to return to a more earth-based spirituality that allows for joy, ecstasy, and the celebration of life.

The universe is alive and pulsing with love. We must let it settle into our bodies, our hearts, our souls, *and* our spirits. Then we must walk it into our relationships, our families, our places of work and worship, our communities, and our earth. Keeping our heart open requires that we ground ourselves in a spiritual wisdom and walk that wisdom into our earthbound love relationships.

SPIRIT, ENERGY, AND HEART

The minute I heard my first love story
I started looking for you, not knowing
how blind that was.

Lovers don't meet somewhere.
They're in each other all along.
                                        —*The Essential Rumi*

Like everything in the universe, we are energy, and energy is a spiritual substance. Energy also contains information. Our bodies are surrounded by this spiritual energy, and, like it or not, we communicate with everyone through this field. In a sense, we cannot hide ourselves. Whether people can literally see someone's energetic aura or not is not the point. Science is confirming spirit. We read these fields all the time, consciously or subconsciously. We stand next to someone and we want to get away. We know when someone is staring at us and whether it is with good or bad intentions. Still others we are drawn to, and we want to remain in their presence. We feel compelled to take a shower after a toxic person bullied themselves into our presence. We talk about good or bad vibes. Some people drain us and others fuel us. There is an explanation if you need one.

Caroline Myss, a pioneer in energy medicine, writes, "I believe that our cell tissues hold the vibrational patterns of our attitudes, our belief systems, and the presence or absence of an exquisite energy frequency or 'grace' that we can activate by calling back our spirit from negative attachments."[2] If Myss is right, how we do our love stories gets recorded right down to our cellular tissues. Indeed, everything we believe, feel, or have experienced in our love relationships is there. Our superstitions are there. So is our wisdom. Profound love experiences are recorded there, and so are our traumas. The emotions attached to all of these experiences can literally make us (and others) sick. But they can also help to heal when we come to a new way of considering spirit in our love relationships. We can create attitudes and experiences that put out a welcome sign to others. Science knows that energy follows thoughts.

To nourish love relationships we must bring in even a small portion of spirit-filled wisdom so that we can not only heal our past right down to the cellular level, but also nourish every relationship we enter—naturally. When we get the miracle of who we are and live it, life is fundamentally changed.

We can go into our hearts and find out how much damage has been done and then muster up the self-love and trust to heal it. Healing does not require that we be happy all the time. Healing means we may grieve for a while, feel our rage for a while, shake off fear for a while, pull up and look at self-loathing for a while—but always with the understanding that it is done in the name of spirit-based love.

To return to a supple heart, to stop feeling needy, to be re-united with Basic Trust, we can reflect on the fact that, yes, we have survived wounds of the heart. Our hearts are strong. Cupid's arrow did not kill us, it woke us up. In fact we are more diamond than black carbon, more gold than lead. Such bravery pumps up the heart and invites us to call in love again and again and again.

Not all love stories are tragic sagas. Some people do get beyond their childhood traumas and return to the heart. Nick's story is one. He went through all the joy and pain of heart healing when he realized that spirit was calling him to rekindle his love for his mother.

Nick is a young man who might never have come into therapy were it not for his girlfriend. She wanted marriage and he did not. She wanted him to figure out why he could not commit to her. They were very drawn to each other physically. They were good friends and enjoyed each other's company. They saw each other nearly every day. She, at least, thought they were soul mates. And though both were spiritually aware, they had differences.

Though Nick meditated every day and had a deep commitment to his spiritual practice, he had a hard time experiencing his heart. Often his heart would not open until after he was sexual with his partner. He knew he was in love on a body and ego level but could not identify a soul or spiritual connection.

In exploring his little story, we found that he had undergone trauma of omission and shock trauma. Though he came from an affluent family that took very good care of his physical needs, supported his education, and gave him good ethical values, he learned a warped sense of love called emotional incest. His father was gone a lot and he became the surrogate man of the house. He took care of Mom, blocking off his own emotions and needs. When you add to this the fact that he underwent a traumatic hospitalization, it's no wonder that his heart often felt cold.

Watching him move back into his body, changing beliefs that locked him to ego-dependent love, reclaiming his soul's gifts, and practicing spiritual meditations with heart was an incredible experience for us both. The most significant thing I saw this young man do was to intentionally love a mother who persisted in being judgmental and distant. He did not get there overnight. He withdrew for a while, he cried for a while, he was rageful for a while, and he was terrified of her for a while. When he had completed these phases, he had nowhere to go but to love. Opening his body he opened his heart. Open spiritually, he touched love directly. He decided to love every bit of his mother with no expectation of anything coming back. It was what freed him to love others as well. Here is his story.

NICK'S STORY

I entered counseling at thirty-two, feeling stuck in virtually every area of my life and feeling that I had much more potential than I was using. I felt helpless to do anything about the situations I had gotten myself into in my life. I didn't enjoy my job, even though I was, from a worldly point of view, successful. I found myself in a stagnant relationship of two years. There were many more things right with this relationship than wrong, but I felt powerless to commit to being with this woman in marriage, which is what she wanted, or to move on and find someone else.

I've always been spiritually inclined. I was raised with a

solid foundation of Christianity, going through Sunday school, confirmation, et cetera. At twenty-five, feeling like I needed more than organized religion to meet my spiritual needs, I found an Eastern path of spirituality that answered all my questions about life, death, and God. I began meditating every day for an hour or two. But even after seven years of meditation, I was unable to find any answers in my life there. The overwhelming feeling of being stuck would not go away.

From a worldly perspective, I had a pretty good life. I had money; I went to work at nine and was off work at two every day. I had freedom; I traveled all over the world. I had a beautiful girlfriend, I was physically healthy, and I spent a lot of time and energy developing my spiritual side. I kept hearing that I had "the life." Well, if I have the life, I thought, then why am I so unhappy and why do I feel so powerless to do anything about it?

At my girlfriend's repeated request I began therapy to help me find my way out of the woods. We began with my earliest childhood memories and started piecing together the map that got me to where I was in my life. It quickly became apparent that many of my issues revolved around an overnurturing mother. I was the oldest boy in a family of four children and was very sick as a child. I suffered from bronchitis, asthma, allergies, and migraine headaches, so I required a lot of time, attention, and energy from my mother. My mother was completely willing to throw herself into the role of caretaker because she wasn't getting her emotional needs met in her marriage. Her children, and particularly me, became her project; with us she gave love, and received love in return. Things were different in her marriage, where she wasn't getting energized at all emotionally. So as a young child I started to become aware of my mother's feelings and her emotional needs and felt responsible for her feeling okay about herself and life. In return I got someone to take care of me when I was sick, someone who was willing to make any decision for me in life.

I felt comfortable with this little contract we had struck up. What I didn't understand is that the contract was based in a fear that if I didn't take care of my mother's feelings, she would leave me when I was sick—and I could die. I absolutely needed her around and couldn't risk her being mad or disappointed with me, so I was a model child and made sure I always agreed with her opinions, was in on time, and did as she said.

The result was that as an adolescent and a young adult I couldn't identify any of my own needs or feelings. I could easily identify with other people's feelings and opinions and would take them on instead of coming up with my own. It was easier, and I really wasn't sure what I felt or needed anyway. So unknowingly I gave my power away again and again. I ceded control of my life to other people. I went with the crowd. What I found is that people love this. I was well liked, but I didn't like myself.

So I began to understand what I needed to do to get the kind of relationship I wanted. I understood that the reason that I didn't tell women how I really feel is that I didn't really know, and that even though I wasn't getting my needs met in a relationship, I couldn't say so. The woman would leave and I would be alone and could die.

I slowly started living in my heart and recognizing basic emotions as they arose: anger, happiness, sadness. I realized as I got more in touch with my feelings that I was harboring a lot of resentment toward my mother. I felt like I was never emotionally prepared for adulthood. I felt used by her to get her adult emotional needs met, and that she should have gone elsewhere to deal with these problems, not project them onto me. These feelings grew and grew and came out in bursts of anger of an intensity that I never knew I was capable of. I blamed her, I hated her, and I cursed her. I went through dark nights of the soul owning this anger. I realized that this anger had always been there; I just had suppressed it.

During this process, my feelings moved from anger to sadness, to grief, to sympathy, then back to anger. I knew that owning all these feelings meant going through them as they came up, and no longer hiding from them. My therapist and I talked about how the fear behind the feelings was a façade. The fear that my mother would go away was only valid to a young child who couldn't take care of himself, not a thirty-two-year-old on his own.

As you can imagine, to undo thirty years of emotional

habit takes time. The groove is deep and new behavior is uncomfortable at first. As I continued to be open to the anger and not run from it, it slowly subsided, and what emerged on the other side of it was a newfound appreciation for my mother. Anger gave way to compassion; grief gave way to hope. I started to feel like I could recognize when I was giving my power away, and no longer had to do so. I now had other options; I was developing tools to get my needs met. Probably the single greatest thing that came out of this was that I realized I loved my mother. I not only loved her, but I wanted her in my life. I realized that she hadn't changed, our relationship hadn't changed, but I had changed. I no longer was controlled by fear, anger, or our childhood contract.

When I was a boy, my mother decided that I would always be a Christian, and that was that. I had always let her make decisions; why would this situation be any different? When I found my spiritual path at twenty-five and began to follow it, my relationship with her all but ended. We would go weeks and months without speaking, and what contact we had was very superficial. To talk about my feelings with my mother was obviously impossible. This went on for eight years, and there was a lot of built-up resentment on both sides until I found myself no longer resenting her, but loving her. I knew I had to try to rekindle our relationship.

What we needed was a new relationship, not the old one. So, armed with compassion and courage, I set out to forge a new connection with my mother. I knew she would resist and it would be hard, but I also knew that compassion and love always win over fear and anger. This must be and always will be true in this world. I knew if I came from my heart with compassion and understanding for her she wouldn't be able to resist me. As we began to talk about our relationship she would try to pull me into the old way and I would gently say we need to move on from there and create a new relationship.

Our relationship now isn't one of best friends, but it is one of mutual respect. Old grooves are hard to change. But after starting this process I believe that if we start to make right choices in our lives and come from places of compassion, empathy, love, and understanding, life begins to work with us and support us. Changes started happening right before our eyes that we couldn't have anticipated. Life starts to reward us for embracing the noble qualities of life and not perpetuating negative ones like anger, hatred, and jealousy.

It's been over a year now that I stopped seeing my therapist, and as I look back I see it as two processes. The first was recognizing and diagnosing the problem and dealing with it: being true to the process of changing who we are and making room for new behavior and a better life for others and for us. This is the hardest part, because we are fighting inertia and many years of repeated behavior.

After you emerge on the other side, you recognize where you lived and that you can't live there anymore. You are spirit, and that spirit knows love and requires we put it out wherever we can. You also emerge with new tools to get your human needs met. The fight isn't over, though. Life doesn't say: "Okay, you did the work, you came out the other side, and here is the prize." Now comes the second test. Life forces you to go into the world with your new weapons of love and understanding, knowing when you are getting your needs met, and when you're not, it challenges you to prove that you are different. You must earn new relationships. You must earn better circumstances. And you can, now, because you have the tools to create them.

Nick's story shows that not only does he have a spirit in his love relationships, but that this spirit is intimately connected with a vast spirit world. He could live in the shadow of body trauma, the emotional incest of the ego's little story, and dark Eros of the soul, or he could live in the cosmic story where we are all one. This generates compassion. In compassion, it does not matter who you learn about love from or what spiritual religion you follow. What is important is that you tap into Love and live it.

THE COSMIC STORY: INVISIBLE CONNECTIONS

In God there can be nothing alien, nothing other.

—Meister Eckhart

The idea that we are all related is no myth, it's reality. In spirit we are one big cosmic community! We contain hydrogen atoms from the big bang. We are star people. Everything above us and below us is in us. We are intimately connected with everything we see, hear, smell, and taste. The work I do—or don't do—on myself affects you and vice versa. If I remain in lust and greed so does the world. If I stay in grids of fear I work against love in the world. Having entered the twenty-first century, we are keenly aware that we develop our personhood in relationships with others, animate and inanimate. With vast networks of communication technology that give immediate bits of information, the world seems to be shrinking. We have more people trying to connect and impose their energies on us via the Internet, Web TV, and telemarketing, to name a few examples. The irony is that we must find time to individuate within and without these relationships (yes, these are relationships, too) so we can form deeper, spirit-based love relationships.

For we, like all other entities in the universe, from molecules to stars, consist of two opposite yet complementary tendencies: to assert individuality and at the same time to be willing to live cooperatively within a larger system. Every relationship has three entities: an "I," a "you," and a "we." The "we" is a reflection of what the "I" and the "you" bring to it. The health of the "we" is dependent on the health of its constituents. Love has a unity consciousness. Physics knows this. In a mature love relationship both the individuals and the relationship are evolving. The whole is always becoming greater than the individual parts alone.

There is a delicate balance between autonomy and belonging. Suppose Oxygen approaches Hydrogen one day and says: "Say, I heard that if we link up we can make this awesome thing called water. How about it?" But Hydrogen, skeptical and afraid of losing his identity (after all, he's supposed to give two parts of himself to Oxygen's one), responds with an antidependent stance: "Sorry. No way will I take a chance at losing myself." Or, feeling insecure because Oxygen seems greater in his oneness, he responds with a classic codependent statement: "I will do it if I can become just like you." Either way, we would not have any water.

This is not unlike many relationships: one person is afraid to

fully enter or willingly gives up his or her identity. Such relationships lack an energetic spirit and die. All creatures swim in a holy
sea of oneness with others. One creature is meant to help sustain
another. It is called symbiosis: a mutually beneficial arrangement
between two uniquely different organisms. It is universal. We are
not objects of love. There are no objects in the universe. There are
only interdependencies and shared energies. Our spiritual self
knows this.

MORPHIC FIELDS

The truth is, we can't possibly be *out* of relationship, whether we
are in close physical contact or not. The universe has already determined that. Science is now willing to catch up with spirit and
cautiously declares that there are invisible connections between
things separated from each other in space and time. There is con-
tinuity between the past, present, and future. We are not just
products of our past; we are constantly being called by our future.

In his book *Dogs That Know When Their Owners Are Coming
Home,* Rupert Sheldrake suggests that animals and humans can
connect and perceive each other beyond the brain memory,
through a mysterious perceptiveness called precognition or pre-
sentiment. Thanks to precognition, events about to happen in
what we call the future affect us now. Since the brain can't remember a future event, where does this knowledge come from?
Though the research is preliminary, Sheldrake proposes the presence of what he calls morphic fields, which link people to people,
animals to animals, and animals to people, even when the creatures are far apart. These invisible bonds allow for continuous
communication. It is as though there is a large, sweeping field
that extends beyond time and space and unites systems.[3] Our intentions, fears, and desires are not only communicated through
words and actions or confined in our head. They resonate
throughout the morphic field, as well. We remain connected with
those we are close to even at long distances. And we even communicate things that have not yet happened that can influence us.
Our ancestors knew this well and relied on it. They could communicate across long distances without phones or the Internet.
They could find their homes on land or sea. In the process of
building civilization we seem to have lost touch with this ability

and now are looking once again at science to prove what has always been true.

This field also seems to have a built-in group memory of past patterns. A giraffe embryo draws on a collective pool of memories that belongs to its species. We too tap into habits, beliefs, and histories of our ancestors. Why do you think it is so difficult changing the patterns in our love lives that have been passed on for generations? Not only do we have body memories, instructions from the ego, and modeling from our souls, but we also have non-localized memories to contend with.

The memory is cumulative. The more often a pattern is repeated, the more habitual it becomes. If fear-based relationship patterns prevail, so does fear. If loving acts prevail, so does love. And yet, even in this morphic field, it appears that patterns are hard to break. To counter the illusions of love that we have created and the fear-based actions that lead to hate and violence, we need a band of warriors with brave hearts. Science is telling us that life-discouraging patterns eventually collapse upon themselves, consuming themselves in the process. As one "cell" in the morphic field, you can bring about change in the whole field by *being* the change you desire. Become love, and others will learn love. A relatively few individuals, comparatively speaking, can alter long-standing patterns. You can become a living bridge to a new way of living and loving.

There is a war going on, and if Love's Way wins, the human race will be a notch closer to its possibility. The point of putting more love into our love life is not merely to satisfy our body, ego, or soul urges; it is about our spiritual evolution, as well. All evolutionary changes come through a creative jump. Maybe this will happen by chance. More likely it will come about because Love's Way will be louder and stronger than the old ways. New patterns do not come out of a vacuum; they come from inherent creativity in the cosmos and in nature. The more often patterns are repeated, the more viable they become. It is time for a creative jump in our evolutionary process, and we are responsible for bringing it about.

Maybe love is intended to be one big morphic field. Maybe it already is. The fact of invisible interconnections is now beyond dispute. Modern technologies depend on them. You are surrounded by bits of invisible information, whether you have a receiver sensitive enough to pick them up or not. Quantum physics has found that particles that come from a common source, like two photons of light emitted from the same atom, retain a mysterious interconnection so that even when separated, what happens to one instantly happens to the other as well. This quality, nonlocality, defined by the Einstein-Podolsky-Rosen paradox, has sweeping implications. According to Paul Davies and John Gribbin, "Once two particles have interacted with one another they remain linked in some way, effectively parts of the same indivisible system. . . . we can think of the universe as a vast network of interacting particles; each linkage binds the participating particles into a single quantum system."[4]

Why is it that our pets can anticipate seizures and can know we are on our way home? Why is a horse a more sensitive therapist than a human? How is it that the Aboriginal people of Australia communicate telepathically? Why is it that Polynesians can travel thousands of miles and always know their whereabouts, without radar or compass? Why have we lost our sensitivity to the invisible world? And how can we get this sensitivity back?

Quantum physics now supports the idea we introduced at the beginning of this section: that how we do relationships affects the universe. If I choose to grow and I am in relationship with you, I nourish your growth. I can compete with you or I can live cooperatively. I can attempt to control you or I can detach with caring. I can be self-absorbed or I can reach out to you in loving-kindness.

The relationship patterns I put out into the universe touch you and come back to me. All the thoughts, feelings, and behaviors about you and myself that I have put out into the world are out there filling the space surrounding you and me at this very moment. It is never-ending. It is one big circle of life.

This totality has a shape, a design, and a color. It is a moving kaleidoscope that only our quantum brain can perceive. Our linear mind is mechanical. It quantifies and calculates life and love. It looks at the cloud and measures its size. The quantum brain sees the shape and movement of the cloud and the figures the cloud makes—the love relationship. What it deems important is invisible to the eye. It is time to understand and use this marvelous and necessary brain.

"I JUST DON'T CARE ANYMORE": RACHEL'S STORY

Let me tell you how I came to understand that we are all connected, through an experiment in isolation, an experiment in the negative. I had been fighting a depression for weeks. After all, I'd just come through a major illness, I'd lost a baby, my mother had died, and I was facing the possibility of divorce. Ashamed of my feelings at first, I jumped into work and caring for others. I became exhausted.

This was my experiment: I gave myself permission to stay with my feeling and deepened it beyond grief and took it to hopeless despair. "What would life be like if I luxuriated in this hell?" I wondered. I allowed myself a day of total immersion in negativity. I went to church and decided everyone there was a hypocrite and not worth my time. I negated people and life. I declared, "There is nothing beyond this material world." I put out no love. I closed my heart and cared about no one, not even myself. I withdrew from any offers of caring. The day got darker and darker and so did I. Then I took the experiment one step further. I imagined everyone thinking, feeling, and acting as I was acting. Life became so bleak that I scared myself. I knew what hell was like.

I had just enough consciousness to ask myself: "What would life be like if everyone stayed where you are now?"

My heart crept through and answered: "If everyone lived in darkness only, there would be no life."

The answer bolted me out of my despair.

"But there is life," I responded.

I never went to the land of the dead again. I did not need to. Oh, I have felt sorrow. I have felt anguish. I have felt anger and fear. But the feelings made sense for the given circumstances, and I let them be a positive, healing experience.

I understood how quickly negativity puts out the light if left unattended. I also learned the importance of caring, which is connecting and acknowledging my connectedness. Caring

was life itself. Without caring and connecting, which is also
love, life lost its luster.

SPIRIT IN OUR RELATIONSHIPS

To keep a relationship healthy, people must be willing to call in
spirit and lend it an ear. Too often spirit has been put in the corner, collecting dust. We must go to our quiet places, drop into our
hearts, and ask spirit to come in and give us answers to the daily
problems that prompt our emotional outbursts.

With wisdom and compassion, spirit will honor the body, ego,
and soul but will not let them get into too much trouble. With
spirit in the driver's seat, what the relationship is to be will
evolve. Spirit brings wisdom, surrender, and sacredness to a relationship. It creates the safe container the wounded human needs.
Spirit does not push us, it draws us to change. It works with the
law of attraction. We then trust that whatever relationship comes
into our life is there for a reason and that the reason will get
clearer as we become more and more willing to learn the lesson.

Sometimes people are threatened when they encounter a
strong, spirit-based relationship and will try to tamper with it. We
must be equally mindful of the toxic intrusions we ourselves
bring in, and own and repair them as quickly as we can. When
spirit is alive and well, there is deep bonding that nothing can
break. When spirit is missing or taken away, we might ignore our
problems or try inept, ego-based solutions.

If we leave spirit out of our relationship equation, our relationships are crippled. We will feel more frantic and act recklessly.
We'll create a vortex that invites anything in to fill it. "The easier,
the better," the ego says, going for control, as it easily does, and
removing the wise, compassionate, all-knowing, caringly detached self that understands higher values, connection, and purpose. Right away we are in romantic illusion, sexual compulsion,
and needy dependency, none of which provide real intimacy.
When spiritual people experience relationship betrayal or outside
interference, they energetically feel the cut.

Spirit is the energy that connects people and gets us beyond
the ego fixations of what a relationship should be. It is bigger than
the primal brain; bigger even than the neocortex. It is greater than

hormones that justify abuse, greater than mental constructs teaching us manipulative ploys to catch someone. Viewed from this perspective, a relationship is directed by spirit and not by the quest of individual ego gratifications. West African teacher Sobonfu Somé puts it quite simply: "The role of spirit in our relationships is to be the driver, to monitor our relationships for the good. Its purpose is to help us to be better people, to bind us in such a way that we maintain our connection, not only with ourselves, but also with the great beyond. Spirit helps us to fulfill our own life purpose and maintain our sanity."[5] Any spirit-filled relationship is green and growing. It is alive.

Perhaps it is the spirit, too, that keeps nudging us forward through the dark times in our relationships, helping us to see beyond our learned limitations and see those we are in relationship with as wounded humans. Thanks to spirit, we can get an eagle's perspective on things. We can bring in compassionate understanding that says, "Never forget the bigger picture." Spirit has no theory to push, no agenda to complete, and no one to impress. It does not obsess about love or attempt to control change in our love life. All it asks is that we be willing to listen and learn and to do our part without judgment. It recognizes that there are two forces, evolution and devolution, life and death—and spirit is a part of both. It invites us into feeling our connection with the great cosmos where all is relationship and all human relationships serve spirit, honor our ancestors, care for our descendants, and give something back to our communities.

All matters of the heart are initiated by spirit, and it is this aspect of self that we need to call on during those stormy and uncertain days. And spirit *is* a comforter. It asks that we be grateful for all the teachers that show up in our lives, thank them all, even the disasters, and be willing to hear why we were brought together, even at the most painful of times. Once we get the lesson, we are done. That teacher will not show up again unless to tease us. We recognize that our lesson was less about personal happiness than about working out the little story lines, showing our soul gifts, getting a better ending to our trauma drama, and, finally, fulfilling our larger purpose.

This is good news, but many will not want to hear it. Our American minds want the quick answer and easy fix, the instant answer to the perennial question "Why?" Since spirit is not a thing the rational mind can eat, it will no doubt be dismissed. If you are reading this book and have gotten this far, you are still listening for spirit. You understand that magnetic force that draws you to something greater than what you already know.

When spirit is experienced in the heart itself, we ennoble the heart and it becomes "Sacré-Coeur." Our relationships are imbued with a down-to-earth practicality and sacredness. The dynamic duo—sacred and secular—produces incredible life-affirming love relationships, family relationships, and friendships that we are challenged to live right now. Every story in this book illustrates this fact.

The more intimately connected we are with our own spirit, the more connected we will be to the spirit in others. Loving intimacy begins with feeding our own spirits. We need walks in nature, encounters with vital natural forces: great waves, active volcanoes, and towering mountains. We need prayer, meditation, rituals and ceremony, wise elders, spirit-based communities, and playtime with children.

Any means by which we can remove ourselves from the demands of the secular world long enough to feel the grandeur of the great universe and the powerful source of life we are a part of will do. Sometimes I can find it in my car on a busy freeway. We can use the freeway for road rage or as the broad highway on which we commune with the great Divine. As we soak up spirit, breathe it in, and restore ourselves, we have the energy to do the hard work that our human love stores demand of us. If we do not do this, we become the walking dead, the vampire, the controller, the addict, the abuser of life and love. We show the worst of the feminine and the masculine. Inflicting violence, we invite more violence.

Our choices for today are quite clear, are they not? Many of the choices we have made in the past have led to dead ends. There is a light at the end of love's tunnel, and it is not an oncoming train. It is a rendezvous with spirit that happens when you honor that part of you that is connected to the divine and have the courage to place it into all of your love relationships.

Spirit means looking at all relationship questions from the top down. Though it's not wise to stay in isolation on top of the mountain, you must stay long enough to learn what it is like up there, and then walk that knowing down the mountain into the swamp of everyday life and light it up with love. Try it—as Robert did.

ROBERT'S STORY

A love relationship is a very precious gift. It is, contrary to how it might feel on some days, the most precious gift you and I can give and receive in this lifetime. How often do you take the spirit's point of view and consider it just that? How often do you thank it for its lessons? Or are you like Robert, a client who had complained to me for a year and a half that he could not access his feelings, yet in the throes of despair talked about the "horrible-feeling situation" he was in with his wife. "I hate feeling this way. Make it go away!" he heard himself say. I reminded him that had things not gotten this bad, he might never have felt and known his feelings and needs and thus would have missed an opportunity to speak to them, as well as an important lesson.

"It's exactly what you have been praying for," I said. "Feelings don't always come in good-news boxes. They don't always make us feel 'up'! That's why we numb out, deny, self-medicate. We only want the good stuff and not the bad stuff. And that was understandable when we were children and we did not have a safe container to come to with our sad, mad, bad, scared feelings. Sometimes our families and friends only wanted the good stuff," I said to him.

"You are absolutely right," he said, and he embraced and thanked his sorrow. "I used to medicate this pain with denial, affairs, or numbing out. But no more. I have been presented with a gift, an opportunity to risk my fear of rejection and be honest with my wife. She's been asking for directness, a show of feeling, for years. My pain is intimacy, too. Okay, she will get them all—my grief and my displeasure as well as my love and compassion. What she does with what I say, I have no control over. I am scared to death, but I know I need to do it." With this he took a deep breath. "Besides, I do know our relationship has a very strong spirit. Why do I doubt and fear? It has always come through for us!"

Robert understands that each relationship has a spirit, a life, a vitality of its own. He knows about Basic Trust and yet, like all of us, would prefer to be in denial about pain and problems when they show up. Recognizing the spirit of a relationship, he knows this makes no sense, and it is the strong spirit of the relationship that sustains it. Beyond the spirit of the relationship itself, in the midst of emotional pain, he called on his spirit in love. Wisdom, detachment, and compassion are the allies he needed and used to get to a transformed understanding of the dynamics of his love relationship with his wife.

When our body and ego are infused with soul and guided by spirit, things are about as good as they can get. We're not only spiritual warriors; we're warriors with heart and we're spiritual lovers. And it is in the recognition of the spirit in our love relationships that we can keep the heart open. Every relationship has a spiritual dimension, whether we acknowledge it or not. An animal has spirit; a tree has spirit. A community has spirit; a creative project has spirit. Every spiritual master has been telling us that we are not human beings having a spiritual experience; we are spiritual beings having a human experience. Sometimes this order gets reversed.

SPIRITUAL SELF-DECEPTION: MICHAEL'S STORY

Spirit is a gift. Some have used this gift to deceive themselves and others. We are hearing this all too often these days. The following story speaks for itself.

> I have a story to tell. I hope you can hear it. I want to tell it because I think it is important and it just might help someone else. Just maybe there is someone out there who needs it and it will make a difference in his or her life. I read the news, I watch television, and I discover there are too many men out there like me and, frankly, it scares me. Maybe my story can prevent disaster for them and help women understand there are men out there who can use them as prey.
>
> I never thought of myself as a predator. I consider myself a very spiritual man. I thought of myself as above most mundane matters. I even looked down and scorned people at times. I am well known and no one would guess my story. Being in

the limelight has its benefits and it has its pitfalls. My problem was self-deceit. It was not the usual intellectual self-deceit. That I could more easily own. Everyone has a bit of that, I told myself. My deceit was spiritual and my duplicity was progressive. I am a holistic doctor and spiritual teacher. I got very good at both. I had children and a beloved partner and I was content.

I will not bore you with the details. You can read between the lines. I had many students and admirers. I kept my boundaries for a very long time. Perhaps it was hitting near fifty that I felt some inner urgency to cross my own line. My life was a smorgasbord of feminine energy. I had many beautiful and not so beautiful but needy women in my life. It was like being in a candy store and being told I could have anything to eat. I was respected, sought after, constantly adulated.

I was able to stay humble and live in integrity for a long time. The shift happened without realizing it. I failed to notice that I began to get a rush from the adoration and I missed it when it was not there. I began to want the high, and all the while I continued my spiritual practice. Without being conscious to the fact, I began using it to satisfy my physical desires and to feed the ego. I would never have acknowledged it then. I would do my meditations and convince myself that my meditations were directing me to another soul mate. I was entitled, I was a spiritual teacher, and spirit had no boundaries or limits. Love was meant to be expressed to everyone, I heard my higher self tell me. I would go to spiritual intuits and listen for permission to get involved and cross my own boundaries. And when I did, I would experience what I told myself was divine love. This life was not meant to limit love. My body was a temple and I was being asked to use it to bring pleasure and love to others. No one owned my body. I was healing and helping, not harming. Surely there could be no harm in this.

I began to forget who I was and how old I was. I became involved with someone much younger than I. Why not? Why shouldn't I? What healthy male would not? It was bliss, it was lust, and it was divine. I knew about dependent personalities but forgot everything. I understood ethical guidelines but did not listen to them. That she had been a student and virtual prey cleverly slipped my mind. I was the soul mate she had been in search of and who showed up in both of our visions.

I was so immersed in my spiritual deceit that I am surprised I survived to tell the story. The crash was inevitable. But unlike many other stories I have heard, it was an inner crisis. I was so removed from my own light that I began to miss it. I began feeling depressed. I knew something was wrong, and I was in too much denial to see clearly what it was. I arranged to do a spiritual retreat. My intention was clear, and I still had enough faith and courage to believe that if I stepped out of the way the answer to my inner discontent would come forth. I asked for total truth and vowed I would do my part with whatever was shown to me. I would sit still and not leave until I had absolute clarity.

I can tell you that I felt a bit like Moses sitting by the burning bush. Only I was both Moses and the untamed in the village. I was hit by thunder and lightning. I got it. I was shown my own deceit, I was shown what love really is, I was shown my future if I were to continue, I was shown forgiveness. My heart flooded and I wept on and off for three consecutive days. I had caused a lot of damage in my blindness. I hurt people who really did love me and whom I could trust. I violated the trust of my students. I had fallen out of grace and certainly love. I had lost my personal integrity. I had become unsafe to myself. I also realized, though I was the predator, that I was also prey to many women who delighted in their seduction and manipulations. That does not excuse me at all. Many were victims.

I was also shown that while it is true that I am master of my body and spirit and love knows no limits, I have chosen to be in a life that has principles that I agreed to and that I must honor those principles for the good of all. My human life is an open book. My spirituality, perhaps unlike yours, considers that there is more than one life. I believe that the spiritual deceit was a profound teacher and that if I had not awakened to the lesson it would haunt me in yet another life. I do not want to redo this lesson.

In the wake of the storm I did lose my beloved partner. That I still grieve. Whatever purpose I served in her life I am grateful for. I am most grateful to her for being in mine and teaching me about love. I was the betrayer, not her. On a human existence the pain is great. But living in integrity again is real and a vital part of my spiritual path. I have many people in my life who hold me accountable. One thing I have learned is how easily we can manipulate even our spirituality to be self-serving.

I look around now and see so much deceit. I wish I could scream out my story, but then each person has to live his or her own lesson. But I do believe we need to pass on our lessons so we can create a more loving human existence.

I really see the male of our species in deep trouble. They are made war heroes, sports heroes, placed in power positions. Yet seldom do they have the networks of other men to say: "Stop! What you are doing is wrong. It hurts you. It plays with others' hearts. It kills the spirit inside. It is not love! Do not deceive yourself." We need men who are not afraid to step up to the plate and tell their stories. We need men to grow up and act their chronological and spiritual age.

Thank you for listening to me. I hope it helped.

THE SPIRIT IN LOVE
The way of love is not
a subtle argument.

The door there
is devastation.

Birds make great sky-circles
of their freedom.
How do they learn it?

They fall, and falling,
they're given wings.
      —*The Essential Rumi*

If it doesn't devastate you, it is not love. For in spirit-based love you are absolutely vulnerable and open. This openness to another is so complete that there are no empty places and there is no hiding out.

Here's the good news: The more complete our love is, the more intimate we allow ourselves to be, and the closer we are to our spiritual core. Spirit in love takes you far beyond yourself to the experience of union with all of life. In that union, you embrace both joy and sorrow as cohabitants of life. When the spiritual core is a part of our relationships, love defies all words. When love comes from the spirit, the soul, the mind, and the body and is run through the heart, we are the Beloved.

This spirit-filled love is an ideal toward which we must strive continually. As we own and shed the darkness in our psyche, we experience more and more moments of spiritual love in our relationships. As we begin to recognize these moments, we can lock them in our human memory bank. We can then count on returning to them again and again.

With all the pressures to be otherwise, it is difficult to sustain such elevated love. Yet, bringing this love into our relationships is probably the only hope we have. For it is the spirit-filled love in us that can reveal previously unknown depths of love and inspire us to love fearlessly. Love with power of spirit is the answer, the living metaphor, for our relationships. Once dormant, now awakened, these spiritual energies produce a feeling of such profundity and magnitude that all at once we feel the best aspects of ourselves. We transcend the pettiness and negativity that have dominated our relationships.

Though spiritual love doesn't need to be defined (it is what it is), it's helpful to know what it looks like when it shows up. We are most likely to get glimpses of it when love relationships are fresh and exciting and we have let our guard down. Our challenge is to bring more of this gold into our love relationships, no matter what our age or the age of the relationship. Love knows no time.

We now know our little story, we now understand we have been traumatized, we now realize life is unfair, mean, and violent at times. We now know that what keeps another from loving us or taking in the love we have to offer is their fear, trauma, conditioning, or ignorance. Living in Basic Trust, we can now take a few more chances. Knowing the importance of the Bigger Story and bringing soul into the picture, relationships liven up. And now we understand there is a cosmic story where our spirit in love dwells.

Relax; settle into the heart of the universe. It is spirit-filled. Tap into it. All the help we need is in that great source. How many times have we been told we are not alone? Alone? In this universe? What do we have to lose? Falling into love is coming home.

We need to stop trying to control our love life and the people around us. Everyone has been in a state of grace and has fallen from it. These inner states of bliss and grace may come and go but we can create stations along the way. The more time we spend at various stations, the more familiar they feel. We are in motion, as is everything else in the universe. Sometimes we are in a traumatic memory, sometimes we are in lust, sometimes we are on the hill, sometimes we are in the valley, and sometimes our hearts are simply bursting with the spirit of love and want to engage in the sacred combat. Mustering up its softness and bravery, it jumps into our love life and shows up as spirit in love.

Here is a recipe for a vibrant, spirit-based love life:

- Find a handful of people who value spirit.
- Add a healthy dose of care, kindness, joy, and celebration.
- See every relationship as a teacher.
- Plant good seeds.
- Nourish and prune as you need to.
- Let only those who have earned it into your space.
- Care with detachment.
- Keep a spiritual curiosity and openness.
- Transcend and transform relationship problems.
- Look for purpose and meaning.
- See others as sacred.
- Offer pain and suffering as a prayer.
- Develop a sense of humor.
- Say thank you, thank you, and thank you.
- Savor the moment.
- Learn the lesson and put it into action.
- Consider love relationships a gift.
- Live from higher values.
- Love with intention and commitment.
- Serve others.
- Make amends.
- Take personal responsibility for the pain you inflict.
- Be tolerant and fair.

- Discern and do not judge.
- Stay humble.
- Develop wisdom.
- Share power.
- Have many spiritual mentors and community.
- Meditate.
- Pray.
- Go to the heart for answers.
- Use love as a laser and only cut when necessary or to stop hurt.
- Build up energy.
- Climb the spiritual mountain and do not isolate.
- Conserve energy.
- Let go of toxic people.
- Be compassionate with yourself and those you love.
- Embrace the inner Beloved.
- Forgive (and don't forget).
- Think and feel: "We are all related."
- Create sacred space where negativity is not allowed.
- Develop your higher, observer self.
- Give without expectations.
- Shift from shame and guilt to regret and remorse.
- Never manipulate another with your spirituality.

MEDITATION FOR THE SPIRIT IN LOVE

I am indebted to my spirit for the wisdom, healing energy, and compassion it brings to all of my relationships. It ensures my connection to the Divine and brings sacred meaning to my love relationships. It helps me to learn the lessons so I may grow from painful events. I will give it the importance due it every day. I will be still and listen.

Memo

To: You

From: Love

You have heard the assignments given to your body, your ego, your soul, and your spirit. I separated these aspects of you because that is the way the ego likes to learn, but they are not meant to stay separate. They are all one, because they are all you. Thinking of them as permanently separate has created the needless pain and suffering you have been experiencing in your love relationships. But let me be clear. Though you are multidimensional, that does not ensure that these parts live in harmony. You have heard the stories. To unify them you must live in your heart. Without heart in the picture, you are a mere multidimensional being. When you bring in the heart you are a multidimensional lover that can accomplish great things.

If you have read this book carefully you know that I enter by one door only: the heart. None of the assignments can be accomplished unless you bring me into the heart. It is not the concept of love that revolutionizes you, it is the actual movement of love through the heart. In that regard, the heart is the most vital of all of your organs.

It is only when two people are at one in their innermost hearts that the illusions of love, the dependencies and addictions that stand in for love, are shattered. The value of a personal relationship—whether it be with a loved one, a friend, a child, a family member, or a peer—is that it creates intimacy that allows me to be lived in all realms as the multidimensional lover. I am like a moving sea. If you have an open heart I enter, and there is a bonding so huge that you step out of yourself and feel the one universal heartbeat.

Your heart is more than a physical organ. It's the bridge between two worlds: the sacred and the secular. When you bring the four facets together, live them from the heart, and are the multidimensional lover, you are a living bridge between the material and spiritual worlds. Your species is the only one on the planet that can experience this great role.

Every relationship will challenge you to live as a multidimensional lover, with the body, ego, soul, and spirit in harmony. I use the word *harmony* and not *balance* for a reason. Balance may imply motionlessness, even stasis. But I am alive, organic. Love relationships have cycles and seasons. There will be times when soul's wetness and wildness must take precedence. There are times when the ego must be in charge and the others need to hold back. At other times the body must be recognized as paramount. Sometimes compassion will be needed, at other times passion. Each part of the self must listen from the heart, because that is where I live. For all the reasons we have already discussed, this harmony will not be easy.

Since the heart is meant to be my home, you must purify it. I realize your heart has been injured, that it aches at times. That's all right; the heart is strong. It speaks to the mind, and the mind speaks to the body. When you let fear control the heart and it becomes tense, I have a hard time entering. And though you must release the many traumatic memories stored there, you do not need to wait to start using it. You must be willing to relax into the heart and go to it for answers, right now. I will be in the answers.

Your great initiation is to live from the heart. When humanity accomplishes this, you will evolve as a species. Can you do it? Of course. The task is noble and great but very possible. You have everything you need to complete the initiation.

The truth is, you cannot afford to fail in this task. Letting one aspect of the self overshadow the others results in great pain. Failure to live from the heart is death. There is a crisis at hand, and there is no more time to waste. If you doubt what I say, read on. The next story speaks for itself.

Thank you.

CHAPTER SEVEN

The Realm of the Heart

■   ■   ■

> Yes, there's suffering, but it doesn't feel like suffering when
> the love is divine on one side, human on the other, and one in
> the loving heart.
> —Robert Bly and Marion Woodman, *The Maiden King*

A WAKE-UP CALL

Her body was strong and mature for a fifteen-year-old. It made a
clear statement: "Don't mess with me." But mess they did. There
was a deadness in her eyes. I could tell she was far away. It
didn't matter how strong she looked, how tall she walked. It did
not matter that she could take me, her therapist, to the floor in a
minute if she wanted to. She had a vulnerability in her that they
found right away. They were predators who delighted in raping
her. One by one, all six took her. It was a male ritual, a "guy
thing." They couldn't care less that she was a little girl not yet
born into womanhood, and that this initiatory outrage would
haunt her forever.

The authorities were not much help. They looked at her as
though she had asked for a gang rape. Why did she agree to get in
the car? Was it really because they had agreed to buy her ciga-
rettes? "Come on," the cops said, "you must have known better."
They took the complaint she filed and forgot about it. They secretly believed she was a whore, anyway.

Yes, she liked drama. Yes, new hormones were raging in her
body. Yes, she was lonely and alienated from her peers and from
her father. It did not matter. Here sat a young girl entering womanhood, ready at last to have her first genuine love experience,

the first great act of her woman soul. Ready to develop the feminine face of her divinity. Ready to learn more about masculine mysteries, the first act of love, the fairy tales promised her that would bring a spiritual ecstasy, proof that there was heaven on earth. How could she have known?

The young heroine is shaken to the roots of her soul. "Where is that 'wonderful something' that was supposed to happen?" she asks in the stillness. Her happily-ever-after story is gone for good. Her new story is one of despair and repair. Is her soul still intact? Is her spirit closed? Will she stay dead to life and keep looking for spirit in dramatic sexual encounters that guarantee a chemical high that can remind her she is still alive? And how many professionals will continue to project their ignorance and fear onto her?

"Help me," she pleaded, "I want to get back into my body."

My heart hurt. I felt a deep ache. Compassion and rage rumbled inside of me. "She could be my daughter," I thought to myself. "No, in the bigger picture of life she *is* my daughter." We are all related. In the bigger picture we are all one another's mothers, fathers, daughters, and sons. If she loses her soul we all suffer. If she develops a warped sense of love, one based on fear, we all are thrown off.

I knew that thinking of her as a daughter, even in the way I meant it, would not be acceptable in the profession. Stay distant, watch for transference, and keep spirit out, says the professional self. Love of client is dangerous. Despite these warnings I knew there was an opportunity to help her get to a transformed understanding of what it meant to be a loving human. And to do so I needed to keep my heart open.

"How do I call her back into a world saturated with warped ideas of what it means to be a man or woman and assure her of safety?" I asked myself. "How do I explain the Bigger Story in a way that makes sense to a child who looks like a woman? How can I compete with what the culture is feeding her day after day, hour by hour?"

I then realized that the point was not to compete at all, not to reinforce a them-versus-us mentality. "This is not a competition," I reminded myself; "this is an opportunity, a sacred moment." I was being challenged to be a warrior of the heart: to express compassion without rescue, to be fiercely proactive, not to judge, and to see the larger problem.

We know there is an opening to sexuality in our adolescence. But we have forgotten that the sexual fire is not the only one kindled at this age. The fire of spirit enters, too, a fire in the heart trying to be birthed. "But in our culture, the adolescent does not see ecstatic religious singers on the street," write Robert Bly and Marion Woodman. "What he or she sees is posters advertising sexual energy."[1] Our adolescents are starving spiritually and filling that need with what the media and advertisers promote. We live in a world that sells emptiness and then rushes in with tasty products to fix it: sex, beauty, and addictive products of all kinds and shapes. And what goes on behind the scenes makes consumerism look like the good guy: drugs, sexual predation, violence. Is it any wonder children grow up to become joyless, mechanical lovers?

Mia's sexual opening was a colossal nightmare, void of love. Where in this bad dream was the hero, the virtuous warrior who knew how to use a sword to slay the enemy and rescue Mia from an awful fate? Where was the good mother, the one who lives happily within her body, her sexuality, and her identity and is not afraid to nourish her child?

Would Mia believe me if I told her there was opportunity in the awfulness of her experience? Would she believe me if I said there is a new and better life for her?

I knew that all the players in the drama were, to one extent or another, cultural robots. My client was the unexpected child agreeing to be the scapegoat who diverted the rage Mom and Dad felt toward each other—the faithful dumping ground for their negativity. Neither parent had full understanding of what it meant to walk in balance, to be the hero with tenderness, the strong mother or father. Dad was a good man, "macho," his identity invested in being a provider and controller. Mom was a struggling "codependent no more"; withholding love was a way for her to feel powerful. What Mia's parents had needed as children to live Love's Way was clearly missing. It is not their fault. They are victims too.

What about the rapists, those predators who apparently got

away with their acts? The perpetrators were victims themselves. Most likely raised in violent homes, living in brutality, they abandoned themselves long ago. Their hearts remain encased in steel, utterly closed off. Unless they learn that they can become warriors with heart, they do not stand a chance of knowing love. But if only one of the six understands and feels disgust at what they did to Mia, he will have moved manhood one step closer to life with heart.

Mia's descent was an adolescent initiation; no doubt she will have more initiations. There may be three or three hundred. We all undergo them. These tests will ruthlessly keep presenting themselves to us until we get it. Our descents are the passageways into and out of our illusions. Most initiations contain a betrayal, a lost love. Mia's lost love was her innocence and her culture, the betrayer. But, paradoxically, here in the awful moment she also had a chance to find herself.

In her young mind she had glimpses of what life and love might be. At the moment of the rape all of these seemed abandoned in a wasteland of sordid perversion and despair. She encountered death. But this was a ritual death, not a literal one, and her soul understands this. Yet her emotional and physical pain might not allow her to rise to a greater self. Without sacred rituals and wise elders to create a bridge to the other side where love is waiting, she may take her symbolic death literally and act on it. Many adolescents do. A warped sense of what some think of as love nearly destroyed Mia. In the chaos of ashes she can create a new understanding for both. So it is with most of us.

How I helped Mia's soul get back into her body is another story. She did get back. The question is, Will she stay? Will she consider this love's failure and live in despair, or will she choose to love herself and cut the ties that bind her? Is there enough in this world for her to nourish her spirit to health and wholeness? Like Psyche, Mia has been to Hades. Will she keep going back? And how can she stay out? In her hell she found a poem:

> Watching the walls of corruption
> They are caving in on me
> Laughing, crying
> In a world of hopeless dreams

I wander above the stars
Content with my invisibility
Not having to see the morbid faces
Laughing, lurking
Above the sky so high
So high
I'm a star
The rest of the world is so small
and nothing matters.

GETTING TO THE HEART OF THE MATTER
Will Mia be able to live with heart again? Will she get from "nothing matters" to "everyone and everything matters"? Will she recognize that we are all related and the healing she does or does not
do will affect us all? Will she protect her reclaimed soul? Will she
stay in her body? Will she love her body or reenact trauma and
abuse it? Will she mourn her loss and reclaim her womanhood?
She has a right to experience love with every fiber of her being—
and that means her body, her ego, her soul, and her spirit.

She also has the responsibility to put love out into the world in
ways that heal, not harm. If she chooses to heal, she can be a
teacher. As a returnee from Hades she will inspire trust in others
who have been forced to make the trip. But will the society she
lives in help her heal enough to be open to love? Or will it keep
her down and under?

Any of us can get hit like Mia—not by Cupid's arrow but by
sorrow and despair. We can take so many different hits: the "once
upon a time" story doesn't get us to the "happily ever after" ending we were promised. A second marriage fails or I discover that I
have a sexual addiction and have been projecting it onto my partner's disinterest in sex or need to control me. It may be that my
nest is empty and so am I. My boss just fired me, after all I did for
the company. He has habits I cannot stand. She is mortal and
aging. I have followed umpteen gurus and read every self-help
book I can find and nothing is working. And where did love go? I
have been chasing it all my life and it keeps eluding me.

It may be a direct hit that sends us into a burning hell. It may
be a shock of insight in the middle of a prayerful meditation that
wakes us up to what love is not. Once we are hit, we are obliged

to notice what has struck us and to realize that we have been looking in the wrong direction for love. It is not in another. It is not in drama. It is not in addiction.

Mia's story is missing one essential ingredient: heart. And what her story tells us is that not one of them—body, ego, soul, or spirit—is of any value in a love relationship unless all four have merged and are vibrating at the core frequencies of the heart. Without heart the body lusts, the ego betrays, the soul wanders off, and the spirit deceives. Not only Mia's story, but every story we have heard so far, speaks to that truth.

Without an open heart we live on the edge of love. We play at it. We live in the lower regions of the heart—in fear, hatred, loneliness, anxiety, and depression. Or we can taste love from time to time, but seem unable to sustain it. Our heart goes on automatic pilot and closes down. Because of the trauma we have experienced, we often remain shut down and put up barriers to keep others out. The tragedy is that not only do we keep toxic people out, we often keep love out, too. Sometimes we need our boundaries, of course. Mia needed them desperately. But it is better to put them up outside ourselves than around our hearts.

The flip side of the coin is that sometimes we foolishly let our guard down when we should not and are perpetrated upon one more time. We're bonded with our betrayer, so we unconsciously submit to her or him once again. The betrayer may be a negligent and distant father or a too-intrusive mother. It could be a sexual abuser or someone who inflicts physical punishment. It could be someone who did not take our emotional needs seriously. Mia must be alert to the fact that as awful as her life experience has been, she did experience intimacy—even, in a distorted way, bonded—with the men who abused her. To get closure she may look for men like them again. Have you ever been attracted to people similar to those who have betrayed you?

It is time to get the message that we need to heal our hearts; in the meantime, we need to do the heart practices that allow us to tap into the heart's intelligence, which we know as love. We cannot afford to wait. On some level we all know this. If we do not do so we will hear more and more stories like Mia's. It is already happening. It is on the daily news. We are so sick of it and yet we sit with hearts hurting and love in the distance calling. We do not know what to do, so we sit waiting for something to drop in our laps, heal us, and assure us that we won't get hurt again. Nothing changes. But since there is no such thing as nonchange, if we do not live in the heart the change will be a downward spiral. We must put a stop to the nonsense. We must create a world with more heart while we still stand a chance. That is what Love has been telling us.

"Happily ever after" is inside. It resides in the realm of the heart. Now that I am conscious of what it is I'm looking for and that it is within me, maybe I will actually get the "happily ever after."

This happily ever after does not mean I leave relationships or stop needing them; it means I can stop placing unrealistic expectation on others for my happiness. I can stop destructive drama. I can stop using others to feed me. I can examine outdated beliefs that limit love. I can look for ways I get lost searching for it. I can look for ways I isolate from it. I can do what I need to do to open my heart physically and spiritually. I can heal and live from the heart. I can stop trying to manipulate the many love relationships I am living and enjoy them for what they truly are: places to be who I am and opportunities to transport as much love through my heart as is humanly possible.

THE INTELLIGENT HEART

Go to your bosom.
Knock there,
and ask your heart
what it doth know.
—William Shakespeare

Touch your breast. Your heart is strong. It works hard keeping you alive on this earth plane. Touch your heart, feel its pulsating rhythm. Thank it. Is it broken, does it leak? Has it failed you? No, it has not. It pulses hour after hour, day after day, year after year. With thirty-six million beats each year, it pumps blood through more than sixty thousand miles of internal piping that keep the body going. More than six hundred thousand gallons of blood flow through it each year. Each second, two million of your blood cells die and are replaced by two million more. Within five quarts of your blood are twenty-two trillion blood cells, and within each cell are millions of molecules that contain atoms that are in perpetual motion. These atoms move at a rate of more than ten million times per second.[2]

There is a reason the heart always comes up when we talk about love. There is a reason we say we have a "heart connection," we "gave our heart away," we carried on an "affair of the heart." Heart and love have an inescapable relationship. We know who has an open heart, who has a brave one or a warm one—and who shows no heart at all. Many spiritual traditions refer to the heart as the seat of the soul or the organ that helps us experience our higher virtues—compassion, courage, and truth. It's especially an emblem of bravery, as when medieval people called a king "lion-hearted," or when inner-city kids today speak of "heart" as the "courage to fight." To the French, *coeur,* heart, means courage. Clearly, the heart is a great deal more than a pleasant spiritual metaphor.

The heart is even more remarkable than we acknowledge. It seems to have intelligence and wisdom of its very own; science is now explaining how this can be. When I was a child I didn't need science to prove it, and I bet you didn't, either. I was sure my heart had a special truth, a special knowledge of who I was, what direction I should take, and what really mattered. My heart told me who was safe and who was not. It told me what was right and what was wrong. It told me who loved me and who was hurtful and why. Often people ask me how I got where I am today. My answer: "By listening to my heart. I have been listening to it as far back as I can remember."

Promising research is proposing that I was on to something when I listened to my heart as a little girl. The heart really is pumping information as well as blood. When two people are together, whether they're aware of it or not, their hearts are always talking. "The heart's electromagnetic field is by far the most powerful produced by the body," writes Doc Childre and Howard Martin of the HeartMath Institute, a research center in central California that is dedicated to studying the heart's intelligence. "It's approximately five thousand times greater in strength than the field produced by the brain, for example."[3] This field can be measured up to ten feet away.

This means that our hearts are broadcasting an energy field all the time, and what is in that field deeply affects those around us. Children under five are keenly aware of this. Dogs are, too. In some cultures guests are introduced to the children first, and the elders watch who the children prefer and how the kids relate to them. Not too traumatized or conditioned as yet, children naturally move toward love and safety. They know who is in the heart and who is not. There is an unspoken communication, a synchronicity.

Physics suggests that when two or more systems have an internal order, a harmony among its components, there is virtually no energy wasted. There is also a phenomenon seen throughout nature whereby systems or organisms out of sync can come into sync. As when two pendulum clocks placed near each other begin to synchronize, two people living with love in a relaxed heart do the same. Their hearts become in tune.[4] We do not need to be with another person to experience this healing power of the heart. Our own body parts benefit from loving heart rhythms. These oscillating impulses resonate throughout the body, and we experience buoyancy, calm, and clarity that draw others to us.

This remarkable organ is surprising in other ways, too. In the fetus the heart starts beating before the brain is formed,[5] "kick-started" by an unknown impetus. As the brain develops, it grows from the bottom up. The primal brain that houses our survival reactions develops first; then the centers of emotion, and then—and only then—our rational brain: "In an unborn child there is an emotional brain long before there is a rational one; and a healthy heart before either."[6] The heart has been there all along. The heart intimately knows body, ego, soul, and spirit. It witnessed and, in part, helped their creation and development. As heart implant surgery is demonstrating, the heart does not need to be connected to the brain to keep beating, but the brain will die if the heart stops. This fact may be all we need to know to realize that we have given too much importance to the traditional IQ, and it is time to give heart intelligence its rightful place. After all, knowledge can be transformed as completely by the presence of the heart as any other human faculty; a heart full of knowledge is nothing less than sacred wisdom.

ENERGY

Before the mind-body split, many ancient cultures and traditions understood that the heart is more than a ten-ounce, multichambered, muscular organ that keeps the body alive. The Chinese character for love includes the character for "heart." The Japanese language has two words to describe heart, *shinzo*, referring to its physicality, and *kokoro*, a sense of "heart" that includes ideas such as honesty, devotion, and essence. In the cabala the heart is the central sphere and touches all the others. Yogic traditions emphasize awareness of the heart. We know of the many references to the heart in indigenous, ancient Hebrew, Christian, and Islamic traditions.

Eastern spiritual traditions and energy medicine say that the human energy field absorbs energy and reradiates it in spiraling vortices located at the root of the spine, along the spine, and above it. We have seven primary vortices, or foci of energy, called chakras, Sanskrit for "wheels." These centers have varying degrees of amplified power. They circulate energy into, out of, and around the body. They are considered to be separate yet intimately connected with the physical body parts, and in alignment with them. Their location varies depending on whether one is oriented to Western or Eastern philosophies and how one utilizes them. These energy distribution centers are points near the body where there is a greater amount of electromagnetic energy, which can now be scientifically measured. Think of the chakra system as the spiritual spine that gathers energies and transforms them so they can be used by your body for physical, emotional, mental, and spiritual purposes.

That the heart sits right in the middle of the seven distribution centers as a connector of body and spirit energies is no surprise. In energy terms it acts as the transformer of knowledge, a two-way communication relay between two worlds: sacred and secular. It connects lower-chakra intelligence of survival, sensation, and power with higher-consciousness intelligence that rests above the heart center—creative, intuitive, and spiritual knowing. In Chinese medicine the heart chakra has been referred to as the Emperor.

Chakras should be thought of as being tangible yet much more subtle than physical. This energetic body has a crucial position between the dense physical body and the formless cosmic energies. In some ways all spiritual teachings are speaking to the relationship of the physical, subtle, and cosmic energy bodies. Most cultures and traditions refer to this energy. Polynesians call it *mana*, medieval alchemists called it *vital fluid*, Hindus call it *ranaa*, the Chinese call it *chi*, the Egyptians referred to it as *ka*, and the Algonquians named it *manitou*—to cite just a few of its many names.[7]

Though the subtle pathways connecting the chakras can be mapped like a rarified digestive system, the system cannot act instinctively as can the physical body. You cannot touch it or weigh it, yet you can experience it through sensations that resonate in your body. Perhaps you can recall a time when you were with someone you loved in front of a fire, sharing an intimate moment. You noticed a warm, radiant expanding sensation coming from the center of your chest that extended outward beyond the body. Your heart center was energized. Or you were meditating in nature and felt a surge of well-being flow through you naturally and effortlessly. A smile came to your face. You could not stop it. You felt opened and calm and had intuitive insights. Sometimes you actually felt a tingling sensation rush through your body as though something had entered it. In all of these situations you were experiencing your energetic body, the chakra network, or what some traditions call the light body or aura field. The halo depicted (and seen) around the heads of saints and mystics signifies that their bodies and chakra networks are open to universal love. Science is now confirming that there is a living, vibratory pulse that exists in the spaces between you and the cosmos.[8]

This awesome statement implies that there is no separation between you and everything that exists. Science is directing us back to ourselves to find answers to big questions. Within us we discover that there is a force that binds all of creation. According to Gregg Braden in *Walking between the Worlds,* each of our quadrillion body cells holds a potential electrical charge of 1.17 volts.[9] I use the word *potential* because whether this energy is activated depends entirely on the way we choose to live and love.

The electromagnetic field that is love, which radiates from the heart, has power, and that power can change our chemistry in a literal "heartbeat." The nebulous state of being "in love" allows that 1.17-volt liquid crystal circuitry of each cell to align with that seven-layered liquid crystal oscillator in your chest called "heart." New data suggests that the DNA in our bodies is affected by our human expression of love and fear. And our DNA determines how the patterns of light, cellular and subtle, show up in our bodies. New studies show that when two people touch in a loving way, their brains light up.

Our ability to experience love, forgiveness, safety, and compassion and, in doing so, to allow others to be who they are is our greatest asset by far. Shifting our perceptions, attitudes, emotions, and responses from hate, jealousy, fear, and control to attitudes that support the energies of love not only helps us to evolve spiritually, it heals our relationships. What stands between you and the power of love is you. Becoming a spiritual warrior with heart and putting that precious heart into every relationship is the way your true power will be realized.

Your greatest teachers will be the human relationships you enter willingly—and unwillingly. As Braden puts it: "Through simply allowing the resolution of each relationship in your life, whether it is the two-minute relationship in the checkout line of a grocery store, or the twenty-year relationship of marriage, you are awakening fragments of your soul that allow your body health, vitality and life giving relationships."[10]

An appreciation of the heart, with its intelligent, powerful, high-speed wisdom, demonstrates again how consciousness and biology, spirit and matter, sacred and secular can come together in human relationships.

As a species we can choose to stay with frustration, suspicion, anger, and fear and perpetuate dependent relationships, love addiction, hatred, and violence. Although they stifle the life force in us, these attitudes provide proximity, drama, and the illusion of love. Or we can choose to come from the heart. Whatever we choose, the corresponding signals will be sent out into the world.

COMING FROM THE HEART

I pray on the subway going home, in the train filled with commuters—just sit there with my eyes closed, breathing in and

out. I let each person I've encountered that day float into my heart, where I embrace them and let them go. Rapid transit is my temple; it maketh me sit down with no phones ringing: it leadeth me through the noise and whoosh of the city of death.
—Alison Luterman, "This Thing about Goodness"

Multidimensional love understands that the heart is a central organizing intelligence for the entire human system—body, ego, soul, and spirit—and goes there for answers. Calling on the heart for answers ensures emotional honesty without the ravaging effects of anger, frustration, fear, and stress. Listening from the heart materializes spirit and keeps compassion alive in all of our love relationships by shining a light on the dark and grungy relationship issues we face many times a day. And going to the heart gives it the exercise it needs to stay strong and open. As the passage in the epigraph says, we do not need to be in a church to practice living from the heart. We can do it many times a day and in some of the most surprising situations, such as at lunch in a crowded restaurant or while stuck in traffic. We can choose "road rage" or active frustration, or we can take a deep breath and fall into our heart in a split second. Any place can be converted into a temple. "Your vision will become clear only when you look into your heart," said Carl Jung, and one of my clients, Marcia, can testify to that truth.

MARCIA'S STORY

I just listen from my heart now. I am so tired of being angry and acting one-up. I caught myself in the middle of one of our predictable power struggles, and suddenly I saw myself persecuting my husband one more time, just as he had invited me to do. And I said to myself and to him: "You know what? I don't want to do this any more. It's crazy." And I just stopped, took a deep breath, and went to my heart.

When I stopped looking outward and judging him for what he has done to me and saw how I actually got off on being a one-up Goody Two-shoes, I dropped into my heart, heard his regret and sorrow, and actually felt compassion for us both. Listening from an open heart eased the tension and promoted the healing we were both in need of. My heart had been hard as nails, and it was easy then to stay with self-righteous indignation. Thinking of him as the jerk, the unhealthy one, eased my initial pain after I learned of his betrayal, but it was also killing me. I was not myself. I learned I could have both an ache in my heart and compassion.

I realized that all of my life I forced actions and decisions because they were expected of me. Now I am becoming in touch with my heart and what feels right from there. When I force things I can feel it in my body. It is tense. I realize that I was making impulsive decisions or having impulsive reactions because I was fearful of others and the power I thought they had over me. I reacted like I did when a child in a home where I felt pretty powerless.

An important lesson in all of this is that going to my heart for answers, I find a clarity that impulses do not provide. I bring more good feelings to my relationships, and my whole body feels better. It is happy. The bonus is that I find more people listening to me. I have more power, not less.

Another client, Maren, got to her heart via an intense dream.

MAREN'S STORY

More than a year ago, when I was struggling with a love relationship, work, and family, I had a dream that was so real, it seemed as though it was a "voice from the divine realm." I knew that the clear messages in the dream were important then, but I had no idea at the time how much strength they would give me. I did not immediately understand them, but I got up and wrote them down. The two messages I remember the voice saying to me were: "Heart hasting; two souls healing" and "To thine own self be true."

With time the messages became clear to me. The first message has proven itself to be true in my life. My relationship ended and I felt deep pain. But in that pain I could sense both my heart and soul healing. I am now consciously aware of physical pain in different parts of my body when difficult issues show up. The physical symptom I am most aware of, which I have never felt before, is in my heart. It aches, feels torn and broken, and yet within this pain I sense a healing, a tugging and pulling. The first indication of a stress is a rapid heartbeat, possibly a "panic attack." When that begins to happen, I know I need to address something that is going on.

But the second part of that first message is that there is a compassionate way of handling situations—at least after a bit of practice. I stop, take a deep breath, drop into my heart, and ask a question. Though the answers vary, they somehow always remind me that we are all one, that we are all perfect in our imperfection, that we are all on a spiritual journey and the pain I feel is a part of that. This helps me to remember that we are all doing the best we can in an attempt to heal ourselves. Everything is as it can be, and I surrender to it. His soul is healing as well as mine.

The second message reminds me to listen from my heart and trust it. It reflects truth. When I do listen I may need to do hard things or say something the other does not want to hear. But if I do so with heart—compassion—I am always brought to a better place in my life, whether I am heard or not. There is a subtle healing, a movement out of the darkness, even if it's only a very minute step. Looking back, those tiny steps were just the ones I needed to get to the next place I needed to be.

What I am learning is that even as I sit with a broken heart, feeling it allows love to come in and to heal it. I had always run from my pain. Now I visualize the wound being penetrated by powerful love. I create a laser in my mind and see that beam of love suturing or healing the cut. I can actually experience my heart heating up. Weird, but true.

Both stories testify to the fact that the most powerful human energy we have is love. And our greatest energy center, our central powerhouse, the heart, mediates that energy. Both Marcia and Maren were in very difficult life situations. Both were fighting depression. Both were in grief. Yet both shifted to the heart, and in an instant, everything changed.

MULTIDIMENSIONAL LOVE
As we really comprehend that the heart is more than a physical organ and also mysteriously gathers the energies of love, we enter the dance, the circle of lovers. When our bodies, egos, souls,

and spirits have united with love via the heart, we truly understand what Love's assignments have been all about. We can join
these four facets together and have sensuality, loving intimacy,
passion, and compassion all at once. We can even feel good while
we are feeling bad, as Marcia and Maren found out. It is bitter-
sweet. It is awesome. When we live with an open heart, when
we harness love, pull it through the heart, and live it in all ways,
we are the multidimensional lover. This is the gift that human life
offers.

Multidimensional love is the greatest symbiosis of all. When
we bring our body, ego, soul, and spirit into symbiotic harmony
by living from the heart, we create a world of amplified power.
This is the real meaning of Love's Way.

Many of us, however, diffuse this power. We separate the components. Separate, our bodies, egos, souls, and spirits may be confused: "Will multidimensional love bring me pleasure?" asks the
body. "Why should I?" asks the ego. "I wonder what it will be
like?" says soul. "What lesson does it have to teach?" asks the
spirit.

But Love has been very steadfast in its message: "Don't fence
me into any one mode. Each of these—body, ego, soul, and
spirit—has a rightful place in your love life. They cannot be separated except in your mind. You delude yourself, and that is how
you have gotten into so much trouble." Love's Way is to play
them all and with heart. And why not? What a trip this earth life
offers us. Through the heart we get to bring love into the total
human experience, into all aspects of self, and into every relationship. And we need to get this message now. If we miss it, we become fragmented lovers who use and abuse and generate more
fear, which generates more trauma, which closes the heart, which
prevents love, which produces the need to feel alive, which produces love's illusions. And then we die.

Think back to the many stories you have heard. If someone
has unresolved trauma in the body and seeks relief in a hyperarousal and depression cycle, has ego beliefs that say he or she is
a "bad seed" or that intimacy is dangerous, has exposure to unlimited or perverse pleasures of the soul, and has suffered from
repressive spirituality or none at all, what is likely to happen to
the person? This is the ruthless killer you read about in the daily

paper. This is the lover who murders his partner. This is the addict who uses and abuses others to feed the sex, romance, or dependent love habit. These are the people who hate, murder, or maim and enjoy it. And this is the person who cannot bond with another human and desperately wants to.

Look around. You will not run out of examples. Trauma, violence, and fear-based relationships are everywhere. Remember what I said at the beginning. Though many will deny that they have fear, it hides out under many disguises: depression, anxiety, isolation, loneliness, rage, hatred, lethargy, jealousy, panic. If you dig deep enough you will find your own version of it. Fear can't be escaped. It is part of a hard-wired survival mechanism.

And what about the person who has had minimal trauma, grew up in middle-class suburbia, is controlled by image and ownership, has very little depth of soul or even denies that soul exists—but who goes to church every week anyway? This person's chances of bringing love into relationships and into life itself aren't much better than those of the more obviously brutalized ones.

Nora, a client, said it so well:

> It is easy for me to be intimate with a leaf or a tree. They have never hurt me. The leaf does not have an ego filled with broken promises and betrayals of the heart. I know how to walk the earth, meditate, and soul travel. But I just can't seem to get the ego to take a risk and open the heart to loving intimacy with my husband. It is time to get my ego involved. I have one foot in the marriage and one foot out the door. And I know it is not about him changing, although I know there are things he can change, too. I need to step in with both feet and both arms, then see what it feels like in there. I now realize that my soul and spirit can't get the lesson unless the ego cleans up its act.

Here's another scenario: A successful businessman, well liked and active in his community and church, a former "perfect child," did not take family-of-origin or addiction issues seriously before he recognized habits that were depressing him. Then he got help. Being who he was, he was sure he could bypass all that. Ted's story is a common one. It describes the inner frustration and even anguish we have when we are not living from the heart.

THE MULTIFACETED CHALLENGE OF LOVE: TED'S STORY

He sat there dumbfounded and depressed.

I can't believe that after two years of intense work on myself I am still struggling with compulsive tendencies. And fighting it is only making matters worse. It can be something as simple or stupid as watching TV compulsively, working at my office till ten at night, or spending hours on the Internet. It is to the point where I am killing myself with lack of sleep. I would love to direct this energy, not have to control it.

Ted was disgusted with himself and finding it very hard to forgive himself. Though he had made great strides in overcoming sexual compulsivity, had freed himself of many limiting beliefs, had stabilized his marriage, and had an active spiritual life, he continued to struggle.

I've fallen into a new compulsive pattern. I am very aware of the physiological aspects of what is going on. I get a rush of adrenaline as I get into cybersex. I feel a longing or urge to keep watching. I hear an inner voice say, "Turn it off!" But the urge to keep watching is ten times stronger. I get another inner response that says, "I can handle it, I'm an adult." But it takes too much effort to stop and so I continue. The hangover is a crabby, tired, beat-up self. "You idiot!" echoes in my head all day long. Now this only happens when my wife is out of town—as if she were my conscience. I feel like a teenager. Spiritually I would like to believe this compulsive self has a gift in it. But my ego wants to kill it. I feel absolutely powerless!

His struggle was not external. It was internal. Recognizing this he began a dialogue with his compulsive self. He got an image of an old, weathered-skinned man, beady-eyed, lurking in the shadows, full of trickster energy. He asked it: "Why are you in my life?"

It responded:

I am in your life because you want me to be. I exploit your weaknesses. You are so dull and numb in your outer life. I provide juice, passion, and enjoyment. You judge me too harshly and see me as a weakness.

I first came to you when you were forced to play sports. You hated it, and the only way you got through it was to become compulsive about it. You could not be honest about how you felt and shut down emotionally. In college you found girls and sex. You felt alive and began a perennial quest for excitement.

As an adult your intellectual self-deception led you to do evil in the name of love. Your dabbling in affairs was all self-serving. You used your charm to escape the Protestant reserve and personal insecurity you grew up with. You wanted to become wild and free—a Rousseauian noble savage. In your self-deception you were convinced the animal self was your higher self.

You were unable to reconcile this image of "poly-fidelity" with your commitment to your wife and family. So with intellectual self-deception you convinced yourself it was acceptable. Secrets were important and they built a sensation of illusionary power, a rush you began to look forward to. But what it created was more isolation and separation. Your satyr role never fit—but you felt alive in it. You have been out of touch with your heart, and you have continued to suppress the gifts of the soul. You have been completing your parents' insecurities. I see your whole family of ancestors standing behind you, applauding you and encouraging you to keep moving forward and doing what they did not know how to do.

But you cannot do it without owning me. I will not die. I will not go away. I am the bucket you put passion into. I need you to take me seriously, to have hope and a sense of purpose. Killing an addiction or a compulsive habit does not mean you kill me. Your parents tried to put the fire out, and I became the carefree punk who said, "I do not need anyone." I was willing to make a pact with the devil himself to keep going. Stopping your addiction was one thing; freeing yourself of the ego constrictions is another. You can be spiritual, but without me you are a dead man. You are afraid of my passionate nature. Your critical ego and your lofty spiritual self have tried to make you believe that a good person cannot be passionate in life. And look what happened.

In the past you have been jealous of others' zest, or you have judged those who have fire in them as "unspiritual." But I am determined to be on earth and to get initiated into the fires of life. If my fire burns, so be it. I need a guide, not a judge.

I feel power straight through my core. This is the gift I give to you. When you shut me off you force me into two places only—the intellect or the genitals. I am not the enemy. I am here to show you how to be alive. You make it so complicated with "should nots" and intellectual theories. So you stumbled a few times. Who cares? It is so simple. Live life. And do it from the heart. When you make your decisions from the heart you will know what to do with me.

Ted was amazed at what he discovered about himself in the dialogue. Like his parents, he was snuffing out his own life force. Though he had stopped acting out sexually, he had not been able to reclaim his sexual and passionate yearning for his wife. Deeply in love with her, he had been confused as to why the slightest movement of sexual energy would bring about a numb-out. He was terrified of his desires. Both longed for the passion they knew was there.

With the insight came forgiveness. The self-judgment stopped. Ted understood how simple love was. He got how the body, ego, soul, and spirit could not *not* be in relationship. This was the symbiosis of all symbioses. He needed to honor the body energy. He needed the ego structure that guided him safely in his relationship issues and worldly concerns. He needed passion, zest, awe, and wonder. He needed a wise, compassionate spiritual self that could guide the soul through the seasons of his life. And he needed to continue living from the heart.

In his own words:

This compulsive self is not my enemy. I have been judging it. It is so clear to me now. The moment I recognized this, I felt a fusion, a vibration from the top of my head to the tips of my toes. It is my power. I felt compassion in my heart. Now I can bring passionate love back into my marriage. It's something we both long for. And I realize something else. As spiritual as I am, I have been out of touch with my soul, and that made it real easy for the body to act out. It was like they were in cahoots. If I had been honoring myself I could have said out loud, "Hey, I am not getting enough passion in my life." But passion is passionate living and with safe boundaries and heart.

As a therapist I hear stories like Ted's every week. They validate for me that a bad habit, even addiction, can be a window into the soul. When trust is lost, the soul appears to go to sleep and stops trusting love. Or it turns to Dark Eros. It will protect itself any way it can. When that happens, the biochemical rush of intoxicating feelings and the soul's need for passionate living often go hand in hand and take over. What is needed are the safe structure the ego can provide and a healthy dose of spiritual wisdom to keep us from harming ourselves or another as we live a vibrant love life. Love, that huge, impersonal energy, wants us to give it a pulsating human form. That requires a benevolent fusion of body, ego, soul, and spirit. Simple, yes. Easy, no.

Love has many ways, not just one. We must not deny any aspect of our humanness or, like the protagonists in the stories we have heard, we will get in trouble or feel love-handicapped.

We live in a body. It has a heart and biochemicals that enhance physical intimacy. Yet, if we have an addiction or a compulsive habit we need to take care of it. If we have a panic attack we will have to get to its source. We might even need the support of medications while we are unlocking trauma in our bodies. We need to eat well, do our yoga, and keep in shape. Our bodies are gifts that help us enjoy life through all of our senses. Though we do not always like them, our primal urges and responses are needed.

We need our egos. They get us around. They help us to organize our love relationships. They communicate. Your ego picked up this book and is reading it so it can be a better parent, have more self-love, and change outdated relationship beliefs and patterns. We have emotions that help us identify wants and needs and allow for emotional intimacy. Yet we know how easily our ego gets conditioned and distracted. We forget who we are and begin living through others. We need to wake up to the fact that we may be living a story that is not ours and that has been around for generations. We must clean up the little story of the ego so we are free to enjoy both physical and soul passion and delights and make room for compassion, that gift of the spirit.

Another essential move toward creating a vibrant love life is claiming our soul. Soul has the Bigger Story, the zest, and the curiosity that allows us to dig deep into our love stories so we end up transformed. It brings heaven to earth. Yet it too can be injured or lost in wicked places. It can be denied by both ego and spirit. It can get lost in desires and primal body urges and hurt others.

And we are spirit. We belong to a great spiritual web of life that has an intelligence that we are just beginning to validate with scientific research. Spiritual masters have been telling us this all along, but because we could not prove it we did not believe it. Spirit aligns with the Great Mind and helps us stay awake to who we are and what matters in our love life. Spirit is the eagle in us that looks at life and love from the highest possible perspective. It brings compassion into the picture. Yet it can be lofty and remove itself from ordinary life, neglecting important parts of our existence.

We need harmony among our four aspects to bring harmony to our relationships. Yet we remain fragmented. Perhaps this is why the world is rife with apathy, abuse, violence, and indifference to others' pain. Fragmented, we desperately search for a love that is at our very fingertips.

Imagine how Mia's story could change if multidimensional love were the norm. Imagine what her recovery might be like if she had bonded with a mother and father who had been given the tools they needed to be the valiant father and good mother and were supported by other adult authorities. Imagine her living in a world where she could be an adolescent and do the exploring and separating that she is called to do, safely. Imagine that her first love experience was sacred, not profane. Just for a moment, imagine.

What happened, happened. Such painful events continue every day. Everyone on earth has a heart, and almost no one uses it to its full potential. It seems it is easier to hurt and hate than to love. What can we do in such a world?

BUT WHAT CAN I DO?

What can you, one person, possibly do? you ask. For starters you can be grateful that love has spoken so directly. These words are not from me. I only support them. Some of the words came to me as a complete surprise. They speak to you as well as to me.

You can then review the assignments you heard. Next, you can work on them a little each day. Some assignments will be harder than others, depending on your life story. You can release the accumulated trauma in your body. You can examine your little stories and change them. You can love soulfully and not worry about the content of the story, but wonder how you are changing as you live the story. You can bring what has been hidden in the dark into the light and love it to death. It will change form! Energy cannot be destroyed, but its form can change. You can muster up as much compassionate understanding for yourself and others as you can tolerate. (And I believe you can increase the tolerance level each day.)

Above all, believe that the assignments are possible—they are, or you would not be in this life. And practice, practice, practice. You will have hundreds of opportunities each day to practice Love's Way. It does get easier and easier with time. I experience miracles each day within myself and between me and those I relate to. I look forward to the day when these seeming miracles are normal daily events.

The heart embodies spiritual wisdom and directs us to walk it on earth—to love the people. Human life without a brave heart does not make it. Spiritual life without heart does not make it, either. If we isolate or judge either, we will have difficulties in our relationships, you can be sure. The love we feel in the heart center cannot be learned. It can only be experienced. Heart power creates an illumined world, and that seems to be precisely what we are being asked to do now. For the heart to run full steam, we must get ourselves together.

Do not be discouraged if you cannot do all of this perfectly. Do you know of anyone who is so put together that they have full trust in self, love, and life, are totally comfortable with their sexuality and sensuality, and are at home with their personal power? I dare say we all have work to do. Please, that does not mean we cannot learn skills and practices that can quickly take us to our heart so that we can make decisions from there.

We are hungry for love because it is the great gift of life. Once it was home. Perhaps reading this book helped remind you of something you already know. It is the only thing that can triumph over fear and hate and stop the needless tyranny we are exposed to each day. Besides, it just plain feels good to be swimming in it. Love's Way is total love. Let's get the message. There is no excuse to be lazy about it any longer. There is no more time to waste!

We need to get how we are all in this together and how each of us can make a difference. If one of our life system organs falters, so do the others. We need to live from an inside that walks the earth and feels its heartbeat; that reaches outside and touches the great something that holds answers we have not been able to get.

This physical heartbeat one day will stop. But there is a bigger heartbeat that resonates throughout the universe and will never stop. Its power is great. You are one of its cells. Within you is the seed kernel of a memory of this power waiting patiently for you to call it forth. It is the promise of all you are capable of embodying in this life. It is not something you earn, nor can it be bought. You must have enough power to see beyond the world that has been created in order to recognize it. When you recognize it you are required to live it. Every relationship is leading you to it. Stop being lazy and waiting for it. Invite it in now.

How lucky we are to be multidimensional. Just think of the experiences we can bring to our love life. Writing this manuscript, I am more keenly aware of what a great creature we are, what wonderful opportunities we have in our complexity. Rather than condemn the body, live in it. Enjoy its pleasures. Enjoy the ego and have a rich emotional and challenging mental life. Join the tribe and serve it well. Bring the soul into everything you do and love with passion. And let the spirit connect you to the wonders and wisdom of the universe that fire up your heart.

Love says: "I am the flow of life. I flow from the Great Spirit to you. I enter through the heart. Harness me. I am the greatest power you can know. Let me in and use me. You must take me to others. Others must take it back to you. This *is* the great circle of life. Go, my friend. Never forget the words: I love you. And now live them."

This is Love's Way.

Here is a recipe for a vibrant multidimensional love life:

- Find a handful of people willing to be lovers with heart.
- Do everything you can to open your heart.
- Nurture childlike innocence, curiosity, and playfulness.
- Be loyal and honor commitments.
- Allow space for contemplation, introspection, and the need to be alone.
- Understand what love really is.
- Get rid of love illusions.
- Experience the sacredness in another.
- Savor heartfelt moments and remember how you got to them.
- Harness love and express it every chance you have.
- View love as the way out of suffering.
- Let body, ego, soul, and spirit be one big happy family.
- Appreciate the gifts each facet brings to you.
- Heal the wounds of the heart.
- Go to the heart with your questions.
- Listen.
- Run everyone you meet through your heart to find out who is safe.
- Think of heart as your emperor and let it run the show.
- Practice the wound of the heart but learn the lesson.
- Be absolutely truthful.
- Know that you are divine love on one side and human love on the other.
- Totally accept the human.
- Greet love with more love.
- See sexual union as love-inspired.
- Dignify yourself and others.
- Stop fooling yourself.
- Let your heart ache—that means it's working.
- Know that every relationship has love in it somewhere.
- Understand that you are a part of one great universal heartbeat.
- Share all of you, from deep in the soul.
- Resolve conflict from the heart.

- Become the "Good Mother."
- Become the "Valiant Father."
- Protect your body, protect your ego, protect your soul, protect your spirit.
- Dance, dance, dance the circle of love.
- Thank your wonderful, strong heart.
- Become a warrior with heart.
- Do lots of down-to-earth loving.
- Get rid of the glut and clutter in all four facets.
- Live your life like an open book.
- Work through any inner fragmentation.
- Give away, give away, give away, and make sure the giving has heart.
- Love fearlessly.
- Radiate love frequencies.
- Bond heart to heart.
- Put Love's Way into the streets.

Shift from fear-based thoughts and emotions to those that come from the heart:

- Appreciation
- Gratitude
- Care
- Kindness
- Passion
- Exhilaration
- Joy
- Tolerance
- Compassion
- Forgiveness
- Awe
- Ecstasy
- Enthusiasm
- Peace
- Serenity
- Happiness
- Equanimity

Memo

To: You

From: Love

By now you have heard my way. It is not easy. Though it's available to everyone, not everyone will choose to live it. It demands that you live with absolute integrity. Your actions must match your words. When they do not, you must own that fact and work to change it. You must become someone you and others can trust. Choosing me is no guarantee that you will not be betrayed. All great spiritual masters suffered betrayals. Some gave up their lives in the betrayal, and their strong spirits live on. In living from the heart, there can be no death. Should you choose my way, at times you may feel like you will die of a broken heart.

You have learned what I am and am not. I am not an illusion. Love illusions are your false dependencies on others, dependencies in which you demand they serve you in some way. I am not a feeling, but rather a huge reservoir of energy that pulsates throughout the universe. And though I am not a feeling, in the rich emotional life you have been given you can pull my energy down to earth and experience me in the higher emotions of the heart.

Nor am I a mere mental construct or a thought. Thoughts have been used to constrain and limit me. You can change your thoughts to those that free me. Likewise I am not your behavior. You have on many occasions misused others in the name of love. Yet you have the ability to act in loving ways. Some of those actions will demonstrate toughness as you stand up for your truth.

I am not a role you play in life's many melodramas. Often in those roles you lose sight of me completely. Yet in the many roles you have been given there are infinite opportunities to express me. Children need a mother and a father who are not afraid to love themselves, each other, and them. The world is in need of bringing me into every role, not just one.

I am not romance. You have misused romance, and it has become a fairy tale you attach to. Romantic love is a place where your virtues and the possibility of human love can be experienced. You need to remember what you look like when you are there, as you will be strong enough to let others in and know you. Sometimes fear creeps in and you close down your heart and become bored, mean, or distant. Your challenge is to keep your heart open and alive so I may mature within you.

I am not sex. Though I can be in your sexual relationships you know that many times I have been absent from them. You often justify sex in your search for me and confuse me with it. While all of life is sexual—male and female—the sex act without love is a chemical high and nothing more; if that's all you're after, please don't invoke my name. You are meant to experience sacred sexual intimacy where I am present.

I am not dependent on a specific object. That should be clear by now. You can experience me all by yourself and everywhere you go. I am not a commodity that you can buy, as your consumer advertising suggests. I do not have a price tag; I am priceless. Nor can I be earned by good behavior, pleasing others, following specific rules. Yet I can be known in these things. I am not limited. No person, love story, religion, spiritual path, cultural group, or gender owns me. And though many try to box me in, I am not a neat little package. I cannot be learned, only experienced. Yet there are lessons that you will learn on the way to knowing me.

And I am not a relationship. Nonetheless it is in relationships that you have your richest opportunities to experience me in all ways: body, ego, soul, and spirit. Nothing in the universe exists in isolation. A lone atom is a meaningless atom. A lone human is a meaningless human. Your relatedness to others is the most important fact of your reality. Yet I don't just appear in relationships. You alone bring me in. You alone keep me out.

It is time to take me to the streets, to put me in all of your relationships. I am certainly needed there. And there is no time to waste. You cannot just dream about Love's Way. It is to be lived. Fear has occupied too much of life. It is as though there is a subtle war going on between the forces of fear and those who believe in my power. It is entirely up to you whether I rule or fear prevails. You cannot afford to sit on the sidelines and wonder. If you are a willing player you need to run onto the playing field and play the best game you can while your heart still beats. It will be a tough game. You cannot afford to wait for others to change. You must get onto the field, wounded heart and all, and engage others in a new understanding of love. That, of course, requires a renewed commitment to know who you really are and get rid of the glut and clutter of life's learnings so I can enter. Remember, though, your life is a sacred mystery—all of it.

Are you willing? You have everything you need. You are one cell of the whole, and as you change so does everything else. What you do and do not do does make a difference. Trust me. "You do your thing and I will do mine" does not work. It separates. Every time you heal your fear, every time you let go of outdated beliefs, every time you stop an addictive behavior, every time you heal your soul wounds, every time you feed your spirit, every time you come from the heart, you bring humanity closer to its possibility.

I have reminded you of that which some part of you has always known. Thank you for taking time out of your precious and full life to listen to me and to take what I have said seriously. *But do not just put the book down and forget about me, as you often do.* Keep it near you, and when you forget about me pick it up, and I will remind you one more time. If you really have heard the message and if you are willing to do the hard work—even a little each day—you will revolutionize yourself and then the world. I do promise you that.

And now, friend, continue on so you can free yourself to live Love's Way.

Good luck.

CHAPTER EIGHT

Taking Love's Way to the Streets

◙　◙　◙

Come, weary traveler, come
Enter these doors of the open heart
Leave the world behind
Sit in the sacred silence—Close your
Eyes as remembrance of
The Beloved is awakened with every
Breath—every word

Feast upon the source of this abundance
Feast upon the words of wisdom to fill
Your cup
Feast, weary traveler, feast—you can never
Be too full for here you are nourished
In the journey of your soul

When you leave all is new—share the
Sweet fruit with all whom your eyes
Gaze in thoughts of grace

Welcome come again and again
Feast in divine remembrance of the Beloved
Feast in the journey of your soul
                                    —Lila-Qadrya

BRIDGING THE SACRED AND
SECULAR WORLDS

And now it is time to do the work. Love's Way recognizes that we
live in two parallel worlds: matter and spirit. We have the physi-

cal body that walks the earth. In that body is the emotional life of the ego. Beyond that, we are soul and spirit. Recognizing that modern living has secularized our life and love relationships beyond what seems healthy, we are challenged to give mystery an honored place again. Love's Way returns the mystery to our human experience. Relationships are appreciated for their uniqueness. Love's Way says we are spiritual beings embodied in a human existence. It supports traditions that understand the relationship between all life forms. It stresses that the healing of our selves, our relationships, our families, and our communities is not for ego gratification but for the health of all of life. It understands that there is only one story, the story of the universe. It recognizes that when we experience physical or emotional pain, there can be injury as deep as the soul wound. It perceives that we are at a critical point in our human development, when we must live from the heart.

As a psychotherapist I was trained to look for pathology and help a person get back into a narrowly defined groove. The intriguing mystery of personhood was often reduced to abnormal behaviors and how to control them. I also learned that ambitious programs for self-help and spiritual advancement often become narcissistic activities in which people get hooked on good feelings.

For many, a schism has opened between the world of spirit and the secular world. Those taking a spiritual path, as we have learned, often neglect healing psychological wounds or ignore addictive processes. This spiritual bypass results in a warped sense of love and causes harm to many. Personal growth, treatment for addictions, psychotherapy, and spiritual practices are not dead ends; they're wake-up calls. They invite us to recognize that the universe is alive, filled with the primordial energy known as love. And to honor our ancestors and guarantee life to our descendants, we need to get and live that message now.

CREATION PSYCHOLOGY

In the seventeenth century a scientific revolution abolished the idea of the soul, leaving a dualistic universe: matter and spirit. Not only was a two-tiered reality created, but also secular and sacred experiences were often kept separate or even seen as opposites. What resulted was a sterility that created a longing in the soul and an aching in the heart. Contemporary manifestations of this cosmic dualism came in the form of addictions, compulsive behaviors, greed, power struggles, depression, anxiety, and unhealthy relationships based on image and ownership. We know the rest. Psychology was called in to fix things.

The word *psyche* originally meant "soul," so psychology was the art of "soul study." But to give psychology reputable status we turned it into a science. In many ways that is good news. Psychology is taken seriously today, and with its help many are guided to a more fulfilling life. But I, and many others in the helping professions, soon learned that a psychology without heart or soul falters.

My humble attempt to understand and address this dilemma culminated in what I call Creation Psychology. Like Love's Way, Creation Psychology is an inclusive model in that it respects and utilizes many psychological models (they're listed below). In learning to respect the intriguing mystery of each person's story, aspects of various models may apply in varying times and ways. There is not a right or wrong path.

There are, of course, innumerable forms and schools of psychology. Here are some major models:

Medical: looks for pathology and defines in pathological terms. Tests and prescribes. Important for diagnosis and detecting biochemical imbalances. Useful in treating addictions.

Behavioral: focuses on behaviors and looks at maladaptive behavior; still focused on pathology. Important in treating addictions and compulsive behaviors.

Psychosocial: explores how we interacted with the environment; family of origin is what matters; still looks for pathology. Primarily an ego level of understanding. Important in uncovering the little story and its learned limitations.

Humanistic: says we are more than our pathology and looks at our possibilities; a growth model. Important in shifting our focus from negative to positive. Often centered on the "I" and not "you" or "we."

Transformational: looks at all life experiences as an opportunity to grow in spiritual consciousness; a nonjudgmental growth model. Can still be too focused on the "I."

Shadow psychology: acceptance of the hidden and dark mysteries of life; a soul-centered psychology. Important to acknowledging and giving soul its place. It brings our dark and murky issues into the light without judgment. Isolated from the other models, it can place too much importance on the soul's darkness.

Ecopsychology: says we can change via strong connection with the earth environment; emphasizes that we must change to save the planet. Important to understanding our symbiotic relationships. An "I," "you," and "we" theory.

Creation Psychology[1]: puts a spirit-filled soul back into psychology. Focuses on the spirit of creativity within all. Integrates the sacred and secular worlds. Understands that there is a mysterious interrelatedness of body, ego, soul, and spirit. It is important because it is an inclusive and evolutionary model. It includes love and the intelligence of the heart.

Love's Way is asking us for a new model of psychology. Love cannot help but be inclusive. It considers both ancestry and descendancy. It respectfully integrates Western, Eastern, and indigenous models of understanding the human story. It considers biology and the effects of conditioning. It still analyzes the impact of life influences and our developmental history. It takes seriously our traumas and our need to heal them. It acknowledges addictions and relationship problems as important. It diagnoses, tests, and prescribes. It includes energy models and holistic healing and believes that process is as important as the content. It has a global view, recognizing that the health of each relationship, each family, and each community depends on the health of each person within it. It is a sacred psychology as it allows for the expression of the pure, uncontaminated self in totality—body, ego, soul, and spirit. It holds in awe the light, dark, creative, and transformative powers that naturally occur in all creation.

As a therapist I consider therapy a sacred process. The person who sits before me is sacred. I am but a witness to another's healing and birthing. I am guide and shaman. My task is to help the person come home. Coming home means having a soul-infused personality. In its first breath, the soul takes in the history of humanity. It brings the collective unconscious into ego life and ensures that the sacred unfolds into matter. The soul's task is to be so close to the physical that a person has instant revelation and instant trust of his or her perceptions.

You too must recognize your sacredness and know your soul's journey. When you do so you will not be inclined to judge or dwell on details but will view life from an eagle's perspective and with compassion. You will know when it is appropriate to pay attention to the body or to the ego and when it is time to address the soul or spirit. You will live from the heart's intelligence. You will know how they are intrinsically interwoven. You will know how to release trauma without creating more injury.

Your commitment to personal change will be an art, and you will trust your intuition, as artists do. You will share power with others in your life, reminding them that you are not the magician, they are; that alchemy is not the process of making something out of nothing. It is the process of increasing and improving that which already exists. You cannot put into them what is already there. Your job is to help claim and use the gifts of the soul in noble ways. A person who wants to be an alchemist must have the magnetic power to materialize the invisible aspects of the soul. The purer the personality, the greater will be the magnetic power to attract that which you want in love relationships.

You will recognize that spirit is within and without all things and manifests in delightfully different forms. Love is like the big bang: You go from a tiny spark to a great being, a universe. And though you may cling to the old ways of self-protection, you gently remind yourself and others that the great work cannot proceed unless old elements die. All great teachers and saviors went through a portal of death.

You need to examine the little story of the ego to see how the soul got lost or injured, how the pathos in your life is an important part of the soul's journey. And in your love relationships you will then feel honored to be entrusted with the care of another's soul. This is a great responsibility, and you take it seriously. There is a precious life sitting in the room with you that may not trust easily or, in its innocence, may be far too eager to trust.

And when there is suffering, you understand that you needed the shattering of the illusion and now need to be with the suffering until you are changed. At first you will only get glimmerings of the soul. And though you may relapse into doubt and fear, your absolute faith and clarity of intention align you with Basic Trust. The truth of who you are will seep through the shattering events, and when that happens you will be grateful for the awfulness of the suffering.

Self-therapy done from a sacred perspective looks and feels much different from the mundane psychological perspective alone. You are not fixated on "what is wrong" and looking for the quick fix. You recognize that the family of origin is likely to contain some dark characters that the fairy tales and mythology speak to and that these characters have ripped at your soul as well as traumatized the body or fragmented the ego via developmental inadequacy and the projections of others.

Perhaps the soul has been maimed or stolen. Love's Way is as much about soul healing as it is about anything. It does not blame or dwell on such darkness, but helps to retrieve the innocent from the monsters. There is empathy and compassion for all the characters of the story, including Mom and Dad. While Love's Way does not excuse the characters' behavior or ignore the release of pent-up emotions, it is more interested in you going through the eye of the needle and coming out with soul intact.

Love's Way never judges life events. It has spirit and compassion. It knows that a sexual addiction, suicidal ideas, and betrayal were teachers and had a place and a purpose. It is how the person uses the experience that's important. Love's Way sets up a curiosity about life and love and asks, "How does this make sense in the person's story?" "What energy does it hold?" "How is this relationship a teacher?" All the events that are put on a person's path will either stand in the way of answering the questions or help answer them.

If Love's Way makes sense to you, it is important for you to find a therapist to whom it also makes sense. This may not be easy, and you may have to choose more than one mentor. If you have an addiction or compulsive behavior, get to someone who is an expert in that area. If you have a biochemical anxiety or depression and are in need of medication, get it. If you have not done family of origin work on an emotional level, do so. Beyond that, find someone to help you heal the injuries of the soul and spirit. You cannot bypass any of these tasks.

I also want to encourage you to create a network of support people, if you do not already have one. It is hard being human and particularly hard to change generations of patterns. Not only do we need our spiritual helpers, we need down-to-earth people who are on the same level of understanding. We have learned that thoughts, behaviors, and emotions are energies. You have been around people who drain energy like psychic vampires. We heal by being around those of equal or higher vibration patterns. Stick with the winners. This is why Christ, Buddha, Mother Teresa, and Gandhi attracted throngs of people to them.

Yes, you are energy, but when you are in pain your walls are down and you need the safety and protection of people who live in love, power, and wisdom. Don't settle for less than you deserve. Some people have chosen to stay in difficult relationships because of commitments and other extenuating circumstances, and have only been able to do so because they have strong networks of like-minded people and healthy internal boundaries that prevent others from zapping their energy. And they have spiritual support.

AND NOW . . .

If you have come this far in the book, you are already on the playing field. Some part of you has agreed to be a warrior of the heart and take love to the streets. Though there are many things you can do and many things you may already be doing, I'm offering a few ideas to add to your portfolio. I've designed the following ideas and activities for use in workshops or in a therapeutic setting. If you find them difficult to do on your own, or if moving through them brings up information or feelings that are uncomfortable, contact a professional counselor or spiritual mentor. Some exercises consist of guided imagery. You may choose to put them on tape and guide yourself through them at a leisurely pace. Many of you are in support groups. Doing these with others has a power of its own, and I strongly recommend that practice. You will need a notebook or journal in which to do the written exercises. Take the time you need to do the exercises. These are not intended to be done in a hurry. Not all answers will come at once, but if you are serious, the insights will trickle in. You can do these in any order, depending upon what is up for you now. Remember that this is a journey and not a destination.

Beginning Meditation

> When the cry goes out,
> There is a response.
> —*The Tibetan Book of the Dead*

Get comfortable. Go to your heart by closing your eyes, taking five deep breaths, and embracing the sensation of gratitude in your heart. Repeat the following:

"I give thanks that I am a radiant child of the universe and that divine love, power, and wisdom flow through me and bring to me all the insights I need to live Love's Way and not mine. My intention is pure, and I have complete trust that I will be shown that which I am ready to know today. With this knowledge I will do my part."

Stay quiet and let the gratitude fill your body. Repeat this each day you tend to the exercises or before each return to an exercise if you are in need of help switching from the distractions in your daily life to your sacred journey.

TRAUMA, TRUST, AND THE BODY

> The biochemistry of the body is the product of awareness.
> Beliefs, thoughts, and emotions create the chemical reactions
> that uphold life in every cell.
> —Deepak Chopra, *Journey into Healing*

Impact of Trauma Exercise

That we have had trauma in our life is an understatement. If we don't create disaster on our own, life and nature will oblige. It is a fact of life. We can do something about the trauma we carry in our bodies. When we do so, we make it easier for new trauma to flow through us without as much damage. The bonus is a more supple heart.

Review the four kinds of trauma in chapter 2. Make as complete a list as you can for each, from the least intense to the most intense. Then honestly review each and note what impact the trauma has had on your love relationships. Examine the fears, belief structures, unresolved grief, behaviors, and compulsive habits that may relate to the trauma. Note what you did to cope or adapt and how this coping pattern keeps repeating in your love relationships. What are you willing to change to allow love in? Remember, there is no judgment; but if you stay in denial, nothing will change. Take these insights to your trusted friends and mentors, including your partner. Tell your story and ask for the support you need.

Trauma of omission: Physical, developmental, emotional, mental, and spiritual needs neglected or not met.

Trauma of commission: Things said and done to you that you experienced as hurtful, injurious, intrusive, or abusive.

Shock trauma: Life events that you and/or your parents were not prepared for: surgery, death, illness, frequent moves, and so on. May or may not be severe enough to meet the diagnosis for post-traumatic stress disorder.

Post-traumatic stress disorder: Life events that were catastrophic and out of ordinary experience: rape, witness to a murder, war, floods, serious accidents, earthquake, and so on.

Listed below are a few examples to give you a starting point.

Trauma of Omission:

Who/what: My parents. They didn't talk to me about life, and when I approached them with my problems, they were too busy to listen. I felt uncomfortable talking to others; I couldn't open up in relationships and never allowed anyone to get close to me.

Fears/belief structure/behaviors: I was afraid to trust. I came to believe that I could and should handle everything on my own.

Coping: Because I had locked inside all of my hurts and frustrations, I drank and used drugs to deal with the pain.

Willing to change: I will stop using and abusing chemicals. I will take a risk and trust others. I will be vulnerable and know that it is okay to have feelings and to talk about them.

Trauma of Commission:

Who/what: My first-grade teacher reprimanded me in front of the class. He said I was no good, I was stupid, and that I wouldn't amount to anything.

Fears/belief structure/behaviors: He was an authority figure, so I began to fear all people in authority. I believed I would not succeed in life. I got into people pleasing.

Coping: I isolated myself and became very quiet. I figured if I didn't say anything, I couldn't say anything stupid.

Willing to change: I am willing to look at myself in a positive light. While I realize I have character defects, I will work on growing through them, rather than dwelling on them and giving them power over me.

Shock Trauma:

Who/what: When I was six years old, I had my tonsils removed. The surgery was frightening; I didn't know what was going to happen to me. No one explained it to me.

Fears/belief structure/behaviors: I felt afraid, alone, and abandoned and decided I wasn't brave enough.

Coping: I tried to be brave by pretending I wasn't scared, a trait that carried over into my love relationships. In relationships, when afraid, I dismissed it.

Willing to change: I'm willing to acknowledge my fears and ask questions until I feel safe.

Post-traumatic Stress Disorder:

Who/what: I witnessed my best friend in college get hit by a car and die. I still have nightmares about that day. I am constantly reliving that instance.

Fears/belief structure/behaviors: If I don't have other close friends it won't hurt if something happens to them. I keep my distance.

Coping: I stay frozen. I haven't made many close friends since then.

Willing to change: I will finish my grief. I will attempt to make new friends, knowing that I may one day lose them, but I will celebrate our friendship and not live in the future or worry about what-ifs.

Trauma Exercise

Love's Way made it clear that we have a body to enjoy the rich pleasures that earth-based relationships offer. Feeling life via the senses helps us mediate life and love. This exercise is intended to help you know what it is like to feel safe and what happens when fear enters. It is important to know the difference. Sometimes we walk around in a state of hyperarousal or tension and we do not even realize it. We often bond with our traumatic experiences and perpetrators and live on the edge of life as we continue to repeat history. We need to get back to relaxed bodies so we can bond with tranquil and safe people just as easily. (By the way, serenity is not boredom! It is a satiation that is bursting with potentiality. In serenity, love can be experienced in the form of grace, awe, celebration, and wonder.) This exercise can be helpful to those who remain bonded to the biochemical rush of trauma and those who live more in the head than in the body.

Close your eyes. Deep-breathe until you are relaxed. If you work with sound that helps drop you into your heart (such as om . . . hu . . . haa . . .), use them. A healthy organism is fluid. Sense the body; listen to and feel the heart.

Imagine being with someone you love and feel safe with. If you cannot think of anyone, bring in a spiritual mentor. You are walking on a beach. Explore the sensations in your body as you feel a warm, soft breeze touching your skin, a dewy wetness in the air, and pleasurable sounds, perhaps birds chirping. Gentle waves are coming up the beach and washing your feet. Feel the sand oozing through your toes. Notice the emotions you feel. Bring a sense of gratitude into your heart. Empty the mind as you immerse yourself in the experience.

It is the next day. You are alone but are remembering the experience of yesterday with your friend. You feel relaxed, comfortable, and appreciative. Your heart is relaxed and full. A smile naturally comes to your face. Suddenly, out of the corner of your eye, you see an enraged stranger running directly at you, screaming. He has a gun in his hand. Notice the changes in your body, your breathing, your heartbeat, your posture, and your muscles. Notice the expression on your face. Notice what you focus on. Stay present to your instinctive response. What does your body do or want to do? Does it want to take flight, fight, or freeze? How long does it take to relax?

Now imagine that your trusted friend appears with others and successfully intercedes. The stranger is restrained; the gun is out of his hand. Now what does your body want to do? Do you let it mobilize? If not, imagine your friend holding you and encouraging you to release the tensions in your body. As you do so, notice what happens. How long does it take to feel safe again? Do you trust at all? Did you like the on-the-edge feeling? To return to Basic Trust we often need to know that there are those we can trust. We often set ourselves up by choosing the wrong people or putting people through unrealistic tests. How many people do you have in your life who demonstrate that they live in Basic Trust or are trustworthy?

It is the next day. You are walking with your trusted friend on the same beach. Are you relaxed? Do you feel safe? Are you in the moment or in yesterday? If you're tense, note how much energy it takes to stay present. Repeat this scene until you begin to feel safe, relaxed, and fully present to your friend and the sensual experience.

WHAT A PERSON LIVING IN BASIC TRUST LOOKS LIKE

Feeling safe is a prerequisite to opening our heart to another. That implies living in Basic Trust, as discussed in chapter 2. While Basic Trust is fundamentally an innate, implicit quality that eludes definition, we can sense when a person is living in Basic Trust by recognizing some or all of the following. Review this list. First assess yourself by noting how many apply to you today. Then look at those significant adults who were responsible for providing the safe container you grew up in. Assess your past and present partners, friends, or anyone in your life that you relate to in a significant way. If you do not have at least five people who live in Basic Trust on your list, you'd better get busy and find them.

A person with Basic Trust

- wholeheartedly engages in life
- is life-affirming
- is authentic
- is courageous
- has a quality of innocence
- understands there is a Bigger Story that includes soul
- knows that separation and isolation are illusions created by the small mind

- views life as basically benevolent
- has ease and confidence
- is willing to surrender to life and love
- trusts that everything is right as it is
- believes in the abundance and generosity of the universe
- is able to simply be; lives in the moment
- is trustworthy
- is willing to live in uncertainty
- has an air of relaxation and openness
- does not fight or attach to pain
- trusts silence, stillness, and just being
- is comfortable living the process of life
- lives from the heart
- views love as the universal container that holds us while we do life

Trust Exercise

We have all been betrayed, and it has left its mark on us. People will continue to disappoint us from time to time. Yet to live Love's Way we must be willing to live in Basic Trust once again. We must be willing to become trustworthy. Refer back to chapter 2 and review the characteristics of human trust. Many people use the words "surrender" or "let go and let God" but still have disastrous relationships. Make a list of people currently in your life who demonstrate the following five characteristics of human trust. Remember that they do not need to be perfect, just willing to own their inconsistencies.

- openness
- reliability
- acceptance
- congruence
- integrity

SELF-TRUST

We seem always to look for safe relationships that make it easier for us to be vulnerable. Yet how safe are we? Do *we* make the Basic Trust list? Do we live in human trust? We need to stop putting the focus outward and do our own inventory. Looking at self might be a more appropriate challenge. To get to trust of self and others we must be brutally honest about the ways we have violated trust in our love relationships. This includes how we have violated self. Trust means we accept that everything in our life is as it should be. It means letting go of power plays and the need for manipulation or control. This should be a clue: How many times have you attempted to change others or control outcomes? Human trust means we are responsible for our own human imperfection and do not project it onto others. We are congruent. Our words and actions match.

- Make a list of the ways you have doubted Basic Trust and attempted to control your love life.
- Make a list of the ways you have betrayed yourself.
- Make a list of the ways you have violated trust in your love relationships.
- More important, what are you willing to change to become safe and trustworthy? Are you willing to start now? If yes, make a list now.

THE EGO IN LOVE

The Little Story: Hologram Exercise

Love's Way made it clear that we each have a little story that we live out unconsciously, and to really get to emotional intimacy, we need to know the story, heal the wounded heart, change destructive story lines, and uncover the secret self-promises that kept us safe at one time but now limit our ability to love. When I work with people I do a very thorough life-script review that helps the client understand that the past, present, and future are all related. We do not need to dwell in the past because it is happening now and creating the future.

Even though the soul lives in the mystery of the drama and really digs the myth, it does not relish repeating history over and over. It would like to get on to a higher level of initiation. So it, too, wants you to get the lesson. After all, the ego is the great pretender. Rather than guiding us to fulfilling love, it tries to ruin it.

That is, of course, until we change our story. The following exercise is intended to playfully help you identify and change aspects of the little story you are living.

The holodeck on board the Enterprise in the television series *Star Trek: The Next Generation* can create any situation in a lifelike 3-D hologram. The crew member who wants to use it asks the master computer to create what she imagines, then walks into the movie. It all seems real. The holodeck voyager can stop the hologram at any point and instruct the computer to change the hologram. She can go back in time and change the future or can go into the future and change the past. Imagine that you have the ability to see your future and you do not like what you see. You go into your computer and delete the old chip in your brain and put in one that leads to the future you want. You have recognized that the past, present, and future are all really one big movie. The holodeck is not that far out. One of the basic discoveries of quantum physics is that we are not merely discovering reality; we are actually participating in creating it. How we see things affects the very thing we see.

Imagine that you have been beamed down to earth life for the experience of it, to check it out, to play a role, to be in a story. The challenge you have is to be in the story but not get lost or controlled by it and always to remember the bigger picture. On deck there is someone who can change the program or bring you back.

Hologram 1: Your Life as It Has Been Lived, Trauma and All
You are in the hologram. It begins before birth. You are pure spirit. You have no judgment. You are asked to allow yourself to be beamed to earth and while you're there to work in the service of love. You agree, even though you are told it will not be easy. But before you enter you want to know what your challenges will be. This is a test. You are to remember your mission as obstacles are placed before you. You accept the challenge. You are confident you will not forget.

You are watching your parents at the time of conception. You notice whether they are planning for you, whether you are conceived in an act of love. You enter the womb of your mother. You hear her heartbeat and the rhythm of her body. You are at one with her. Then you are born. You have your first bonding experience in the secular world. You notice how men and women feel different. You explore your world with all of your senses as you continue to grow.

Little by little you begin forgetting your mission as you adapt to the world you are in. You notice how people talk, touch, relate. You follow their rules. You have no choice. You need others for physical and emotional survival. You begin to experience trauma. Some needs are not being met. There are surprises and even shocks. You feel trapped in the body and ego. By age two you have lost Basic Trust. You even wonder how important you are. Sometimes you are led to believe you are most important. You notice who has the power in this world and how they get it. You notice your gender and its limitations.

You learn there are definite rules about love. You begin to believe it is something you earn, that it is only available in relationship, and that it can be bought. Some convince you that a doctrine or a specific culture owns it. Suppressed, you start playing the game of love to feel alive.

By age seven you have developed a story line that keeps your life predictable and defines who you are. You are the hero or the forgotten one. You carry this role forward in your life. You begin to repeat history in spite of yourself. You are in adolescence, your twenties, your thirties, your forties, your fifties, your sixties, your seventies, your eighties, and beyond. You have hundreds of relationships. You notice patterns you have acquired. You are one up, you are one down. You love, you withhold love. You are betrayed, you betray. Your life keeps repeating itself. You ask: "What is love?" "Where is love?" You have forgotten you are love and it is everywhere. You feel crazy. You want out of the holodeck. "Computer, end program. Exit."

Hologram 2
Hologram 1 has not met your expectations. You do not like it. You tell the computer to change the program and you describe the future you want to be in, the program you want to create. It is Love's Way.

The computer says, "It is done." You reenter the holodeck. You are in the new program. It is delightful and challenging. All kinds of characters show up to test you. There is no magic. But in this scenario you never forget what love really is. That keeps you grounded, and you walk through life knowing that everything is as it should be and ultimately truth and love will prevail. That basic knowing gets you through human suffering. You are determined to learn the lesson. You are feeling challenged by love's obstacle course. Even when you make a mistake, you catch yourself and get back up. Since the past, the present, and future are one, as you changed the future, the present and the past changed, as well. It's time to return to deck. "Computer, end program." You exit. Now that you're back on deck you have this memory going for you. And you have an option you can always use: You can tell the computer to change anything, anytime, and it hears you. There is relief in that.

Take time with this imagery. Visualize it with your mind's eye or write it out. Get clear about where you have been and change those things that interfere with the future you say you want. The more clarity you can get, *and the deeper you feel the experience*, the more likely it will be that it will show up. Science and spirituality say so.

Gain from Pain Exercise

In this life there is suffering. All the coping mechanisms in the world will not change this fact. So the best advice I can give you is to learn how to use the pain wisely. We scripted ourselves in dramatic or traumatic moments of painful intimacy. We are bonded with the negative experience because of that. At the moment life betrayed us we moved out of trust and into a highly charged emotional experience. Though we may have later numbed out, at the time of emotional pain we likely made a protective self-promise or came to a black-and-white conclusion that now is locked in our hearts and minds and is limiting our ability to be open to love. So it makes perfect sense that when we recreate an old trauma drama and are in a feeling state once again, we use that vulnerable time to give ourselves a positive message. We reprogram ourselves for Love's Way this time. We are older and wiser, we can care for ourselves, and we have established a healthy support system. There is no longer any excuse to keep repeating the drama.

It is when we *feel* something deeply *and change it* that the change gets recorded in our nerves. For example, it is easy to say, "I deserve love" as a mental mantra when things are going well. Yet it is far more potent to say, "I deserve love" when we are having a feeling-memory of someone hurting us or are in the presence of deep grief caused by a betrayal. When we are in a feeling state we are raw and open. We can use our feeling and add to it a bit of wisdom and compassion. Whatever we tell ourselves in an intense emotional moment becomes our future.

When we're betrayed we usually want to tell ourselves how stupid we have been or convince ourselves never to trust and certainly not to get too close again. We unwittingly prepare ourselves for disaster. Now, as adults, we must be wise enough to say: "I will grow from this pain," "I believe in love," "I will grieve but not personalize the betrayal," or a hundred other affirming statements that ensure love's presence. Pain presents us with an opportunity to create the future we want. Pain is a natural indicator that something is wrong; without it we would never know what lessons we need to learn. It also gives us the opening to practice living from our heart. I don't mean to sound like Pollyanna, though. It is also the most challenging time to stay true to love's call.

EMOTIONAL HONESTY

Relationships often skimp on emotional intimacy. Many people know how to be physically or socially intimate but are afraid to tell each other who they really are and what they feel or why they cannot feel. More important than pleasing or trying to fix someone is being present to them. As one person I know said to his partner after being told he was not expressive enough: "I know you want me to be more expressive with my feelings, but all I can tell you is that I am here and this is what is going on with me. I feel numb right now and I hate feeling numb. I wish I had your fire right now. I do not and I cannot manufacture it." We crave safe containers: relationships that hold us while we tell our stories. Judgmental or discounting comments such as "Don't let it get to you," "I don't want to talk about it," "Just forget about him (or her)," "You should be over it by now," "Why can't you feel more, talk more, be more?" don't help us.

Sometimes all we need is our partner or one good friend to say, "I hear you" or "I'm sorry you're hurting." We need someone to see us right down to the core of our being. Children who have one adult whom they can count on to listen and accept without discounting them are less likely to personalize the betrayal of others or carry trauma in their bodies. They grow up being good listeners, too! We have unfinished business stored inside because we did not have support for our emotional needs when we needed it. When we are heard, trust—the very thing we need to bring love into our relationships—is present.

Discuss and practice the following in your relationships:

- Go to your heart.
- Be totally present.
- Listen attentively.
- Keep your agenda separate from the other person's.
- Accept with open-mindedness.
- Wait for them to finish.
- Refrain from urges to defend, fix, criticize, judge, or cajole.
- Affirm that you have heard.
- Ask how you can support them. You may discover you already have, just by being there.

Developing a Healthy Inner Parent

The ego has accumulated a lot of faulty parenting models and messages over the years, and these contribute to the emotional hurt and pain so pervasive in our relationships. We likely missed out on important models and messages as well. Our ego goes on automatic pilot, and, though it wants to be more loving, it says and does things it regrets later. Most of our parenting has been critical, controlling, permissive, or rescuing. That is enmeshment, not love! It is abusive or mushy. We try to fix people, and, since that never works, we begin to criticize or judge. We look to others to parent us or fill in the gaps and remain unconscious that we're doing it. We even scheme to get what we want.

Since we have an ego and emotional bonding is one of its treasures, we are challenged to develop an internal structure that creates a safe container for ourselves, our children, our partners, our friends, and others we relate to daily. There are times in our adult relationships when we genuinely need parenting. This is what healthy support groups, friends, or lovers provide. Father/mother love is important. It can be soft or tough. The father/mother is inside each of us, regardless of gender, and needs to be developed. Here are two lists that describe a healthy-ego father/mother structure. Check off the items from both lists that you have developed and note those that could be improved upon. And get rid of what you have been using that hurts, maims, limits, or stunts growth.

The Good Mother: Our Inner Mother
  gives nurturing physical touch
  gives verbal strokes
  makes special time
  holds our hands
  trusts
  provides intimacy
  gives strokes for being
  listens
  comforts
  kisses
  hugs
  gives gifts
  provides home cooking
  rocks her children
  understands
  consoles
  affirms
  gives permission
  smiles
  shows concern
  is empathetic
  acknowledges feelings
  provides a nurturing environment
  is attentive
  massages
  encourages
  provides unconditional acceptance
  appreciates aesthetics

affirms needs
invites equality
soothes
nurses
yields
has patience
serves
sets no conditions
is compassionate
shows appreciation
gives kindness

The Valiant Father: Our Inner Father
sets structure
organizes
sets healthy limits
keeps world safe
is potent
is firm
prioritizes
shows caring discipline
affirms equality
acknowledges responsibilities
honors commitments
sets consequences
clarifies what to do and what not to do
stops hurtful behaviors
clarifies values and protocol
earns respect
guides
is consistent
provides options
is believable
is reliable
is trusting
shares power
clarifies what is important
clarifies boundaries
has strength of character

is well organized
is effective
has firm handshake
makes direct eye contact
has upright posture
is appropriately assertive
has positive self-image
has quiet confidence
gives appropriate conditional strokes
expresses anger appropriately
has consistent expectations

How did you do? Is it easier to parent others than yourself? A wise and caring inner father/mother is needed as we let go of addictions and compulsive habits, heal our traumas, and set healthy boundaries in our relationships.

THE SOUL IN LOVE

Betrayal Exercise

This exercise can be done via guided imagery, letter writing, or two-chair dialogue. I suggest lying on a mat in a safe and secure setting with no interruptions so that you can release without prohibition.

This exercise will guide you back in time and both claim and release betrayals. Some will seem minor and others will hit deep. Whatever comes up for you will be what's ready for release. Let it go. Allow the feelings to ripple through your body. They have been holding you up for a long time. A good cry or wail will not hurt you. As you have learned, blocked energy has kept you from the full experience of love. Trust that your psyche knows what you are ready for. You are not being pushed or coerced into knowing. If nothing happens, nothing happens. This exercise can be done with a trusted friend, your partner, or a therapist, who can act as the wise mentor who is willing to take your pain and release it.

Note: When people do emotional release work I remind them that emotions and thoughts are energy. Since there is more than enough negativity being projected outward these days, I ask people to state a clear intention. The intention is always to release fear, anger, and grief to make way for forgiveness and other forms of love to come into our lives. We ask the universal forces to take the pain and transmute it into something positive, in the same way that the big bang ultimately resulted in the stars, earth, and the beauty known as life.

You have an observer or higher self. Imagine that the higher self is speaking with your human self—the one who has been betrayed in love relationships. The higher self will ask repeatedly, "Tell me how you have been betrayed." Begin by sharing the most recent betrayals or those least threatening.

Continue going back until you hit a deep feeling-experience, and describe it to your higher self. When you are finished, the guide will ask, "Will you forgive the person now?" You may or may not be willing. Forgiveness may include anger, grief, or fear. Forgiveness is a process. Remember that our spirit may be willing, but our body and ego may need more time. Take it. Denial only breeds more denial. The challenge is to feel without being attached to the feeling. With your spirit self overseeing the process, you can be both in the pain and detached from it.

SOUL LOSS

And Jesus said: "For what is a man profited, if he shall gain the whole world, and lose his own soul?"

—Matthew 16:26

Love's Way suggests that in addition to treatment for an addiction, traditional psychotherapy, and Twelve Step work, we may need a process by which soul injuries are healed and the soul is integrated back into self. Common traumas associated with soul loss are coma, rape, sexual abuse, accidents, war, verbal and physical abuse, addictions, toxic shaming, illness, near-death experiences, surgery, codependency, and love addiction.

The following may indicate soul loss, especially when they persist beyond treatment or psychotherapy: dissociation, emotional numbness, apathy, chronic depression, persistent immune deficiency problems, chronic illness, memory gaps, chronic struggles with addictions, looking outside oneself to fill a void, or feeling stuck after a major life change such as divorce or death of a loved one. There are many ways to heal the soul, and I offer you this one:

Reclaiming Our Soul

There have been many times in our lives when we were drawn to live soulfully and we were shamed for it or the urge was denied. We've all had urges to play in the mud, to steal the apple, to explore the unknown or the forbidden. Rather than receiving wise guidance or permission, we may have been punished or stopped by some well-meaning authority figure. Go over each of the following words slowly: *wet, raw, deep, passionate, earthy, juicy, murky, longing, creative, soulful, melancholy, dark, wild, daring, erotic, wonder, zestful, curious.* Repeat until you reach a word that stands out for you. Feel it down to your bones. When you have the word you resonate with, close your eyes and let yourself remember a time in your growing-up years when you were living or being drawn to live the word. If you do not have a time, create one in your mind. Be fully in the experience.

Then imagine someone coming in and shaming you or sharply denying you the expression of your soul's desire. Notice what happens to that part of you. Separate your wise man or woman self from the part of you being shamed. How do you feel about what is happening to him or her? As your higher self, enter the scene and explain to the child and the authority figure who you are and what you feel about the shaming or criticism. Ask the child if it is willing to leave the scene and come home with you. Explain how you will benefit by a relationship with it. Take the child to a safe place. Hold it. Welcome it back. Ask it three questions: What more can you tell me about yourself? What gifts do you bring back? How can you feel safe with me so you can express your gifts? Tell the soulful child what you are willing to do to honor what it brings back to you and to help it express that in good ways.

Repeat this using other words.

RELATIONSHIPS AS CONTEMPORARY INITIATIONS

Religious historian Mircea Eliade has written that ancestral initiation rites—once a vital part of most cultures—must now take place inwardly via dreams, visions, and stepping fully into painful life experiences. The basic patterns remain the same: first, torture at the hands of the spirits; second, ritual death; third, resurrection to a new mode of being. According to Eliade, "Initiation is equivalent to a basic change in existential condition; the novice emerges from his ordeal endowed with a totally different being than that which he possessed before his initiation."[2]

When we are in the midst of a painful situation we forget that we have been here before. Looking at the history of your relationships, take yourself through the steps of initiation. Take one event at a time. You may find yourself actually feeling grateful for the experience. Remember that a relationship takes many forms. We have relationships with surrogate lovers like food, alcohol, drugs, pornography, affairs, and codependency. You may be in the first or second stages of initiation now. If so, know there is a resurrection ahead for you. You must be willing to let go to get there. This is total trust and letting go of control.

Torture: The time of extended pain, uncertainty, temptation, distress, or suffering.

Death: Hitting bottom, the final blow, the fall, the ruin, the collapse, the end, letting go.

Resurrection: The time of renewal, recovery, upswing, and resurgence.

Now look at how you were transformed in the process. How are you different? How was this relationship or event important? What gifts are in it for you? (*Note:* Events may repeat themselves, and, assuming you are doing your work and learning the lessons, the time you spend in each recurring event will be noticeably shorter each time.)

THE SPIRIT IN LOVE

Compassion and Our Observer Self

The great mystery of our personhood is that we are both human and divine. These qualities are not in opposition. If we drop either side of this paradox we are in trouble. It is at the *center* of this tension that our *hearts open.* That is what love has been telling us all along.

Suffering does not feel like suffering when we bring spirit into it. In fact, we learn to transcend and transform it. We develop compassion. We forgive. Then and then only do we get to experience the great love we have been talking about. When we grasp this point, love breaks through and we are able to love the sickness in us. Rather than hate our inner addict, our inner betrayer, we can work through the pain and turn it into a new life form. That is the magic of it all, and the point of this meditation.

Choose an aspect of yourself that has been giving you trouble in your love life. It may be the dependent lover self, the sex addict self, an antidependent character self who refuses to commit or be vulnerable, or the loner who lives in fear of intimacy. It could be any part of you that has locked up life energy in an annoying habit. Whatever it is, separate it from the self that is wise, all-knowing, and compassionate, has a sense of humor about it all, and is willing to forgive.

You can do this via writing, two-chair work, or imagery in your mind. For our purposes I offer guided imagery.

Get in a comfortable position. Relax, deep-breathe. Let go of any distractions or clutter in the mind and allow yourself to be fully present. When you are relaxed, become the human who is tired of his or her behavior, thought pattern, or feeling mode. Perhaps it does not like its body. Whatever it is, feel the exhaustion, disappointment, disgust, grief, fear, anger, shame, or anything else that's present. This human knows where it has been, it knows how it sabotages life and love, but it seems unable to stop. Or if it has stopped, it still feels shame, grief, and uncertainty about itself.

Bring in the wise inner guide. Become the guide. Observe the pitiful human. Feel compassion in your heart, yet be strong in your resolve. Does this human hang on to pain, addictions, and hurt? Does it hurt others? How? What do you notice about it? What does it need to let go of so it can move forward with its life? Does it trust you? Begin the dialogue. With candid and kind honesty, talk to the human. Explain who you are and why you are here. Tell it what you see in its future if it persists. Ask what it needs in order to listen to you and work with you.

Become the human and respond. Tell the wise one how you came into being and why you are afraid to leave. How has this behavior, feeling, thought, or body symptom been serving you? What do you need to release the energy and let it become something else? You have been here for a very long time. Are you ready to let go? What do you need to work on with the wise one?

Continue the dialogue until you experience inner friendship or alliance. Keep the reunion going. Inner dialogue helps to restore inner harmony. Inner harmony leads to outer harmony in our love relationships. It also presents a united front. United we stand, divided we fall.

This process can also be used when you are struggling with relationships or having difficulty letting go. While the ego can delude us, our inner wisdom will be more objective and tell us with compassion truths that we may not want to hear.

Level of Spiritual Awareness

This chart has been of help to me in my life. It reminds me of how and why there are moments, hours, days when my spirit seems to slip away. It helps me understand why I cannot be around certain people for any length of time. It helps me realize how my hellish days affect those around me. Some days I am in divine love. Other days I am in the swamp of darkness and pain and I cannot even meditate or pray with meaning. Most days I try for neutral or one notch above it. Knowing these states helps to remind me why I need to get out of hell if there for even a moment. Use the chart in ways that you can. Not only is there individual spirit consciousness, but also each relationship has a spirit consciousness of its own. Some pull us down and others elevate us. Remember we are spiritual energy! Here are questions to explore:

- Where is your spirit's consciousness today?
- Does the energy of your primary relationship elevate you and support your moving into higher spiritual states?
- Does your relationship pull you down?
- What relationships in your life invite spiritual growth?
- What relationships in your life hold you back?

Note: Use this like a daily thermometer. You may find it helpful to chart yourself for a month and note your fluctuations and what they are related to. You can even do a daily chart and notice how your consciousness changes on an hourly basis and why. Patterns will be noticeable. (The chart is adapted from a more comprehensive chart presented in I. K. Taimni's *Science of Yoga*.)[3]

States of Consciousness

States of Consciousness	Description
+4	Classical satori. Fusion with Universal mind, with God.
+3	A point source of pure energy, light and love, astral travel, out-of-body experience, and spiritual energy. Lucid dream state.
+2	Blissful state, receiving divine grace, cosmic love, cosmic energy, heightened bodily awareness, highest function of bodily and earth consciousness, being in love.
+1	Functioning well, higher self awareness, soul lost in positive or pleasurable activities that one knows best.
0	The neutral state, doing teaching and learning with maximum facilitation, neither in a positive nor negative state, neutral. Feel grounded on the earth.
-1	Doing what one has to do but in a state of pain, guilt, fear; the state of slightly too much alcohol; the first stages of lack of sleep.
-2	Extremely negative body state where one is still in the body, as in an intense migraine attack, awareness is only in the present in one's pain, cannot work or do one's usual duties; one is isolated, a bad inner state.
-3	Extremely negative, a purgatory-like situation; fear, pain, guilt in the extreme; meaninglessness prominent.
-4	Like +4 in that one is fused with other energies but all bad, and one's self is bad and meaningless; quintessence of evil, the deepest hell of which one can conceive; can be extremely high energy state lasting eternally though by the clock time one is there only a few minutes.

THE REALM OF THE HEART: THE
MULTIDIMENSIONAL LOVER

Appreciation

Appreciation is a step to love. It is energy giving. You have
learned that you have been gifted with various dimensions of
yourself that contribute to the multidimensional lover. How often
have you stopped to thank each dimension for the many ways
they have enhanced your life and love relationships? Take time
now to do so. List all that you appreciate, and the ones you are in
awe of too. Thank each for the gifts they bring, especially to your
love relationships. Put aside for now the ways they might have
failed or disarmed you. Today we're doing it Love's Way.

Body

Ego

Soul

Spirit

Living from the Heart's Intelligence

Your heart contains intelligence, and you can call on it at any
time. It is the cheapest therapy around. Deep heart listening has
been proven to be good for our health and our relationships. We
know that love's frequencies are healing and fear-based feelings
are not. Appreciation and gratitude elevate our energy levels.
Waiting to complete our trauma work, change our story lines, or
learn our souls' lessons before we live from the heart is not necessary or even wise. While it is true that we find it easier to live
from the heart as we move through the necessary changes, there
are many simple things to do right now. We can get to our heart
much quicker than you may think.

Here are some quick and effective heart tools I have been
using for years. Even as a kid I knew that most prayers were ego

beggings and that when I opted to give thanks instead, a shift took place. I experienced the intelligence of the heart directly. So can you. These meditations can be accomplished as you sit on an airplane, ride in a car, wait for a client, relax on a beach, or take a break from a shift or a board meeting. Going to your heart does not take time, but it does take a decision. Once you have the routine down it takes only a few seconds. The trick is to get out of your head and into your heart. Remember that the heart is not intellectual. It has direct flow of insight and awareness. When you're in your heart, love speaks to you directly.

1. Close your eyes.
2. Take a deep breath. Focus on your heart.
3. Think of something in your life that you are deeply grateful for.
4. Breathe the sensation of gratitude into your entire heart and body.
5. Stay with the sensation. It is the energy of love you are experiencing.
6. Tell yourself: "This is real; remember how you got here. Never forget the importance of the moment." (You are scripting your body, ego, and soul to join you for the enlightened experience.)

Variation: Now ask your heart what you need to know about.

• what is happening in your love relationship
• what in this awful moment you can be grateful for
• how you can handle stress more effectively

Or ask about any other question you want answered.

Go to your heart whenever fear shows up. Fear creates an energy deficit, and though you may need to let it go through you, you do not want to dwell there.

Go to your heart to release anger.

Go to your heart to release resentments and grudges.

Go to your heart to forgive.

You do not need to go to your heart with an agenda. You can go there for a visit or to say thank you.

Meditation for Energizing the Heart

We know that many hearts have been wounded—our own and the hearts of others we care about. This meditation is designed for heart healing.

Begin with a deep breathing exercise: inhale, exhale, hold. Do it five times. Breathe in a circular motion—no beginning, no end. Bring the breath into the heart center until a feeling of warmth and fullness is present. Now look at your heart. Is it wounded? Is it armored? As you dwell on your heart, deepen the experience by embracing awe, compassion, and gratitude—human expressions of love.

If you're having difficulty, reflect on something in your life you are truly grateful for. Experience love as a laser beam that heals the wound of the heart or melts the wall encasing it. Let love fill and then expand outward from the heart to your skin. Allow the tingling sensations to penetrate every cell. Then extend that energy out beyond the body until you merge with something greater than yourself. Experience the endlessness of the energy known as love. Hold the experience. If there are places in your body in need of healing, penetrate those areas with love's energy.

Now, extend that love to someone you know whose heart has been injured. Be sure you have the person's permission. (If a person is not physically available, or is in a crisis or in a coma, send your higher self to his or her higher self and ask for permission.) See your energy penetrating the other and approaching the area of the heart. Is there armor around it? If so, get permission to enter. Do you see atrophy? Wounds? Again, with love and permission, melt the wall, fill the atrophied heart, and let love heal the wound.

Now place your left hand on your heart and your right hand on your belly or power center. Imagine breathing a circle between your hands. Feel these two centers connected—love and power in balance. Let that strength ground you. Slowly come back to the here and now. Return to a normal state of mental alertness while maintaining the love/power experience.

Increasing Your Energy Field

You are matter and spirit. Matter is an atomic structure consisting of protons and electrons in constant motion. Because of that, all matter has an energy field sometimes referred to as an aura. The human aura is the energy that surrounds the physical body. It is three-dimensional—egglike, in fact. While the average field is eight to ten feet wide, it has been said that spiritual masters can extend their energy field for miles. The energy field is related to both physical and spiritual health.

It is said that there are two aspects to the human field. One is the subtle body that surrounds and interpenetrates the physical energy field. The other is the physical aura that comprises sound, heat, light, and electromagnetic energy. The more vitalized your energy field is, the more energy you will have to attract, protect, and accomplish Love's Way.

I do daily practices to enhance and protect my energy field. Under stress I do even more. Review these for yourself.

Ways to Increase Your Energy Field

- Spend time in nature, among the four elements: water, fire, air, and earth.
- Have at least five primary relationships that feel safe and energize you.
- Form healthy communities.
- Create—art, music, writing.
- Pleasure and feed the senses.
- Do daily heart meditations.
- Take care of your body.
- Listen to the heart.
- Practice living from the heart.
- Do deep breathing exercises.
- Love yourself.
- Clean out addictions and compulsive habits.
- Feel without attachment.
- Let go of the inner critic, rebel, tyrant, and complainer.
- Never hold a grudge.

- Make gratitude a daily experience.
- Clear your mind of negating and limiting beliefs.
- Pray and meditate daily.

Ways to Protect Your Energy Field

- Remove yourself from toxic relationships.
- Return or remove items that relate to toxic people you've let go of.
- Call in spiritual protection every day.
- Visualize permeable protective boundaries.
- Never misuse your sexual energy.
- Say no when you need to.
- Let go of fear and unrestrained desires.
- Cut energetic cords to others who are draining you.
- Admit into your space only those who have earned the right to be there.
- Ask friends and mentors to pray for you.
- Live from and project your deepest values.
- Use grounding rituals and ceremonies.
- Create a sacred place or altar with totems that are meaningful to you.
- Establish your bottom line and stick to it.

HEART-TO-HEART BONDING

When you can bond with another human on the body, ego, soul, and spirit levels all at once, you have arrived. You are the multi-dimensional lover. If you have not, or if you on occasion relapse into fear, do the following. I included it in the revision of *Is It Love or Is It Addiction?* Because it really does engage the many dimensions of love, I've brought it forward again. To call it an exercise demeans it. It *is* intimate love.

It has been suggested to partners wishing to renew their heartfelt bond after much hurt and betrayal of trust within their relationship or in past relationships. It has also been suggested to couples working toward an experience of sacred sexuality when recovering from a sexual addiction. In that regard, becoming comfortable with sharing our hearts precedes sexual intimacy. If there is a history of betrayal and abuse, this will have to be done one step at a time. It is essential that there be no expectations and that participants stop when they feel uncomfortable.

Though this is a profound and simple exercise, surprisingly, it has not been easy for many partners to complete. Many have balked at it. I understand. Recovering sex addicts and rape or incest victims have violated or been violated—starting with the body. This experience is based on the premise that at the basis of relationship problems is a violation of trust. The first developmental task we had to complete as children was to trust ourselves, others, and life. When the heart is injured by a betrayal of that trust, we are reluctant to ever again share it fully, even though the more inspired part of us wishes to do so. Yet to really live Love's Way we must be willing to be vulnerable. This is no easy task, but let's try:

Create a safe and nurturing environment that will allow for privacy and uninterrupted time. This should be mutually discussed and agreed upon.

Lie down side by side in a way that allows the physical heart of one person to make contact with the heart of the other.

Breathe deeply and relax. Do not speak. Feel the heartbeat of the other person. Stay with the experience.

Observe any fear, distancing, or limiting thoughts without judgment. A broken heart takes time to heal and trust again.

Continue until your body flows naturally and easily and there is a strong exchange of heartbeats.

With intention, generate and share love heart to heart: sensual pleasure, emotional bonding, passion and awe, reverence and healing.

Closing Memo

To: You

From: Love

You have learned by now that I am far greater than you imagined. I am the air you breathe and the blood running through your veins. I am a wave pulsating throughout the universe. I am life itself. I am the beauty in a newborn's face and the passion between two lovers. I am the power that heals and guides humanity into a new form of being. I am the Beloved you seek. *I am you.*

I have given your body, ego, soul, and spirit each a challenging assignment that guides them to know me. You have heard them and have been given guidance about what you can do to complete them. Each of these facets of you contains its own unique power, which is realized as you live the challenge. Bonding these powers in the heart provides you with the ultimate human love experience. It is my gift to you. It is Love's Way.

Walk into the world newly united and expanded. Then express your newfound unity to everyone you meet. Bring me into every task, every thought, every action, and every feeling. Summon me into the heart and let me heal your emotions. Use me to bond with others heart to heart. Take me into the tasks you have avoided. Take me to your faults and failures. Take me to your gifts and blessings. Take me to those who have betrayed or failed you. Take me to your stress and discomfort. Take me to your fear and anguish. Take me to your hatred and perversions. Use me!

Use my power to forgive. Use it to bring as much gratitude, joy, awe, compassion, and passion as you can take. With me you will not fail. You will experience a power beyond anything you have known. Share Love's Way any way you can think of, and when this human life ends you will know you did what you were here to do.

Go, my friend. Pass on what you have learned.

Good luck—and thank you.

Resources

Brenda Schaeffer: www.loveandaddiction.com

The National Council of Sexual Addiction and Compulsivity: www.ncsac.org

The Foundation for Shamanic Studies: www.shamanism.org

HeartMath Research Center: www.heartmath.org

Peter Levine and the Foundation for Human Enrichment: www.traumahealing.com

International Transactional Analysis Association: www.itaa-net.org

Hazelden Information and Educational Services: www.hazelden.org

Notes

□   □   □

INTRODUCTION
    1. Diane Ackerman, *A Natural History of Love,* 118.

CHAPTER ONE: WHAT IS LOVE?
    1. Kahlil Gibran, *The Prophet,* 29.
    2. Sara Paddison, *The Hidden Power of the Heart: Discovering an Unlimited Source of Intelligence,* 284.
    3. Edith Hamilton, *Mythology: Timeless Tales of Gods and Heroes,* 36.
    4. Rumi, Maulana Jalal Al-Din, *In the Arms of the Beloved* (New York: J. P. Tarcher, 1997).
    5. Edward Emerson, ed., *The Complete Writings of Ralph Waldo Emerson,* 185.
    6. Walt Whitman, *Leaves of Grass* (New York: Signet, 1958), 114.
    7. Sobonfu Somé, *The Spirit of Intimacy: Ancient Teachings in the Ways of Relationships,* 22.
    8. Lama Surya Das, *Awakening the Buddha Within: Eight Steps to Enlightenment,* 140.
    9. Howard Cutler and the Dalai Lama, *The Art of Happiness,* 114.
    10. Ibid., 114–15.
    11. Lama Surya Das, *Awakening the Buddha Within,* 225.
    12. Caroline Myss and C. Norman Shealy, *The Creation of Health: The Emotional, Psychological, and Spiritual Responses That Promote Health and Healing,* 337.
    13. 1 John 4:8.

14. Arthur William Ryder, *Bhagavad Gita.*

15. A. J. Arberry, *Sufism: An Account of the Mystics of Islam* (London: Allen and Unwin, 1990).

16. Kabir E. Helminsky, *Living Presence: A Sufic Way to Mindfulness and the Essential Self.*

CHAPTER TWO: THE ILLUSIONS OF LOVE

1. Edith Hamilton, *Mythology: Timeless Tales of Gods and Heroes.*

2. Mark Laaser, *The Secret Sin,* 21.

3. Patrick Carnes, *Don't Call It Love: Recovery from Sexual Addiction,* 109–11.

4. Erich Fromm, *The Art of Loving,* 18, 52.

5. Gregg Braden, *Walking between the Worlds: The Science of Compassion,* 67; Sara Paddison, *The Hidden Power of the Heart.*

6. Braden, *Walking between the Worlds,* 94.

7. A. H. Almaas, *Facets of Unity: The Enneagram of Holy Ideas,* 40–41.

CHAPTER THREE: THE BODY IN LOVE

1. Og Mandino, *The Greatest Miracle in the World,* 95.

2. Diane Ackerman, *A Natural History of Love,* 140.

3. Harvey Milkman and Stanley Sunderwirth, *Craving for Ecstasy: The Consciousness and Chemistry of Escape,* 45.

4. Ackerman, *A Natural History of Love,* 143.

5. Sobonfu Somé, *The Spirit of Intimacy: Ancient Teachings in the Ways of Relationships,* 84.

6. Jennifer Schneider, "Effects of Cybersex Addiction on the Family: Results of a Survey," *Journal of Sexual Addiction and Compulsivity* 7, nos. 1 and 2 (2000): 31–58.

7. Helen E. Fisher, *The Sex Contract.*

8. N. Kalin, 137.

9. Robert D. Phillips, *Structural Symbiotic Systems: Correlations with Ego-States, Behavior, and Physiology,* 29.

10. Peter Levine and Ann Frederick, *Waking the Tiger: Healing Trauma,* 19.

11. Phillips, *Structural Symbiotic Systems,* 24.

12. Patrick Carnes, *The Betrayal Bond: Breaking Free of Exploitive Relationships,* 88.

13. HeartMath Research Center, *Research Overview: Exploring the Role of the Heart in Human Performance.*

CHAPTER FOUR: THE EGO IN LOVE

1. Eric Berne, *What Do You Say after You Say Hello?* 33, 106, 213.

2. Antonio Damasio, *Descartes' Error: Emotion, Reason, and the Human Being*, 6.

3. HeartMath Research Center, *Research Overview: Exploring the Role of the Heart in Human Performance*, 6.

4. Doc Childre and Howard Martin, with Donna Beech, *The HeartMath Solution*, 145.

5. Eric Berne, *Transactional Analysis in Psychotherapy.*

CHAPTER FIVE: THE SOUL IN LOVE

1. Thomas Moore, *Soul Mates*, xv.

2. Kahlil Gibran, *The Prophet*, 29.

3. Sandra Ingerman, *Soul Retrieval: Mending the Fragmented Self*, 1.

4. Mircea Eliade, *Rites and Symbols of Initiation: The Mysteries of Birth and Rebirth.*

5. Joseph Campbell and Bill Moyers, *The Power of Myth.*

CHAPTER SIX: THE SPIRIT IN LOVE

1. James Hillman, *A Blue Fire: Selected Writings by James Hillman*, ed. Thomas Moore, 112–13.

2. Caroline Myss, *Anatomy of the Spirit*, 25–26.

3. Rupert Sheldrake, *Dogs That Know When Their Owners Are Coming Home*, 280.

4. Paul Davies and John Gribbin, *The Matter Myth: Dramatic Discoveries That Challenge Our Understanding of Physical Reality* (London: Viking, 1991), 217.

5. Sobonfu Somé, *The Spirit of Intimacy: Ancient Teachings in the Ways of Relationships*, 12–13.

CHAPTER SEVEN: THE REALM OF THE HEART

1. Robert Bly and Marion Woodman, *The Maiden King: The Reunion of Masculine and Feminine*, 21.

2. Og Mandino, *The Greatest Miracle in the World*, 94.

3. Doc Childre and Howard Martin, with Donna Beech, *The HeartMath Solution*, 33.

4. Ibid., 266–67.

5. Ibid., 9.

6. Ibid.

7. John Mann and Lar Short, *The Body of Light: History and Practical Techniques for Awakening Your Subtle Body*, 105.

8. Ibid.

9. Gregg Braden, *Walking between the Worlds: The Science of Compassion*, xiv.

10. Ibid., vi.

CHAPTER EIGHT: TAKING LOVE'S WAY TO THE STREETS

1. Trademark pending.

2. Mircea Eliade, *Rites and Symbols of Initiation: The Mysteries of Birth and Rebirth.*

3. I. K. Taimni, *Science of Yoga.*

Bibliography

Ackerman, Diane. *A Natural History of Love.* New York: Random House, 1994.

Adams, Kenneth M. *Silently Seduced.* Deerfield Beach, Fla.: Health Communications, 1991.

Almaas, A. H. *Facets of Unity: The Enneagram of Holy Ideas.* Berkeley, Calif.: Diamond Books, 1998.

Berne, Eric. *Transactional Analysis in Psychotherapy.* New York: Grove Press, 1961.

———. *What Do You Say after You Say Hello?* New York: Bantam, 1972.

Bly, Robert, and Marion Woodman. *The Maiden King: The Reunion of Masculine and Feminine.* New York: Holt, 1998.

Braden, Gregg. *Awakening to Zero Point: The Collective Initiation.* Questa, N.Mex.: Sacred Spaces/Ancient Wisdom, 1994.

———. *Walking between the Worlds: The Science of Compassion.* Bellevue, Wash.: Radio Bookstore Press, 1997.

Breton, Denise, and Christopher Largent. *Love, Soul, and Freedom: Dancing with Rumi on the Mystic Path.* Center City, Minn.: Hazelden, 1998.

Campbell, Joseph, and Bill Moyers. *The Power of Myth.* New York: Doubleday, 1988.

Capellanus, Andreas. *The Art of Courtly Love*. Ed. Frederick W. Locke. New York: Ungar, 1957.

Capra, Fritjof. *The Turning Point*. New York: Bantam Books, 1983.

———. *Uncommon Wisdom*. New York: Bantam Books, 1989.

Capra, Fritjof, and David Steindl-Rast. *Belonging to the Universe*. New York: HarperSanFrancisco, 1992.

Carnes, Patrick, *The Betrayal Bond: Breaking Free of Exploitive Relationships*. Deerfield Beach, Fla.: Health Communications, 1997.

———. *Contrary to Love: Helping the Sexual Addict*. Minneapolis, Minn.: CompCare, 1989.

———. *Don't Call It Love: Recovery from Sexual Addiction*. New York: Bantam Books, 1991.

———. *Out of the Shadows: Understanding Sexual Addiction*. Minneapolis, Minn.: CompCare, 1983.

———, ed. *Sexual Addiction and Compulsivity: Journal of Treatment and Prevention* 1, no. 1 (1994) and 7, nos. 1 and 2 (2000).

Childre, Doc, and Howard Martin, with Donna Beech. *The HeartMath Solution*. New York: HarperSanFrancisco, 1999.

Cutler, Howard, and the Dalai Lama. *The Art of Happiness*. New York: Riverhead Books, 1998.

Damasio, Antonio. *Descartes' Error: Emotion, Reason, and the Human Being*. New York: Putnam, 1994.

Eisler, Riane. *The Chalice and the Blade: Our History, Our Future*. San Francisco: Harper and Row, 1988.

Eliade, Mircea. *Rites and Symbols of Initiation: The Mysteries of Birth and Rebirth*. New York: Harper and Row, 1958.

Emerson, Edward, ed. *The Complete Writings of Ralph Waldo Emerson*. New York: Wise, 1929.

Estés, Clarissa Pinkola. *Women Who Run with the Wolves*. New York: Ballantine Books, 1992.

Fisher, Helen E. *The Sex Contract*. New York: Quill, 1982.

Fox, Matthew. *Original Blessing*. Santa Fe, N.Mex.: Bear, 1983.

———. *Passion for Creation*. New York: Doubleday, 1995.

Frankl, Viktor E. *Man's Search for Meaning*. New York: Pocket Books, 1963.

Fromm, Erich. *The Art of Loving*. New York: Harper and Row, 1956.

Gibran, Kahlil. *The Prophet*. New York: Random House, 1951.

Goulding, Robert, and Mary McClure Goulding. *Changing Lives through Redecision Therapy*. New York: Brunner/Mazel, 1979.

———. *The Power Is in the Patient*. San Francisco: TA Press, 1978.

Hamilton, Edith. *Mythology: Timeless Tales of Gods and Heroes*. New York: Little, Brown, 1969.

HeartMath Research Center. *Research Overview: Exploring the Role of the Heart in Human Performance*. Boulder Creek, Calif.: Institute of HeartMath, 1997.

Helminsky, Kabir Edmund. *Living Presence: A Sufic Way to Mindfulness and the Essential Self*. New York: J. P. Tarcher/Perigee Books, 1992.

Hillman, James. *A Blue Fire: Selected Writings by James Hillman*. Ed. Thomas Moore. New York: Harper Perennial, 1989.

Ingerman, Sandra. *Soul Retrieval: Mending the Fragmented Self*. New York: HarperSanFrancisco, 1991.

Johnson, Robert A. *Femininity Lost and Regained*. New York: Harper Perennial, 1991.

———. *He: Understanding Masculine Psychology*. New York: Harper and Row, 1986.

———. *She: Understanding Feminine Psychology*. New York: Harper and Row, 1997.

Kalin, N. "The Neurobiology of Fear." *Scientific American*, May 1993.

Kasl, Charlotte D. *If the Buddha Dated*. New York: Penguin Putnam, 1999.

————. *Women, Sex, and Addiction: The Search for Love and Power.* San Francisco: HarperSanFrancisco, 1990.

Khalsa, Subagh Singh. *Anatomy of Miracles: Practical Teachings for Developing Your Capacity to Heal.* Boston: Tuttle, 1999.

Krishnamurti, J. *On Fear.* New York: HarperSanFrancisco, 1995.

Laaser, Mark. *The Secret Sin.* Grand Rapids, Mich.: Zondervan, 1996.

Lama Surya Das. *Awakening the Buddha Within: Eight Steps to Enlightenment.* New York: Broadway Books, 1998.

Levine, Peter, and Ann Frederick. *Waking the Tiger: Healing Trauma.* Berkeley, Calif.: North Atlantic Books, 1997.

Levine, Stephen, and Andrea Levine. *Embracing the Beloved.* New York: Anchor, 1995.

Lindbergh, Anne Morrow. *Gift from the Sea.* New York: Pantheon Books, 1975.

Lowen, Alexander. *Fear of Life.* New York: HarperSanFrancisco, 1980.

Mandino, Og. *The Greatest Miracle in the World.* New York: Bantam Books, 1977.

Mann, John, and Lar Short. *The Body of Light: History and Practical Techniques for Awakening Your Subtle Body.* New York: Globe Press, 1990.

Matt, Daniel C. *God and the Big Bang.* Woodstock, Vt.: Jewish Lights, 1996.

McArthur, David, and Bruce McArthur. *The Intelligent Heart.* Virginia Beach, Va.: A. R. E. Press, 1997.

Milkman, Harvey, and Stanley Sunderwirth. *Craving for Ecstasy: The Consciousness and Chemistry of Escape.* Lexington, Mass.: Lexington Books, 1987.

Moore, Thomas. *Care of the Soul.* New York: HarperCollins, 1992.

————. *Dark Eros: The Imagination of Sadism.* Woodstock, Conn.: Spring, 1994.

————. *Soul Mates.* New York: HarperCollins, 1994.

Moyers, Bill. *Healing and the Mind.* New York: Doubleday, 1993.

Myss, Caroline. *Anatomy of the Spirit.* New York: Three Rivers Press, 1996.

Myss, Caroline, and C. Norman Shealy. *The Creation of Health: The Emotional, Psychological, and Spiritual Responses That Promote Health and Healing.* Walpole, N.H.: Stillpoint, 1993.

Needleman, Jacob. *A Little Book on Love.* New York: Dell, 1996.

The New Oxford Annotated Bible: New Revised Standard Version. New York: Oxford University Press, 1995.

Paddison, Sara. *The Hidden Power of the Heart: Discovering an Unlimited Source of Intelligence.* Boulder Creek, Calif.: Planetary, 1998.

Palmer, Helen. *The Enneagram: Understanding Yourself and Others in Your Life.* New York: Harper, 1988.

Pearson, Carol. *The Hero Within.* San Francisco: Harper and Row, 1993.

Peck, M. Scott. *People of the Lie.* New York: Simon and Schuster, 1983.

Phillips, Robert D. *Structural Symbiotic Systems: Correlations with Ego-States, Behavior, and Physiology.* Chapel Hill, N.C.: self-published, 1975.

Rubik, Beverly. *Life at the Edge of Science.* Philadelphia: The Institute for Frontier Science, 1996.

Ruskan, John. *Emotional Clearing: Releasing Negative Feelings and Awakening Unconditional Happiness.* New York: Wyler, 1993.

Ryder, Arthur William. *Bhagavad Gita.* Chicago: University of Chicago Press, 1929.

Sardello, Robert. *Facing the World with Soul: The Reimagination of Modern Life.* New York: Harper Perennial, 1992.

Schaeffer, Brenda. *Corrective Parenting Chart.* 5th ed. Minneapolis, Minn.: self-published, 1998.

———. *Is It Love or Is It Addiction?* Center City, Minn.: Hazelden, 1997.

———. *Loving Me, Loving You.* San Francisco: HarperCollins, 1992.

Schneider, Jennifer, and Burt Schneider. *Sex, Lies, and Forgiveness: Couples Speaking Out on Healing from Sex Addiction.* Tucson, Ariz.: Recovery Resources Press, 1999.

Sheldrake, Rupert. *Dogs That Know When Their Owners Are Coming Home.* New York: Crown, 1999.

Somé, Sobonfu. *The Spirit of Intimacy: Ancient Teachings in the Ways of Relationships.* New York: Morrow, 1999.

Steiner, Claude. *Scripts People Live.* New York: Grove Press, 1974.

Swimme, Brian, and Thomas Berry. *The Universe Story.* New York: HarperCollins, 1992.

Taimni, I. K. *Science of Yoga.* Wheaton, Ill.: Quest Paperback, Theosophical Publications, 1967.

Wauters, Ambika. *Chakras and Their Archetypes: Uniting Energy Awareness and Spiritual Growth.* Freedom, Calif.: Crossing Press, 1997.

Weed, Joseph J. *Wisdom of the Mystic Masters.* New York: Parker, 1968.

Welwood, John. *Love and Awakening: Discovering the Sacred Path of Intimate Relationship.* New York: Harper Perennial, 1997.

Whitfield, Charles L. *Memory and Abuse.* Deerfield Beach, Fla.: Health Communications, 1995.

Yogananda, Paramahansa. *Autobiography of a Yogi.* Los Angeles: Self-Realization Fellowship, 1993.

Index

◼ ◼ ◼

ABOUT THE AUTHOR

Brenda Schaeffer, D. Min., M.A.L.P., is a licensed psychologist, certified addictions specialist, communications consultant, and author of the best-selling *Is It Love or Is It Addiction?* which has been translated into four languages. She holds a doctorate in Creation Spirituality from the University of Creation Spirituality in Oakland, California. Additionally, Dr. Schaeffer lectures and presents workshops internationally. She unites a wide range of topics in her repertoire of presentations, including Western psychology and various world philosophies. She believes that painful life events are wake-up calls and that therapy can be movement forward on a soul's journey. Her style is direct and compassionate.

Dr. Schaeffer is a member of the National Council of Sexual Addictions and Compulsivity, International Transactional Analysis Association, and the International Association of Enneagram Teachers and is clinical director of Healthy Relationships, Inc., Minneapolis, Minnesota. Her other publications include *Loving Me, Loving You: Balancing Love and Power in a Co-dependent World; Signs of Healthy Love; Signs of Addictive Love; Power Plays;* and *Addictive Love: Help Yourself Out.*

For media interviews, speaking engagements, workshops, retreats, or consulting, Dr. Schaeffer can be reached at the following:

Brenda Schaeffer, D. Min.
Healthy Relationships, Inc.
Box 844
Chanhassen, MN 55317
Phone: 1-952-903-9215 or 1-888-987-6129
E-mail: brenda@loveandaddiction.com
Web site: www.loveandaddiction.com

HAZELDEN INFORMATION AND EDUCATIONAL SERVICES is a division of the Hazelden Foundation, a not-for-profit organization. Since 1949, Hazelden has been a leader in promoting the dignity and treatment of people afflicted with the disease of chemical dependency.

The mission of the foundation is to improve the quality of life for individuals, families, and communities by providing a national continuum of information, education, and recovery services that are widely accessible; to advance the field through research and training; and to improve our quality and effectiveness through continuous improvement and innovation.

Stemming from that, the mission of this division is to provide quality information and support to people wherever they may be in their personal journey—from education and early intervention, through treatment and recovery, to personal and spiritual growth.

Although our treatment programs do not necessarily use everything Hazelden publishes, our bibliotherapeutic materials support our mission and the Twelve Step philosophy upon which it is based. We encourage your comments and feedback.

The headquarters of the Hazelden Foundation are in Center City, Minnesota. Additional treatment facilities are located in Chicago, Illinois; New York, New York; Plymouth, Minnesota; St. Paul, Minnesota, and West Palm Beach, Florida. At these sites, we provide a continuum of care for men and women of all ages. Our Plymouth facility is designed specifically for youth and families.

For more information on Hazelden, please call **1-800-257-7800.** Or you may access our World Wide Web site on the Internet at **http://www.hazelden.org.**